The Task-Centered System

The Task-Centered System

William J. Reid

Columbia University Press · New York

Library of Congress Cataloging in Publication Data

Reid, William James, 1928–
The Task-centered system

  Bibliography: p.
  Includes index.
  1. Social case work. 2. Social group work.
I. Title.
HV43.R378   361.3   78-2488
ISBN 0-231-03797-X

Columbia University Press
New York   Guildford, Surrey
Copyright © 1978 Columbia University Press
Printed in the United States of America
9 8 7 6 5 4 3 2

To my father (in memory), Sophie, Valerie, and
Steven

Contents

Preface   ix

  1 An Evolving Practice System   1
  2 Problem-Oriented Theory   12
  3 The Nature of Psychosocial Problems   20
  4 Problem Formation and Resolution   42
  5 Intervention Strategy   83
  6 Problem Specification and the Service Contract   113
  7 Task Planning and Implementation   138
  8 Ending   179
  9 Conjoint and Group Treatment   189
10 A Study of Effectiveness   225
11 Systematic Case Information   272
12 Dissemination   294

Appendix I Typology of Target Problems   309

Appendix II Activities and Techniques Coding Schedule   315

References   331

Author Index   347

Subject Index   351

Preface

The task-centered approach is a system of social work practice designed to help people with problems of living. Clients are helped to solve problems through their own actions, or tasks, which they select, plan, and carry out with the assistance of the social worker. The service offered is short-term, structured, and empirically based.

The foundations of this practice system were set forth in an earlier volume, *Task-Centered Casework,* published in 1972. Since that time a great deal of effort has been devoted to improving the system. The theoretical base of the approach has been considerably expanded. New intervention strategies and procedures have been designed and subsequently tested through a controlled experiment. Methods of recording and utilizing case information and of training practitioners have been devised.

This book incorporates these developments and presents a generally revised formulation of the task-centered practice system. I hope that the volume, like its predecessor, will be used by students and practitioners who are interested in applying the task-centered approach to their work. In addition, the book may be of value to other readers: those interested in theories of psychosocial problems and problem solving; or in clinical studies of treatment processes and outcomes; those in search of a general framework for adapting research-based methods to social work practice; and those who may derive some ideas and stimulation from a book that deals, in one way or another, with most aspects of clinical social work.

The use of "we" rather than "I" throughout much of the book

reflects the collaborative effort that made its creation possible. The treatment approach presented in the book would still be only a partially conceived daydream had I not had the good fortune to join forces, some years ago, with Laura Epstein, who helped create the task-centered model and built the educational program that has proved so crucial to its development. Only a small part of her contribution to the present volume is contained in its final chapter, of which she is the senior author.

The development and testing of a treatment model in an educational setting requires supervisors skilled in both clinical teaching and research. This blend of talent was amply supplied by Eleanor Tolson, Lester B. Brown, and Ronald H. Rooney, who not only made the model work in the field but who contributed significantly to the evaluation of its theory and method.

Measurement of how well the model worked proved to be one of our most challenging tasks. Anne E. Fortune, who designed and supervised the complex measurement operations used in our principal field test, proved equal to this challenge as well as to many others that she undertook in her role as research associate. Gerald Bostwick contributed his knowledge and skill to the coding and computer analysis of the data yielded by this test. I am also indebted to the many research assistants who served on this and other projects in our research program. Those who assumed major responsibility for different phases of our work and deserve special mention are Carol Swartz; Richard O'Connor; Richard Dougherty; and Christine Beard.

The work reported in this book was made possible by two essential forms of support: financial and institutional. A grant from the Social and Rehabilitation Service, the Department of Health, Education, and Welfare gave us the wherewithal to carry out the major field test of the model previously referred to. A generous gift from Lawrence and Mildred Schuerman enabled us to enlarge the dimensions of that study. The School of Social Service Administration has provided an optimal environment for our program. For this I owe much to the school's principal administrators, Dean Harold A. Richman and Associate Dean John R. Schuerman.

Special thanks are due to several persons who helped me put my ideas and words into final form: to John R. Schuerman and Cheryl Zeigert for their perceptive reviews of drafts of chapters of the book; to Tina Rzepnicki for her thoughtful searches of the literature; and to Gwendolyn Graham and Gloria Jones for their skilled and industrious typing of the manuscript.

Finally I should like to express my gratitude to the many students who have participated in classes and projects on task-centered practice. The book would not have been written without the empirical data, case examples, and intellectual stimulation they provided.

William J. Reid

The Task-Centered System

Chapter 1
An Evolving Practice System

Social work practice with individuals, families, and groups is a remarkably diverse enterprise. Much of it is concerned with face-to-face work with people to help them effect changes in attitudes, feelings, and actions, but a good part involves efforts to alter destructive environmental conditions or to arrange for the provision of needed services, personal care, or mutual aid. Social work practice may be directed at helping individuals or families with self-defined problems or may deal with persons who wish no help but whose behavior violates social norms. The change target may be the behavior of an individual, the interaction of family members, or a complex field of individuals and organizations. Practitioners may work with persons one by one, in family or other natural groups, or in groups formed by some common concern. They may combine efforts at these levels with attempts to bring about change in larger social systems. In carrying out their work they may assume a variety of roles: therapist; teacher; collaborator; consultant; group leader or facilitator; coordinator; and, at times, something akin to an officer of the law.

Perhaps the common thread in this variegated fabric is the effort of the social worker to help people resolve difficulties through direct interactions with them and their social systems. To this process the terms "clinical social work" or "social treatment" are commonly applied. I shall use them henceforth with the understanding that the processes of individualized social work are not confined to the consulting room and are better characterized as collaboration with than as treatment of people.

Practice Systems

Innumerable ways of carrying out this practice have been described and advocated in a half-century of literature. Writing on social work methods has reflected the viewpoints of different schools of treatment, or what I call general systems of practice. Such systems, which usually consist of loosely organized bodies of values, theory, principles, and techniques, provide guidelines for practice over a wide range of clinical situations. The most notable example to date has been the psychoanalytically-oriented (psychosocial) system of casework, a school that has dominated clinical social work for the past four decades (Hamilton 1951; Hollis 1972). Other examples include functional casework (Smalley 1970), the problem-solving approach (Perlman 1957, 1970), crisis intervention (Rapoport 1970; Parad 1965), and behavioral treatment (Thomas 1970; Schwartz and Goldiamond 1975; Fischer and Gochros 1976).

Most social work practice systems have borrowed considerably from other disciplines and in some instances are related to practice systems within' those disciplines—for example, the psychosocial approach can be seen as one of several offsprings of psychoanalytic treatment theory and practice. What gives a system a social work stamp is an articulated relation of theory and method to the special concerns of social work. Thus, some psychotherapeutic systems, such as transactional analysis or Gestalt therapy, have not given birth to distinctively social work practice systems even though they have been applied in various ways in social work.

General systems of practice have proved attractive as vehicles for teaching and clinical work because they incorporate broad principles that, once learned, can be applied to a wide variety of situations; moreover, they offer means of synthesizing otherwise fragmented pieces of practice theory and method. But this mode of organizing treatment has certain characteristic weaknesses. A system may be extended by its adherents to situations in which its application is ineffective or even dysfunctional. In its emphasis on general principles, a practice system may have little to say about specific types of clients or problems or may cause practitioners to view them from a narrow, systems-blinded perspective. Moreover, practice systems tend to multiply. As they do, and as each advances its own claims to superiority, teachers, students, and practitioners find themselves in quandaries about which to use for what purposes. The rapid proliferation of treatment systems in clinical social work and psychotherapy in recent years has made these dilemmas particularly acute.

It is hard to find anyone who is satisfied with the present balkanization of social treatment; nevertheless, for the time being a "schools approach" seems unavoidable, given our wide variation in beliefs about the purposes and methods of treatment and our lack of hard knowledge about how it works and what it can do.

Since we must contend with a variety of practice systems, we need to find means of coping with diversity. The solution may lie in viewing any system as potentially useful in two ways. First, a system can be employed in its entirety by certain practitioners, in certain settings, or for certain types of cases. In this usage the fit between the offerings of the system and the needs of the practitioner, setting, or case must be relatively good. A system can also offer a cohesive package of theory and methods that can be taken apart by discerning practitioners who can select from it those pieces of value to them. The latter use is probably the more important, at least in today's practice. Practitioners seem to be solving problems of choice among competing systems by becoming increasingly eclectic. Even if they tend to be primarily oriented toward one system, they have no qualms about supplementing it with elements of others for particular purposes. Practice systems are constructed to be dismantled, a pardox their designers should not forget.

This book is an attempt to extend and develop one system of social work practice—task-centered treatment—that may be used in these two ways. It is not written to win converts to a cause or to proclaim the superiority of that approach over any other. Rather, its purpose is to present a set of ideas and methods that some practitioners may use as general guide for their work and that others may draw from for particular purposes. Since this work is not the first to appear on the subject, I should like to trace briefly the evolution of this form of practice and to indicate what will be added by the present volume.

The Beginning

The task-centered system of practice was developed in the early 1970s (Reid 1972; Reid and Epstein 1972). The system consisted of (1) a *model* of brief, time-limited casework, with a model defined as a set of guidelines or directives for the conduct of practice; (2) an underlying practice theory; (3) a set of value premises; (4) a body of emprical data supporting the theory and model. The model itself (the how-to-do-it part of the system) incorporated the time-limited, structural aspects of an earlier form of brief casework (Reid and Shyne 1969), elements of Perlman's (1957, 1970) problem-solving approach, Studt's (1968) conception of the client's task, and prior work on the articulation of casework methods (Hollis 1973; Reid 1967).

In its first comprehensive formulation (Reid and Epstein 1972), the model resembled a number of structured short-term approaches already in use in social work and related fields. It was addressed to specific problems that clients expressly agreed to work on and could alleviate through their own actions. Once agreed-on problems were pinned down, the practitioner and client formulated courses of problem-solving action, or tasks, the client could undertake. In actual use, tasks tended to be defined for the client in rather general terms, such as "to improve performance at school," "to obtain a job," or "to work out a plan for a mentally retarded daughter." Thus, tasks were equivalent to goals the client had agreed to work toward.

The practitioner's efforts were directed largely at helping the clients achieve such tasks. To do so, practitioners made use of traditional casework techniques (including exploration, advice giving, encouragement, helping the client increase his understanding of his own behavior and his social situation, and environmental intervention). The period of service was limited to a range of sessions (eight to twelve) to take place within a two- to four-month period, although provisions were made for extensions of these limits.

The model was supported by a limited theory that defined an array of target problems, outlined certain dynamics of problem change, and suggested a general strategy for problem alleviation. Two value premises were central. One emphasized the primacy of the client's expressed, considered request—what the client says he wants after considering his needs in relation to the practitioner's offerings.* The client's conscious wishes, not the practitioner's or other's assessment of what he "really" wanted or needed, was to control the helping effort. The other asserted the supremacy of research-based knowledge over knowledge acquired from other sources, such as practice wisdom or untested theory. The empirical foundations for the model consisted largely of the results of studies of the outcomes of short- and long-term casework, counseling, and psychotherapy (as reviewed in Reid and Epstein 1972, pp. 82–93; Reid and Shyne 1969, pp. 176–93). Generalizations derived from these studies included the following: (1) recipients of brief, time-limited treatment show at least as much durable improvement as recipients of long-term, open-ended treatment; (2) most of the improvement associated with long-term treatment occurs relatively soon after treatment has begun; (3) regardless of their intended length, most courses of treatment turn out to be relatively brief. These generalizations provided empirical grounding for our position that brief, time-limited models were generally preferable to lengthier forms of intervention. To this base, we added the results of some modest tests of our particular form of short-term treatment, results that compared favorably with other tests of short-term approaches (Reid and Epstein 1972).

* The masculine pronoun is used throughout only for convenience. I regret the inequity this usage connotes.

A Program for Development

During the past six years, a continuing program of testing, research, and study has been carried on under the direction of the author and his colleague, Laura Epstein, to refine, expand, and improve this system of practice. A good deal of this effort has been conducted at the School of Social Service Administration, the University of Chicago, in conjunction with the training of graduate social work students. As a part of a year-long sequence in task-centered treatment, from 20 to 25 students each year have applied the model to more than 1,000 cases in school, psychiatric, and other settings. A smaller number of these cases (200) have been part of formal research projects, including controlled experiments, in which systematic data have been collected on treatment processes and outcomes. Additional projects relating to aspects of the model have been conducted by master's and doctoral students at the school.

Another part of our program of model development and testing has consisted of applications of the task-centered approach by professional social workers in a number of research projects, both in this country and abroad. These projects, conducted in consultation with the author and Laura Epstein, have yielded data on several hundred cases in a variety of settings and have led to a variety of modifications and innovations in the approach.

Finally, we have provided consultation and training to numerous agencies that have applied the task-centered model in their programs. Our most ambitious effort to date has been a two-year staff development undertaking with a state department of social welfare* interested in adopting the model as a basic counseling service. Case reports from practitioners who have used task-centered methods in the course of training have proved to be a rich source of insight into the operation of the model under a wide range of practice conditions.

* The South Dakota State Department of Social Services.

Information resulting from applications of the model has been combined with theoretical studies and literature reviews relating to various aspects of the task-centered system. Our objectives here have been to expand and strengthen the theoretical base of the approach in a manner consistent with our own data and to incorporate into our approach promising and compatible methods tested by others.

Previous publications have reported on some of this work. Garvin (1974) and Garvin, Reid, and Epstein (1976) presented the foundations of a group-treatment form of the model. Korbelik and Epstein (1976) discussed the task-centered training program at the School of Social Service Administration, and Epstein (1976) analyzed skill requirements in use of the model. Reid (1975) set forth the results of a field experiment testing the efficacy of a set of activities for helping clients achieve specific tasks. Cormican (1977) devised a task-centered approach for work with the aged. Applications of the task-centered model in a variety of settings were described in a volume, *Task-Centered Practice* (Reid and Epstein 1977), to which 19 authors contributed papers. While all of these publications have dealt with innovations in the task-centered approach over the past five years, none has provided a comprehensive and detailed statement of developments in its theory, intervention strategies and techniques, and empirical base during this period.

The present volume will present these developments and attempt to build upon them. In essence, the book is an effort to push forward the evolution of a system of practice that by design was meant to change in the light of new data, new ideas, and new demands.

Guidelines for Development

Developments in the task-centered approach in recent years have been guided by our desire to create a demonstrably effective system of practice fitted to the requirements of social work. In order to put our work in proper perspective, this twofold purpose needs to be considered with some care.

The need for demonstrably effective methods is critical at this juncture in the evolution of clinical social work. Before the 1960s, few systematic tests of methods used by social workers had been conducted. In the absence of any rigorous evidence, it was assumed that these methods, principally casework, were effective, an assumption buttressed by uncontrolled studies and case reports. This assumption, or perhaps faith, was finally put to the test through a number of controlled experimental studies of casework treatment (see reviews by Fischer 1976; Mullen and Dumpson 1972). The results, as we know, were not encouraging: taken as a whole, they provided little evidence that intensive casework treatment could accomplish any more than clients could achieve on their own or with minimal help. To be sure, none of these studies was free of methodological flaws, and they were limited largely to "nonvoluntary" clients, such as delinquent youth and families receiving public assistance. It has been argued (Polemis 1976) that they did not provide an adequate test of the efficacy of social treatment. Still, by their failure to demonstrate the potency of the methods tested, the studies created a climate of skepticism about the effectiveness of clinical social work. Ebbing confidence in traditional methods has brought about a search for new technology. Though promising alternatives have been introduced, most practice is still built around methods whose efficacy is open to serious challenge. The only way to answer this challenge, in my judgment, is to develop and disseminate methods of demonstrable effectiveness; that is, methods whose effects can be demonstrated through research of acceptable rigor. Only then can we offer treatment to clients with justified confidence that it will, in fact, make a difference in their lives.

To be maximally useful in the practice of clinical social work, an approach must not only be demonstrably effective; it must also be fitted to the requirements of that practice—to its purposes, clientele, and auspices. These requirements cannot be definitely stated, since the function and boundaries of social work itself are by no means clear or settled. Moreover, it is possible to propose quite different roles and contexts for social work than exist today (Piliavin 1968; Morris 1977) and thus deal with a radically different set of practice conditions. In this book, however, I am concerned with fashioning a system that takes into account the typical demands placed on clinical social work as we now find it.

At least some of these demands, and their implications for practice systems, can be identified. First, a central function of clinical social work is to help people alleviate problems. Although other goals, such as prevention and the facilitation of personal growth, may also be important, problem reduction is cited most consistently in various statements of the objectives of the profession of which clinical social work is the major part. Not surprisingly, this purpose is the first of three stated for the profession by the National Association of Social Workers: "To assist individuals and groups to identify and resolve or minimize problems arising out of the disequilibrium between themselves and their environment" (1958). Although the characteristics and limits of these problems cannot be precisely defined, most problems dealt with by clinical social workers seem to involve distress over interpersonal or situational concerns; thus, the widely used term "psychosocial problem" seems an apt characterization.

Second, clinical social work is largely a product of a complex organizational network that comprises not only agencies offering social work services but also organizations that provide financial support and sanction for these services. As a consequence, the practice of clinical social work is shaped by the purposes and requirements of multiple organizations. A growing emphasis on accountability in social work practice (Briar 1973) appears to be heightening these organizational influences.

Third, social work provides individualized services to large numbers of people who are poor, who may lack a high degree of verbal facility, who may not be motivated for help, and who are often in need of a variety of services. How to serve best this clientele has been traditionally one of the profession's greatest challanges.

Fourth, though we may wish it were otherwise, much, if not most, social treatment is carried out by practitioners with limited training. For many, particularly in the public services, training may consist largely of brief, in-service programs. For many others, it is confined to undergraduate courses. In the light of recent trends, one might expect an even greater share of responsibility for direct treatment to be assumed by workers without professional graduate training. Finally, clinical social work is part of a larger profession. The "other half" of social work uses different methods—including community organization and development, social planning, and social action—to effect problem alleviation and social change on a broad scale. These different arms of the profession are being brought together increasingly in collaborative efforts to alleviate particular social problems as well as in generalist training and practice.

This configuration of conditions, which gives clinical social work its distinctive character among the helping disciplines, suggests the need for systems of practice that are addressed to alleviation of psychosocial problems, that take into account organizational sponsorship of service, that are suited to work with a lower-class clientele of uncertain motivation and with multiservice needs, that can be learned and used by practitioners with limited training, and that are related to other methods of the profession.

A practice system may lack a social work orientation and still be quite helpful to social workers, since it may provide a useful technology that they can adapt to their purposes. A distinctively social work practice system has certain advantages, however: it is more directly relevant to the kind of case situations and organizational contexts characteristic of social work practice; it can be better integrated into training and intervention strategies that involve other aspects of social work. More generally, in our striving to build a unified profession we need to develop, at all levels of intervention, conceptions of practice that reflect social work as a whole.

Plan for Book

The first section of the book (chapters 2, 3, and 4) will develop the problem-oriented theory that underlies the task-centered model. The general strategy of intervention used in the model will then be presented (chapter 5), followed by a detailed explication of how this strategy is carried out (chapters 6, 7, and 8). Variants of the model developed for use in the treatment of family systems and in work with clients in formed groups will be the subject of chapter 9. A controlled experiment in which the efficacy of the core methods of the model was tested will be reported in chapter 10. If an agency-based practice system is to be employed successfully, ways must be found to collect and utilize systematic case information and to train and supervise personnel in the approach. These aspects will be taken up in the final two chapters. The final chapters will also provide additional detail on the structure of the model and the skills required for its use.

Chapter 2

Problem-Oriented Theory

Any system of social treatment is supported by a body of theory. The supporting theory defines the objects or targets of treatment, provides an accounting of how these targets originate and change, and shows how the methods of intervention prescribed by the system contribute to these change processes. The theory component of a system can be distinguished from its practice principles and techniques that in our terms make up the treatment model. A theory consists essentially of definitions and propositions: it defines, explains, and predicts but does not direct. In contrast, a model prescribes what the practitioner is to do under given circumstances. Thus if we say that a mother who has given birth to a deformed baby is depressed because she is unconsciously grieving the loss of a wished-for normal infant and that her depression will be relieved if she can gain conscious awareness of this source of grief, we have made certain theoretical statements but have not as yet prescribed a method of intervention. If we set forth a set of procedures to be used by practitioners to help the depressed mother gain awareness of her grief, we have described an element of a treatment model. As can be seen, a theory essentially provides a framework, direction, and rationale for the prescribed practitioner behaviors that make up the model.

Numerous bodies of theory have informed models of practice used by clinical social workers. Among the most influential have been psychoanalytic theory (particularly ego psychology) and theories pertaining to problem solving, social roles, communication, socialization, crises, small groups, social systems, and learning. Although such theories have enriched clinical social work, it cannot be said that any one, or any combination of them, yet provides an adequate base for professional practice. Most propositions from most theories have not been sufficiently tested. None has the scope or depth to cope with the manifold complexities of clinical situations. Theories, like the models they inform, provide the practitioner with limited guidance at best.

Need for Problem-Oriented Theory

If we accept the position that a major concern of clinical social work is to alleviate *problems* of individuals and families, then we should focus our attention on the development of theory designed to explain how such targets of intervention come into being and can be resolved (Reid 1977b). Take for example a common problem dealt with by social workers in child welfare: natural parents not visiting children in foster placement (Fanshel 1975, 1977). A social worker confronted with this problem would be helped considerably by a theory that would provide explanations for nonvisiting and would suggest conditions that might make contact between children and parents more frequent.

Traditionally, we have approached understanding of problems of living through theories designed for other purposes—to explain personality dynamics and disorder, learning, the functioning of social systems, and so on. While such theories have an important role in the assessment and treatment of problems, they are not addressed to the particular properties of most difficulties social workers deal with. Personality or learning theories, for example, do not tell us how problems are perceived by clients and others, do not account for the complex interplay of personal and environmental factors so characteristic of problems of living, and consequently offer an insufficient base for developing remedial strategies. Consider a woman who lives in a high-crime area and whose problem, as she sees it, is her fear of leaving her apartment. Using a theory of personality or personality disorder, one might interpret the problem as a phobic reaction (possibly an expression of displaced anxiety) or perhaps as symptomatic of an incipient paranoid state. If a theory of learning were employed, her difficulty might be seen as a function of the adverse consequences of previous forays from her home. Neither theory in itself would be likely to lead us to a systematic accounting of her conception of the problem, how it affected her life, what she had done or would like to do about it, or the range of immediate personal *and* situational factors that might be producing or aggravating it—for example, realistic fears of being mugged on the street. While a practitioner might use one or the other of these theories and still be able to assess these other elements, the theories themselves would not help him do this.

In the example above, as in so many others, no available theory quite fits the problem. Thus the practitioner faces a dilemma in the use of possibly relevant theory. If he relies exclusively on one body of theory, he may overlook important factors that fall outside the scope of that theory. If he uses multiple theoretical perspectives, he usually must make uncertain choices about how these perspectives can be best combined and applied to the problem at hand.

When he encounters a problem for which available theory exists, another kind of dilemma occurs. There are often competing theories to explain the same problem, and these theories are usually outcroppings of larger bodies of diagnostic and behavioral theory which in themselves need to be understood at some level before one can grasp the derivative theories relating to the specific problem. Consider, for example, the many theories of depression.

For now, I can see no real solution to these dilemmas. The construction of a general theory of psychosocial problems with branches for a wide range of specific difficulties is clearly beyond our grasp. Theory building toward that goal may still have value, however. In particular, we need formulations that would help social workers define and assess the kinds of human problems they confront in their daily work and would offer some guidance for their remedial efforts. A central function of such a theory at this point would be to provide means of organizing the existing welter of theories and data relevant to psychosocial problems. If it did nothing more than facilitate an orderly and generative analysis of psychosocial problems, it would be of great value.

Testability

Ideally, a theory should have convincing empirical support before it is used as a basis for practice methods. Given our present state of knowledge and practice, this requirement seems unrealistic. We can at least demand, however, that a theory be cast into testable form. This means that theoretical formulations need to be accompanied by a specification of how they can be tested. It should be clear what kind of evidence is needed and how it can be obtained to support or reject hypotheses drawn from the theory. These criteria would not only apply to the original formulations of a problem-oriented theory but also to existing theories that it may draw from.

Evidence from systematic research could then be marshaled to demonstrate that the hypotheses in question hold, or do not hold, for specified types of clients, problems, situations, interventions, and the like. Hypotheses receiving empirical support would still need to be tested for fit to the case at hand. Research-supported hypotheses seldom express invariant relationships: usually the number of deviant cases—those that do not fit the hypothesis—is substantial. Moreover, the case situation facing the practitioner usually differs in important respects from the case populations that have been used in formal tests. As a result, research-tested hypotheses are useful to the practitioner largely for heuristic purposes—to give helpful starts in promising directions.

Thus a practitioner may be referred a young child who has just been hospitalized. One empirically supported theory he might use would predict that children in this situation will go through several stages in working through their separation from their parents and their adaptation to the hospital (Bowlby 1969). But this prediction, while generally true, may not hold for this child. To test the applicability of the theory to the case, the practitioner would need to determine through interaction with the child, observation, and interviews with ward personnel whether or not these stages were occurring. To do so he would need to be able, like the researcher, to spell out the hypothesis in measurable terms and collect data, albeit crude, that would bear upon it. If the hypothesis is genuinely testable, he should be able to make a judgment as to how it applied in the case. If he uses theory as we think it should be used, he should be able to say, in the face of contrary evidence, that the hypothesis does not seem to apply in this case and to try to locate others that might help understand the child's reactions. Testing of this kind assumes greater importance when we consider that most clinically relevant hypotheses have at best ambiguous research support.

Much of the theory we use in clinical work is not readily testable by either the researcher or practitioner. Consider the following variant of crisis theory:

> When an individual's coping mechanisms are unequal to solving problems created by a stressor event, he will feel anxiety, and in this situation he will be in a state of active crisis. He may mask his anxiety by means of inner defensive operations so that an outside observer cannot tell that he is in a crisis. He may employ the defense of denial so that he himself is unaware of his anxiety. [Lukton 1974]

If neither an outside observer nor the person himself can identify the "crisis state," it is hard to imagine how the condition could be measured and how the theory could be tested. One can readily think of less extreme examples that are either untestable or highly resistant to testing through systematic data collection. Consider theories of practice concerned with "reestablishing ego boundaries" or "restoring family homeostasis" in which there are no measurable indicators for these target conditions nor even any specification of the kind of data needed to describe them.

The crux of the argument, then, is that the practitioner should pin down theory to empirical events in the case at hand and that he should have theory that enables him to do so. Those who accept this position would use highly speculative, untestable theory (of the kind illustrated above) with great caution, if at all. Such theory may provide practitioners with some intellectual titillation, but by its nature cannot produce evidence either that it works or does not. Very often it produces little more than reified fantasies in the mind of the practitioner, who sees ego defenses crumbling or system boundaries expanding as if such pictures really captured the realities before him.

I do not assume that reliance upon testable theory would provide any more than a fraction of the answers to the tough clinical questions with which practitioners must continually struggle. I do assume, however, that its use would help avoid pseudoanswers to these questions (or pseudoanswers to pseudoquestions). But uncertainty would be more the rule than the exception, and perhaps more often than not the practitioner would say, "Some evidence may be found for my interpretation of the problem, but I am really not at all sure if it is correct." If the practitioner is to eschew untestable formulations for the limited guidance that empirically demonstrable theory can afford, where can he look for guidance in uncertain situations? He should turn, I think, to his common sense, which one would hope to be less common and more sensible than the layperson's, since it should be buttressed by a greater fund of hard knowledge—facts essentially—about human problems and behavior. Common sense should not be glorified by being labeled "practice wisdom" or other synonyms for sagacity. It is simply a basis for making decisions in the absence of tested knowledge—a better basis, I submit, than untested theory.

Theory for Task-centered Practice

The need for problem-oriented, testable theory in clinical social work has guided our efforts to develop the theoretical base of the task-centered model. In our initial formulation (Reid and Epstein

1972), we proposed some very limited formulations concerning the nature, origins, and duration of psychosocial problems typically dealt with by social workers. We suggested that these problems generally reflected temporary breakdowns in problem coping that set in motion forces for change. These forces, principally the client's own motivation to alleviate his distress, operate rapidly in most cases to reduce the problem to a tolerance level, at which point the possibility of further change lessens. If so, then clients might be expected to benefit as much from short-term treatment as from more extended periods of service. Placing time limits on the brief service might be expected to enhance effectiveness by mobilizing efforts of both practitioner and client. Effectiveness would be further augmented by concentrated attention on delimited problems in which practitioners, using traditional casework techniques in a highly focused way, would help clients formulate and carry out problem-solving actions.

This theoretical base has been considerably enlarged by the development of formulations for understanding the nature and dynamics of psychosocial problems and the role of human action in their alleviation. These formulations, which have been inspired by the work of Goldman (1970), a philosopher, will be summarized at this point. They will be presented in detail in the following two chapters.

Both our initial and subsequent theoretical work has been based on the premise that the essential function of task-centered treatment is to help clients move forward with solutions to psychosocial problems that they define and hope to solve. The primary agent of change is not the social worker but the client. The worker's role is to help the client bring about the changes the client wishes and is willing to work for.

Much of our recent theoretical work has thus been concerned with understanding how client-defined problems arise and how they get resolved. We assume that such problems are always the expression of something the client wants that he does not have, whether he desires something as concrete and humble as a warm coat or as complex and elegant as self-actualization. The usual and most effective way to obtain what one wants is to take action to get it. Since the client is a human being, his action is guided by a sophisticated set of beliefs about himself and his world, beliefs that help him form and implement plans about what he should do and how he should do it. Since his problem is psychosocial, his plans and actions usually will involve others—the individuals, groups, and organizations that make up his social system. These actions will be in turn shaped by his evaluation of the responses of this system.

Our theory does not attempt to deal with remote or historical origins of a problem, but rather with those factors that are currently causing it. Our attention is further focused on those factors that the client or practitioner can act to change. These factors become, in effect, obstacles to problem resolution that can be modified through the collaborative efforts of client and practitioner. Such obstacles are found in the same matrix of forces that bring about problem resolution—in the client's actions, beliefs, and social system. Dysfunctional patterns of action and belief and deficient or uncooperative social systems provide the usual barriers to problem alleviation. In this view, problems are created by the same elements through which they are solved. Both problem causation and remediation can then be understood in terms of a common set of concepts.

These formulations, more than some others that guide social work practice, stress man's autonomous problem-solving capacities—his ability to initiate and carry through intelligent action to obtain what he wants. In this conception, man is seen as less a prisoner of unconscious drives than he is in the theories of the psychoanalyst and less a prisoner of environmental contingencies than he is in the views of the behaviorist. Rather he is viewed as having a mind and will of his own that are reactive but not subordinate to internal and external influences. We think those human problem-solving capacities—complex, ingenious, and, in the main, quite effective—deserve more prominence than they have received in theories of helping. We have tried to build our theory accordingly.

Chapter 3

The Nature of Psychosocial Problems

Perhaps the first question that a problem-oriented theory must consider is, "What constitutes a problem?" Most clinical social work practice is concerned with the alleviation of psychosocial problems; yet there is considerable variation, and often insufficient clarity, in how such problems are conceptualized. In this chapter I shall attempt to set forth our current thinking on how problems are defined within the task-centered framework. In some parts the chapter will be an updating and extension of previous writings (Reid and Epstein 1972, 1977). The core of the chapter, however, will present new material on the definition and structure of problems. I shall begin with a review of the major criteria used to identify a target problem, as they are currently used in our practice.

Client Acknowledgment

In the typically complicated clinical situation, a critical initial question that must be answered is, "For whom is something a problem?" We often bypass this question in clinical work by defining some problem for the client and simultaneously giving him possession of it. The client may or may not be informed of our definition of his difficulties. We write in our summaries, "Mrs. A's problem is that she overprotects her child," or, "Mr. A has a problem of underlying depression." Unless the clients themselves claim ownership of these problems (as is often not the case), the only sense in which they "have" them is that someone has *at-*

tributed these problems to them. *Attributed problems* boil down to the statement, "I say that you have a problem."

A problem that the client himself says he has may be thought of as an *acknowledged* problem. Operationally defined, an acknowledged problem consists of statements about his problems that the client volunteers, provides when asked, or agrees with when presented to him. "My wife and I quarrel all the time"; "My son is unmanageable"; "I agree with what you say—I am not doing as well in my studies as I would like to." To be considered "acknowledged," a problem must be explicitly stated. To say that the client really is troubled by this or that but cannot verbalize it is another form of an attributed problem.

This distinction may not be important when acknowledged and attributed conceptions of the problem are relatively close. In clinical social work, however, acknowledged and attributed problems may differ greatly, particularly in work with the socially deviant. A clinician may work on an attributed, unacknowledged problem, but it is important that he recognize what kind of problem he is working with. If a problem is not acknowledged, the practitioner cannot rely on the problem-solving capacities of the client to the same extent as with an acknowledged problem; this limitation must be taken into account. If practitioners proceed as if the distinction were of no consequence, then the result may be the kind of unproductive "clash of perspectives" between worker and client reported in several studies of social work practice (Mayer and Timms 1970; Silverman 1970; Rhodes 1977).

The present theory is concerned primarily with acknowledged psychosocial problems. In fact, we will have only such problems in mind when we use the simple term "problem." This decision results from our general focus on the role of client action in solving psychosocial problems. If the client's actions are to play a central role in alleviating a problem, it is assumed that they must be directed at a problem that he himself recognizes. Moreover, within the value framework of the task-centered system, it is considered a violation of the client's rights to act on his behalf for a problem he has not acknowledged.

Haley?

It should be made clear that this emphasis does *not* leave out "involuntary clients." The social worker may do a variety of things to help such persons recognize problems, or he may find areas of concern to them not immediately related to reasons for their referral. Nor does it mean that the practitioner uncritically accepts whatever tumbles out of the client's mouth. In most cases the client's raw perception of his difficulties will need to be explored, clarified, and refined. In some cases it may need to be vigorously challenged. But whatever is done, the client should still be able to say, "Yes, that is my problem."

The injunction of the model—to work only with acknowledged problems—means that an explicit agreement must be reached on what the problem is before the practitioner takes remedial action. Unlike some other forms of practice, treatment does not proceed on the basis of the practitioner's attribution of what is really bothering the client or on the assumption that certain actions must be taken for the "client's own good."

In restricting the model to problems acknowledged by the client, we must resolve complex issues that arise in situations involving a variety of potential problem definers. A child is referred to a school social worker because he is "acting out" in class. Who has what kind of problem, and who becomes the client? The teacher may attribute a problem to the child; the social worker may attribute a problem to the child and his parents; the parents and child may acknowledge no problem but may attribute a problem to the teacher. The social worker might end up working with the teacher as client about her acknowledged problem (perhaps the only one on the scene) about how to cope with the child.

As this example illustrates, it is possible within the framework of the model to work on an acknowledged problem in which the source of the difficulty is defined as the behavior of another person. This circumstance frequently arises in work with families: a particular family member may be helped to cope with the behavior of another family member who may not be seen at all. The acknowledged problem in such cases is the client's inability to deal with the behavior of the other to his satisfaction. While the ensuing treatment strategy may involve efforts on the part of the client to alter the behavior of the other, the problem still remains with the client. The behavior of the other person simply provides the basis for the client's acknowledged problem. As a rule, an effort should be made to engage the other person or "change target," to use the phrase of Pincus and Minahan (1973). If that person is not willing to be a party to treatment, then he should at least be informed by the practitioner or client that they will be working together in ways that might affect him.

Relief through Independent Action

Our interest is centered on those problems that clients can alleviate through independent action, that is, action they can perform on their own, outside the treatment session. Thus, a person can act to resolve a family conflict, to improve his performance as a student, to control his eating, and to obtain a job. He may not be able to take independent action to rid himself of his stuttering or his ulcer. Certain actions, such as seeking expert help or taking medication, may be instrumental in relieving difficulties of the latter sort, but an external agent would provide the principal medium of relief. Some problems, of course, may be alleviated either through the person's actions or through external agents. A person may relieve a reactive depression by engaging in structured activities, by taking a pill, or by doing both. Furthermore, within any category of problem one may find some cases in which client action is sufficient to effect solutions and others in which it is not. Some problem drinkers can shut off or control their alcoholic intake; others cannot. In general, a problem that is *potentially* resolvable through the client's action falls within the domain of the present framework; even though the action in particular cases may not prove sufficient to solve the problem.

Specificity

The model is addressed to target problems that are relatively specific. Problem specificity is always a matter of degree; we have not yet developed precise criteria by which we can determine how much is optimal. Our aim is not to rule out problems that are globally stated at the outset but rather to try to break down such problems into reasonably clear, manageable units before beginning intervention.

A problem may be considered specific if it is explicitly defined and delimited. To be specific, a problem should be spelled out in terms of its particulars, that is, referents at a low level of abstraction. To say simply that a father and son "have a disturbed relationship" is to make a global statement of their problem. The statement becomes more specific when the interactions that make up their difficulty are more explicitly defined: for example, "they quarrel over the son's use of the family car." Additional specificity is obtained if we observe that quarreling over the car occurs about twice a week when the son wants to use it to drive to a nearby city to visit a girl friend. This level of explicitness might be considered sufficient for purposes of a working definition of the problem, though more detail might be desirable: what they say to one another, for example. Similar explications are in order when the problem involves feelings or environmental circumstances. If a person is depressed, one wants to know what he is depressed about, how often, and so on. If a tenant is dissatisfied with her apartment, what specifically is bothering her? Noise? Lack of heat?

Certain problems are broad in scope. Their explication might result in an extensive enumeration of particulars. A second requirement for specificity involves limits in the range of the problem. To take our earlier example, the problem of father-son interaction might be spelled out in terms of a large number of referents that could be grouped into particular problem areas. Our conception of a target problem in the case would relate to one of these areas—quarreling over the car, father's upset over the son's smoking, and so on. Although it would be possible to define more than one problem in their interaction, the difficulty in their relationship as a whole would not be viewed as the problem.

Global definitions of problems may be of value in isolating some general area of difficulty but are too vague and imprecise to serve as a guide to the kind of problem-solving action a person might take. If someone acknowledges that his problem is his inability to get along with his peers, that is a beginning step; but it does not give him much of a clue about how his relationships might be bettered. Problems put at a more specific level are more informative. If the same individual were to say that he tends to be overly critical of his peers' work or that his boasting about his accomplishments tends to drive them off, then he has stated his problems so as to suggest possible courses of remedial action.

We assume that clinical efforts to assist the client's problem-solving actions are more effective when addressed to relatively specific problems. This assumption has received a good deal of support from research on the outcomes of interpersonal treatment (Reid and Shyne 1969; Mullen and Dumpson 1972). Generally, when the effectiveness of treatment has been clearly demonstrated through controlled studies, the problems dealt with have been rather specifically defined as particular behaviors, symptoms, relational difficulties, and the like (Sloane et al. 1975). Because of limits on the effectiveness of treatment methods at their current stage of development, we can perhaps help people resolve "small" problems but not "large" ones. It makes sense, I think, to expand the scope of our interventions gradually through demonstrable success with limited difficulties—at a level at which the effects of treatment processes can be more clearly perceived. Bringing about change in a specific problem may in fact be a strategic route to the alleviation of more general concerns. As Perlman has observed: "The more beset the ego the narrower its capacity for coping. Thus some carved out piece of what is often felt as an overwhelming larger problem is less threatening to the person who has it; it feels more manageable to him. Within that piece it is usually possible to find a miniature representation of the whole" (1970, p. 149).

Problems as Unsatisfied Wants

Up to this point we have mentioned characteristics that problems must have in order to be regarded as a legitimate target of task-centered treatment. Having isolated such problems, we shall examine their ingredients more thoroughly.

Almost everyone would agree that a person who acknowledges a problem is dissatisfied: with his own feelings or behavior, with the behavior of others, with his life situation, and so on. But dissatisfaction can be experienced only if one has some sense that things can be different. A person who is dissatisfied, then, *wants* something that he is not getting. Therefore, an unsatisfied want is a necessary condition for an acknowledged problem. If there is no want, there is no problem. Two overweight persons may weigh exactly the same, but one may be experiencing a problem of "being too fat" because he wants to be thinner; the other may not be concerned about his corpulence because he has no wish to lose weight.

This is not to say that a problem can be reduced completely to a frustrated desire. As will be shown, problems must also have reference to unwanted conditions, such as the excess poundage in the example above, which can be objectively described. The essential point is that these conditions only have *meaning* for problem description when the person experiences them as undesirable.

The concept of a *want,* which is central to this way of understanding problems, merits analysis. The concept, used by Thorndike (1935), among others, to describe an individual's strivings or motives, has been recently elaborated in detail by Goldman (1970). A want may be usually thought of as a cognitive-affective event consisting of an idea that something is desirable and a feeling of tension associated with not having it. But a want may also be expressed in negative terms—as a wish to be rid of something seen as undesirable. A want can always be recalled and described to others in words. "I want to feel better about myself"; "I want my husband to talk to me more"; "I want to improve my school grades"; "I want my wife to stop nagging me."

When a want is experienced without means of satisfaction at hand or in sight, one has the sensation of "having a problem." In the course of everyday living, countless problems are sensed and, in one fashion or another, resolved. I want to be on time for an appointment, but in driving there I encounter a traffic jam and with it the realization that my want is jeopardized—a traffic problem. I try to make up lost time by driving faster when I get the chance, but when I finally reach my destination I cannot find a place to park—a parking problem. I arrive a few minutes late and receive an unexpected frosty greeting from a person I normally want to please—an interpersonal problem. And so on.

In some instances problems arise because a want is experienced and then blocked. (I wanted to find a parking place but could not.) In others, the want is consciously experienced after it has been blocked. Thus, I sense a problem when greeted in an unexpectedly cold fashion when I arrive late. I do not arrive with a conscious wish to please this person but have rather a general desire to do so, which is expressed from time to time in consciousness. The realization of being greeted coldly brings this want to consciousness. The extent to which we want something is often appreciated only when we are deprived of it, a sentiment summed up by the common expression: "I did not realize how much it meant to me until. . . ." To put the distinction in Goldman's terms, wants can be "occurrent," that is, occurring in one's consciousness, or "standing," that is, having been experienced and open to being reexperienced but not occupying one's attention at the moment. One can recall standing wants, however, when asked about them. In the psychoanalytic framework, they are preconscious rather than unconscious.

The unsatisfied wants that define psychosocial problems that clients bring to social workers or agree to work on tend to be persistently occurrent. In other words, they occupy a good deal of the client's attention much of the time. And they occur with sufficient intensity to prompt the client to seek the social worker's help.

The inability to satisfy a persistent and intense want normally produces some degree of emotional distress, usually self-labeled as feelings of frustration, anger, anxiety, or depression. The particular negative affect associated with a problem will depend on what the want means to the person. Usually the emotional distress is perceived as distinct from, and secondary to, the blocking of a particular want. Thus, a student may be anxious about whether or not he will pass, a worker may be depressed over his job performance, or a father angered over his son's taking drugs. The student, worker, and father would doubtlessly see their distress as being relieved if they could get what they wanted. In some cases, however, the upset itself may be in the focus of attention, such as when a person cannot identify external causes of his wants. In such cases the person wants simply to be rid of the unpleasant emotions. He may not be clear as to why he is upset but knows that he wants to feel better.

The operational definition of a want would require a self-description of what the person desires. In this way the concept of a want differs from such concepts as "motivation" and "drive" when they are used to define inner processes from the perspective of outside observers. For example, one can study a person's motivation through inferences made about his behavior. A want is close to (though not synonymous with) a "need" when the latter is an expression of the person's wishes, as in "I need a job," but not when "need" is used to express an outsider's evaluation of what a person should have, as in "He needs help."

This distinction is particularly important given the traditional emphasis in social work on the second meaning of "need." Historically, social work programs have been based on professional and agency conceptions of the needs of different classes of people—the poor, the mentally ill, delinquents, troubled families, and so on. In the process, not enough attention, in my judgment, has been paid to what people *want*. It is hoped that the central position given to wants in the present framework will help serve as a corrective to one of the primary occupational hazards of social work—acting on the basis of what we think is good for clients.

A focus on wants rather than needs may give us a different perspective on the "unmotivated client." Usually, he is unmotivated to be what social workers or others believe he ought to be. He lacks "motivation" to be a better spouse or parent, or to be more law-abiding. To our dismay we see vast numbers of people who do not have motives for self-betterment, as we define it.

While many clients lack motivation in these terms, few lack wants. If the client's wants are our concern, then the essential questions become: What does the person want? Can we help him get it? Should we do so? Should we try to create wants he does not have? If so, by what means? Such questions are not easily answered, but they may help clarify our position and thinking about the many people who are less than enthusiastic about our efforts to help them.

The definition of problems as unsatisfied wants serves more general functions. It helps provide an explanation for the common observation that psychosocial problems are an inevitable fact of human existence. Externally defined needs can be met, but wants never cease—when one is satisfied, another usually takes its place. A young man may desperately want to marry a particular woman. ("She's all I want in the world.") Once this want is satisfied, others will arise. ("I want her to learn how to play golf"; "I want her to go with me on Sundays to have dinner with my parents.") If one is fortunate and resourceful, he may get most of what he wants but usually not all, or forever. Wants that cannot be satisfied become the problems of life.

The notion of problems as unsatisfied wants may also help explain why acknowledged problems, as we have previously argued, tend to be short-lived (Reid and Epstein 1972). From the perspective of an outside observer, a problematic condition may appear to remain constant over a long period of time, but what a person affected by the condition *wants* to do about it may fluctuate considerably. He may accept it for a period, want to change it for another period, then accept it again. Or he may bring about small changes in the condition (imperceptible to an outsider) that may eliminate his wanting to change it further. As wants wax and wane, so do perceived problems. All of this fits well, of course, into a rationale for short-term service programs.

Finally, stress on wants forces attention from the beginning on the kind of change that the client expects would alleviate the problem. What the client is striving for can be made clear. The problem can then be analyzed in terms of desired changes and what may be involved in obtaining them. It may then be modified or reformulated in the light of the kind of change that seems possible to achieve. In general, the direction is charted for work toward feasible solutions that will prove satisfying to the client.

Constrained Wants

A want, as the term is used here, is not necessarily what a person might desire in the absence of constraints. It is, rather, a signal that a given action, object, and so on, is desirable under whatever circumstances prevail. This point can be seen most clearly in actions taken under duress. In general, a person acts under duress when he faces limited alternatives, none of which may be desirable. Confronted with a Hobson's choice, he must decide which alternative he wants to pursue. Thus, a parolee decides he wants to see his parole officer (a mildly disagreeable alternative) rather than take a chance that his parole will be revoked (an even more disagreeable alternative). One might say he wanted to see his parole officer to satisfy another want—to stay out of prison.

The parolee might say, of course, "I will see him, but I really don't *want* to." This is a popular usage of the term "want," to express what we would prefer to do if we did not feel under certain constraints. We often use "want" as opposed to "have to," "ought to," "should," "must." This usage is vague, however, because it is not always possible to evaluate the influence of constraining factors on one's wishes. Suppose the parolee must see his caseworker before a certain date to maintain his parole status. With the date at hand, he may want to see his caseworker (in the popular sense of the term) and might go to any length to do so.

In the present context, a want informs the person that "X is desirable" regardless of the constraints, pressures, or other factors that may have caused this particular thought. This formulation is not to ignore the importance of these factors in human choice. Our intent is only to exclude them from the concept of "want." It becomes, then, possible to separate *what* one wants from *why* one wants it.

Acknowledged problems may then be said to be the expression of unsatisfied wants that are shaped by constraints of various kinds. A youngster may want to improve his grades in order to please his parents, or an abusive father may want to control his aggression against his child because of an agency's threat to remove the child from his home if he does not. It is important to understand how such pressures influence wants. A want resulting from constraint will disappear when the constraint is removed, thus putting an end to the acknowledged problem. In general, wants that are dependent upon external constraints (pressures from family members, agencies, and the like) tend to be unstable and short-lived. Such wants are real, however, and can produce genuine problem change.

So far we have discussed situations in which the client *wants* to change some fundamentally troublesome condition, even though his desire may result from some constraint. A client so motivated should be distinguished from one who wants *only* to placate those putting pressure on him to change. His acknowledged problem (if he were to reveal it) might be expressed simply in terms of getting someone "off his back," and he might be expected to act accordingly, for example, by giving a false impression of change. To illustrate the distinction, suppose in one case an alcoholic husband wanted to stop drinking to preserve his marriage. Although his want arises from constraint, it still pushes him in the direction of forsaking alcohol. Another alcoholic husband may want only to keep his wife from scolding him about his drinking. His want directs him toward actions that would reduce the scolding, not necessarily the drinking.

In many cases, of course, it is the practitioner himself whom the client wants to appease. This situation arises most frequently in work with socially deviant persons (such as delinquents or neglectful parents) in which the practitioner has a legal obligation to supervise the client's activities. The social worker becomes the problem if the person's unsatisfied want is essentially the worker's presence in his life. His problem-solving actions are then directed, logically enough, toward eliminating this presence, rather than toward the goals the worker has in mind.

Such acknowledged problems are acceptable within the framework of the model, although it must be recognized that their solution may bring about only temporary change that might leave a number of interested others, including the practitioner, dissatisfied. This kind of problem definition is presumably reached after attempts have been made to persuade the client to accept a definition that would lodge the problem at least to some extent in his own behavior. The choice, then, becomes either to work with the client on very limited terms or not at all.

"I'm Glad You Didn't Listen to Me"

Sometimes, when a practitioner ignores a client's express wants and proceeds according to his own conception of what the client needs or what is best for him, the client later recognizes that the practitioner was "right" after all. He may say that the practitioner helped him realize what he really wanted or that he appreciates whatever is now different about his life. Such occurrences naturally raise questions about the validity of our position. I would argue, however, that they are infrequent and that the good they exemplify is outweighed by the mischief resulting when the client's expressed wants are brushed aside. The number of clients who were glad they weren't listened to is dwarfed, I think, by the number who say later, "My social worker did not give me the kind of help I wanted." That kind of complaint at least emerges with some force from several assessments of social treatment (Lake and Levinger 1960; Mayer and Timms 1970; Silverman 1970). It is hard to find other than anecdotal evidence attesting to the satisfaction of clients whose wishes were not followed.

Manifestations of the Problem

As noted earlier, a problem is more than an unsatisfied want. A problem must also be defined in relation to the conditions that are deemed to be undesirable. These conditions spell out the manifestations or content of the problem—the reality that needs to be changed in order for the want to be satisfied. They may describe the client's overt behavior, private events, or his life situation. What happens and when are the essential questions. A man is not doing well on his job and wants to do better. His wanting to do better is necessary to make his job performance an acknowledged problem. But in order for the problem to be adequately defined, we would need to know about the particular aspects of his performance he is dissatisfied with.

A problem, then, refers to a set of conditions a client wants to change. It may be operationally defined through an oral or written statement of these conditions. A problem may be summarized through a problem statement—a single sentence that states the conditions to be altered, with the client as subject of the sentence. This grammatical form helps to put the problem in terms of the conditions the client finds undesirable, whether or not he is responsible for them.

Thus:

Miss A does not have an adequate social life.
Mr. B has been refused public assistance even though he appears to be eligible.
Mrs. C constantly loses her temper with her daughter.

In the present framework, such statements always refer to what the person (the subject of the sentence) wants altered. If Miss A did not want a fuller social life, if Mr. B did not wish to receive public assistance, or Mrs. C did not desire to control her temper with her daughter, their problem statements would be invalid. Although imprecise, the problem statement provides a shorthand expression of the problem for purposes of convenience in communication.

The next part of the operational definition is a more complete and more precise delineation of the specific conditions to be changed. For example, in the case of Miss A, specification would consist of a delineation of present inadequacies in her social life and might include specific data on number and type of friends and the frequency and nature of her social activities. For a condition to be included, one would need to establish her desire to change it. But one would not include possible indicators of inadequate social activity (such as lack of membership in organizations) if that particular lack was of no concern to her.

Common and Interdependent Problems

Problems have been defined thus far as individual phenomena. Much clinical practice, however, is concerned with problems that involve more than one person. Our framework must, therefore, be extended.

Two or more individuals may acknowledge the same kind of problem, one that is an expression of similar unsatisfied wants. A husband and wife want to pay off their debts, or parents may be dissatisfied with their child's situation at school. Such difficulties may be thought of as *common problems,* even though there may be significant variations in how they are perceived by the individuls who share them.

Frequently, however, individuals have problems that are clearly different in character but are so intertwined that the fate of one controls the fate of the other. Problems of this kind may be regarded as *interdependent.* Examples abound in family interaction. A wife may define her problem as her husband's not backing her up when she disciplines the children. The husband sees a problem in her being an overly severe disciplinarian. In this kind of situation, the *acknowledged* problem of each partner is a problem attributed to the other. It is also clear that the solution of one problem may well be dependent upon the solution of the other: the wife may only act differently if the husband does.

Calling this entangled set of difficulties simply a problem of human interaction glosses over the inescapable fact that distinct, and in some ways quite contrary, problem definitions exist. Obviously, the two people are interacting, and, as will be shown, the concept of interaction is essential in explaining their difficulty. Nevertheless, an analysis of how each acknowledges and attributes problems is important in devising strategies to alter their actions toward each other. For example, the practitioner may try to help each partner acknowledge problems in his/her own behavior or in their interaction, or failing this, to get each to agree to act reciprocally to solve the problem of the other.

Problem Classification

The range and type of acknowledged problems addressed by the task-centered model is defined by a problem-classification system originally presented in Reid and Epstein (1972). A condensed, revised version of the typology is presented below. The revised scheme is given in greater detail in appendix I, together with data on its reliability as a coding instrument.

1. *Interpersonal conflict.* Problems centered on the interaction of persons. For this category to apply, the persons affected must define the problem in terms of their interaction—"We fight all the time"; "We don't get along." Subtypes include marital, parent-child, sibling, peer, and teacher-student conflict.

2. *Dissatisfaction in social relations.* The client is dissatisfied over some aspect of his relations with others in general or with some particular person. Unlike problems of interpersonal conflict, the difficulty is located in one person (the client): the client may center the problem in himself ("I don't have enough friends"; "I am too aggressive with others") or on the behavior of others toward him ("Other kids pick on me"; "My wife nags me all the time").

3. *Problems with formal organizations.* Difficulties in the cient's relations with such organizations as agencies, hospitals, residential institutions, and schools ("The court is on my back"; "They won't let me return to school").

4. *Difficulty in role performance.* The client's main concern is his difficulty in carrying out an ascribed social role to his satisfaction ("I can't hack math"; "I need to learn how to control my children"). Such

types are differentiated according to the role involved; such as parent, spouse, employee, student.

5. *Decision problems*. Problems in reaching particular decisions, usually involving contemplated change in a role or social situation ("I don't know if I should stay in school or drop out"; "We have to decide whether or not to have another child").

6. *Reactive emotional distress*. Problems centered on emotional upsets precipitated by some event or situation ("I'm down because I have lost my job"; "I'm worried about my health"). Major subtypes are depression and anxiety.

7. *Inadequate resources*. Lack of money, food, housing, transportation, child care, job, or other tangible resource.

8. *Psychological or behavioral problems not elsewhere classified*. A residual category that includes habit disorders, addictive behavior, phobic reactions, concerns about self-image, and thought disturbances. Problems placed here cannot be classified in preceding categories and should meet other criteria previously discussed—client acknowledgment, capability of being relieved through independent action, and specificity.

Two categories merit comment. "Decision problems" (5) replaces "problems of social transition" in the original scheme. It was found that the key, distinguishing element in problems involving change in a role or situation was the client's need to make decisions about contemplated changes. Other problems involving social transitions could be more conveniently classified under other categories—such as problems in role performance or inadequate resources. The final category, also an addition, was needed to classify problems not originally included that practitioners using the model were nonetheless treating, often with apparent success (Brown 1977b). Although it is not well limited, this category has not been used that often, since it receives only problems that cannot be more specifically classified. Eventually it needs to be replaced with more discriminating categories.

The typology has proved most useful in providing a general map of the territory covered by the model and in classifying cases for instructional and research purposes (see, for example, Grinnel and Kyte 1975; Ewalt 1977; Brown 1977b). As a clinical tool, its chief utility has been to help practitioners clarify complex problem situations, locate specific problems, and define these problems in ways that may suggest possible courses of remedial action. The scheme's usefulness for clinical purposes is illustrated by the case of Mr. and Mrs. Harris. Mr. Harris sought help at a family agency "in a panic" because his wife had just "walked out," leaving him with the care of their two young children. In a subsequent joint interview, it was revealed that her leaving was precipitated by his procrastination in breaking off a year-long affair. She was not sure she wanted to remain married to him in any event, given the many long-standing difficulties in their relationship. Mr. Harris, in turn, maintained that these difficulties had "pushed" him into the affair. His wife was unwilling, however, to agree to work on these issues until he gave up his girl friend. The problem-classification scheme proved helpful in sorting out these interrelated problems and arriving at a treatment plan. Mrs. Harris agreed that, whatever her husband did regarding the girl friend, she had to reach a decision about whether or not to return to give the marriage another try. Mr. Harris, anxious to get his wife back, saw his immediate problem as breaking off with the girl friend and demonstrating in other ways to his wife that the marriage was worth saving. Accordingly, it was agreed that the partners would work on their different problems in a series of separate sessions: Mrs. Harris on her decision problem; Mr. Harris on his acknowledged deficiencies in carrying out his role as husband. With the categories of the system in mind, the practitioner was able to move quickly to help the Harrises formulate their problem in these terms. Without such a scheme, the practitioner might have made a premature effort to treat the problem as if it were simply one of interpersonal conflict.

The usefulness of such systems is limited, however, by the state of knowledge about psychosocial problems and the kind of processes necessary to resolve them. At present, we often do not know enough to help clients disentangle complex problem situations, particularly those involving elements of several categories. As they stand, the problem categories tend to be too global to be of great use in mapping intervention strategies. Although these categories can be broken down into subcategories, it is frequently hard to discern what the breakdowns should be or, more importantly, what interventions should be used with particular subunits. These limitations notwithstanding, we need, I think, to continue the process of developing more discrete problem categories and intervention strategies to accompany them.

To illustrate the kind of specification that is needed, consider one subcategory: difficulty in role performance, student. This classification comprises a vast assortment of distinguishable difficulties. In breaking this category down, we might begin by sorting out the student's role at different levels (grade school, high school, college). Taking the grade school branch, we find such difficulties as poor academic performance and disruptive behavior in class. Under the former categories can be located such problems as poor study habits at home, inattentiveness in the classroom, and learning difficulties in relation to particular subjects. At this level we begin to attain a useful kind of specificity. For example, in one study (Polster 1977) poor study habits at home was in fact isolated as a specific problem and an intervention package addressed to the problem was designed and implemented (with good results).

This problem-classification strategy could produce hundreds of specific problem categories along the various branches of the system. The numbers of entities should not necessarily be a cause for dismay, confusion, or retreat. The multitudinous disorders of plants, animals, and the human body have been somehow put in order by botanists, biologists, and physicians. A beginning attempt to identify and catalogue specific problems and tasks related to them is presented in chapter 11.

Whose Problem?

However they are defined, the problems addressed by the model are the problems of clients. It may be well to make clear what is meant by a "client" within the present framework, particularly since the term is used with various and conflicting meanings to describe a variety of persons within the orbit of the social worker's attention. In current usage, a client may be someone asking for or receiving help from a practitioner; someone not seeking help but nonetheless seen by a social worker (the "involuntary client"); someone who is not seen but whose welfare is of concern to the worker (as in references to an infant being the "client" in a child-abuse case); or to sundry collections of people ("The family or community is my client"). Moreover, certain usages result in some rather remarkable anomalies. A person fighting off the overtures of a social worker tooth and nail may be nevertheless dubbed a "client," or the label may be applied to a family member who may not be at all aware of his "client" status. It is hard to justify calling either kind of person a client under commonly accepted usages of the term outside of the field of social work, especially in most professions, which define a client as one who engages the services of a professional.

Within the present framework, the designation of "client" is, strictly speaking, applied only to persons who have accepted a social worker's offer of help with problems of concern to them. Thus, a person becomes a client through an explicit contract with the practitioner. This definition is in accord with prevailing use of the term in other professions and with the value premises of the present model, which calls for social treatment to be offered only to persons who make it clear they are willing to accept it.

Our definition of the social work client is by no means novel. Perlman (1963) and Pincus and Minahan (1973), among others, have suggested similar limitations of the term. What needs to be additionally provided, however, are ways of handling the consequences that arise from an adherence to a limited definition of client.

First of all, if the concept of client is limited in the manner suggested, we then need to develop terms to describe persons in "preclient" stages of contact with the social worker. Perlman (1963) has suggested the word "applicant" be used for persons seeking help prior to the development of a contract. Perhaps another term needs to be created for the individual whom the social worker seeks out or who comes in prodded by one or another person in authority. The usual designation "involuntary client" would be a contradiction in terms, and "applicant" would be obviously misleading since there is nothing he is applying for. I would suggest, for want of anything more descriptive, the term "respondent," since the person can be thought of as responding to the social worker's exploration of his situation or offers of help.

The limited concept of client may help clear up some of the fuzziness about who is the client in work with families. Thus, if an offer of help is accepted by only one member of a family, only that member would be considered a client, even though other family members may be seen as collaterals for purposes of obtaining information needed in work with the client. To refer vaguely to all members of a family as clients in such a situation may result in confusion in the practitioner's purposes, since he may think (erroneously in my judgment) that it is incumbent upon him to help all members of the family with whatever problems he may regard them as possessing, or may pursue some ill-defined goal having to do with "improved family functioning" or the like. As I shall argue subsequently, the practitioner should usually try to involve other family members *as clients* if the problem presented to him is family-related. But if he cannot, or does not, he should be clear about who his client is and consequently about whose problems he is trying to resolve. Only if more than one family member becomes a client can one properly refer, I think, to working with a "client system."

The restriction on the term "client" within the task-centered framework helps clarify the status of persons who have not agreed to accept help as well as the social worker's role with such persons. With an individual in an applicant status, the practitioner's immediate function is to determine what kind of help he wants and how this can be provided. For a person designated a respondent, the social worker needs to provide a rationale for any contact beyond the initial encounter. Sustained work with respondents— for example, in correctional or child-protection settings—would fall outside the present system of practice.

Although these discriminations between "clients" and "non-clients" may be enlightening, they create a terminological difficulty: we are left without a generic term to describe a person who may be occupying any of the statuses we have just described: applicant, respondent, or client. Given the discriminations among terms that have been suggested, the semantically correct solution would be to invent a new generic term for applicant-respondent-client. A more practical solution, and the one I shall adopt, is to retain the term "client" for this purpose. Since this usage is so embedded in the vocabulary of social workers, it sems unlikely that any novel term would prevail. I will still limit this usage, however, to the generic case of persons who may be at various stages of the engagement process. Thus, any reference to a client in this generic sense, as in "how the client perceives the social worker is always an important consideration," will denote clients (in the narrower sense), applicants, and respondents. When more careful discriminations need to be made, the stricter meaning of client will be employed, as in, "After an initial discussion of her problems with the social worker, Mrs. A decided not to become his client." The context of usage should make it clear to which meaning the statement pertains. Although the term remains somewhat ambiguous, it has been shorn of several confusing and imprecise referents.

Chapter 4
Problem Formation and Resolution

If the role of the task-centered practitioner is to help clients resolve psychosocial problems, he should understand the forces that either facilitate or impede problem resolution. In keeping with the orientation of the model, my focus will be on factors promoting or retarding actions the client may take to alleviate his problems. I shall not attempt to present a comprehensive, detailed theory, but rather a limited set of formulations that may be useful in themselves and may serve as a basis for organizing much larger and more complete bodies of knowledge.

The development of this theory has been guided by two assumptions that should be made explicit. First, it was assumed that the theory would be most useful if it attempted to elucidate factors underlying both problem causation and strategies of remediation. One might then avoid the dichotomy identified by Fischer (1978) between "causal knowledge" and "intervention knowledge." In arguing, correctly I think, for greater stress on the knowledge of the latter type, Fischer observes (also correctly) that knowledge of the causes of a problem does not provide one with the conceptual tools to solve it. In fact, causal knowledge may not be necessary at all if a definition of the problem itself suggests an effective solution. It is not necessary to learn why a man is drowning in order to know enough to throw him a rope. Certain problems have standard or commonsense solutions that may be applied regardless of cause; moreover, intervention knowledge, even if limited, may be more advanced than knowledge of causation.

Causal knowledge becomes important when it helps one

choose and shape courses of remedial action. Thus, if a child is having difficulty concentrating in class, it may be essential to know if the reason for his inattentiveness is lack of sleep or lack of comprehension of the subject matter. Yet, for the clinician, such knowledge of problem causation is useful only to the extent that it can be related to intervention knowledge; we need to know what to do about the "cause." These two kinds of knowledge can be brought together most effectively, I think, through a theory concerned with how problems get resolved *and* the obstacles that prevent their resolution. In this formulation, knowledge of obstacles is equivalent to knowledge of causation. A cause of a problem can be thought of as whatever is preventing its resolution. The crucial question is not what brought the problem about but rather what is keeping it active.

The potential range of factors that might facilitate or impair problem resolution is almost limitless. To develop an encompassable theory useful in clinical work, I decided to emphasize those factors susceptible to the combined influence of client and practitioner, that is, those that might be considered modifiable through their interventions. Thus, causes of problems embedded in the history of the individual, in his genetic and physical makeup, or in broad social and economic forces may be beyond the power of either to affect. While in certain situations it may be as important to know what cannot be altered as what can be, priority must be given to understanding what *can* be changed if the practitioner is to move promptly and efficiently to help the client bring about desired changes. It is proposed that modifiable factors can be found in the client's current wants, beliefs, emotions, actions, and in the social system of which he is a part. Although these elements influence one another in a reciprocal manner, for the sake of orderly exposition they will be taken up seriatim.

Wants and Motivation

It is commonly accepted that a person's motivation for change is a central factor in actions he will take to resolve his problem. In our framework, motivation arises principally from the unsatisfied want that defines the problem. This conception is similar to Ripple's definition of motivation as "what the person wants and how much he wants it" (1964, p. 25). In a series of studies, Ripple found that motivation defined in these terms was the single best predictor of case outcome.

Motivation, as Ripple's definition suggests, has two aspects: *direction* (what the person wants) and *strength* (how much he wants it). The direction of motivation needs to be examined in relation to the feasibility of the client's obtaining what he wants. A want may be intense but unrealizable. The strength of a person's motivation must be evaluated in relation to the problem at hand. We do not ask, "How well is the client motivated?" but rather, "How strong is his motivation for resolving a particular problem?" Even when so limited, the strength of motivation is not easily assessed. Perhaps our best evidence is obtained in clinical work by asking the client how much he wants whatever it is that would resolve his problem and by carefully attending to his answer.

In assessing motivation, the want defining the problem must be seen in relation to other wants that might either facilitate or interfere with problem-solving actions. Standing wants for effectance or mastery (White 1963) and for approval from others are among those that may augment the want directly related to the problem. A mother wishes to resolve a conflict with her son not only because she wants a better relationship but to prove to herself and others that she can master the difficulty. The value of such motivation is sometimes discounted in clinical work because it may be seen as producing temporary or false solutions to the problem. But to the extent that it augments a want unique to the problem itself, it can become a constructive force for change.

Other wants may also conflict with problem-solving actions. The want that defines the problem may be overshadowed by another or may be realizable only at the frustration of another. A father wants to regain custody of his children, but he also wants to be free of the responsibilities of fatherhood. An addict wants to kick the habit but has from time to time an irresistible desire (occurrent want) for the drug. Because wants may be contradictory, we cannot say that the want defining a problem will necessarily lead to sustained action to resolve it. It must compete with others in the welter of motives that drive the human organism.

Conflicted wants explain why many psychosocial problems are not satisfactorily resolved. Obstacles created by such conflicts are not always, of course, modifiable by either the practitioner or client. To the extent they are, modification must generally take place through the individual's belief system, as will be subsequently made clear.

Beliefs

Although wants initiate action, how the action is carried out depends on how a person views himself and his world. These views, as we shall see, in turn shape the wants themselves.

Nature of Beliefs

Following the work of Goldman (1970), Murray and Jacobson (1971), Bem (1970), and others, I have chosen the concept of *belief*—or *belief system*—to depict these views. In the present usage beliefs comprise self-concepts as well as constructions of external phenomena—in general, the individual's storehouse of perceptions, knowledge, expectations, hopes, and opinions.

The totality of a person's beliefs corresponds closely to Miller, Galanter, and Pribram's notion of an image (1960):

> The Image is all the accumulated, organized knowledge that the organism has about itself and its world. The Image consists of a great deal more than imagery of course. What we have in mind when we use the term is essentially the same kind of private representation that other cognitive theorists have demanded. It includes everything that organism has learned—his values as well as his facts—organized by whatever concepts, images or relations he has been able to master. [p. 17]

A belief system is also close to Frank's assumptive world. As Frank has put it:

> In order to be able to function, everyone must impose an order and regularity on the welter of experience impinging upon him. To do this, he develops out of his personal experiences a set of more or less implicit assumptions about himself and the nature of the world in which he lives, which enables him to predict the behavior of others and the outcome of his own actions. The totality of each person's assumptions may be conveniently termed his "assumptive world."
>
> This is a short-hand expression for a highly structured, complex, interacting set of values, expectations, and images of oneself and others, which guide and in turn are guided by a person's perceptions and behavior and which are closely related to his emotional states and his feelings of well-being. [1974, p. 27]

The basic unit of analysis in this scheme is the individual belief, which may be thought of as a statement a person might make to himself or others that could logically begin with "I believe." For example, I believe that the world is round, that physical violence is wrong, that I will be unhappy if my work is ignored. Beliefs, like wants, can be represented, and hence operationalized, by verbal statements. I assume that people can tell us what they believe through their own statements or through their responses to prepared statements, as in objective tests. There are always uncertainties, of course, over the correspondence between such statements and the cognitive events they purportedly represent.

Beliefs may be based on what one perceives to be facts (factual beliefs) or, as Bem (1970) observes, may be value judgments (evaluative beliefs). Factual beliefs are in the nature of hypotheses about external reality or of one's own capacity that can ultimately be tested by some form of data gathering. A mother's belief that her son is taking drugs can be so tested, even though it may be difficult to obtain the necessary information. An evaluative belief expresses judgments about what is good, bad, undesirable, desirable, and so forth, and hence is not directly capable of empirical verification. One cannot use data to verify whether or not a person is unworthy or whether or not he should behave in a certain way. Evaluative beliefs may be based in part, however, on beliefs that can be tested. For example, the evaluative belief that someone is "vicious" may rest on factual beliefs about that person's conduct.

The concept of belief provides a building block from which other cognitive concepts can be constructed. A belief about the probability of the occurrence of an event may be thought of as an "expectancy" (Rotter, Chance, and Phares 1972). The belief that a person occupying a particular social position should act in a particular way becomes a "role expectation." Evaluative beliefs describe the cognitive component (the aspect usually measured) of attitudes (Bem 1970). More generally, the concepts of belief and belief system serve to link the present theory to a broad and active field of theory building and research in cognitive processes (Korman 1974; Mahoney 1974).

Beliefs and Wants

Wants are well-known shapers of beliefs, a relation aptly suggested in the phrase "wishful thinking." Less apparent, but perhaps more important, is the influence of beliefs on wants. Most wants of a social character have their origins in our belief systems. Thus, what we want from our spouses, parents, friends, and others who occupy vital social positions in our lives is largely determined by beliefs about what they can and should do for us. If Mr. A believes a wife ought to be primarily a homemaker, he may want his spouse to remain at home and care for the children. If Mr. B believes a wife should contribute to the family income, then he may want his spouse to seek employment.

It follows, therefore, that a change in a person's beliefs can produce a change in his wants. This principle underlies much of the effort expended to motivate individuals to change. Consider a high school student who is failing a subject without apparent concern about the consequences. We may try to activate a standing want, say to "be somebody," by trying to persuade him that passing the subject will increase his opportunity for success by enabling him to graduate and get a job or to go to college. If he begins to indicate that he wants to do better in the subject, we may try to increase or sustain his motivation through nurturing beliefs that he can succeed; that he will be able to get help, and so forth. Through such means we attempt to create belief structures—consisting of perceived incentives and rationales for acting on a problem—that will foster or maintain motivation.

Similarly, we attempt to affect wants that may be unrealizable. A widowed mother wants her socially active 18-year-old son to stay home in the evening and be a companion to her. There is little chance he will do this. Her want is in part a product of her lack of other relationships but is also influenced by her belief that a grown son should sacrifice his own interests for his mother's welfare. An attempt to affect this belief is made through raising questions about the legitimacy of her expectations.

If wants are to be affected in clinical work, the means of influence is necessarily through the belief system. Just as there is no disputing tastes, there is no disputing wants, at least not directly. We do not accept others' definition of what we want but may find our wants affected by redefinition of what we think is true.

Beliefs as Guides to Action

Beliefs provide the intelligence that guide problem-solving action. Having experienced a want, we depend on our cognitive system to provide directions for its satisfaction. One set of beliefs that may be brought into play concerns how problems in general may be best solved. A person's beliefs may follow some standard rational problem-solving paradigm, like Dewey's (1938) or the one set forth in the present volume (when faced with a problem, one should spell it out, then come up with alternative solutions, etc.). Or one's beliefs about how to solve problems in general may be highly idiosyncratic (when faced with a problem, the first thing to do is talk it over with my sister). We really have very little idea about problem-solving paradigms that people actually use or that work best, although many of us have faith in rational approaches and try to impart them in one form or another to clients.

Whether or not a person uses such a paradigm, his actions are inevitably guided by specific beliefs about how the problem can be best solved. His beliefs may cause him to try various alternative actions on his own, to turn to others, or to challenge the validity of the want itself. Thoughts about how to solve a particular problem are in turn influenced by beliefs about the importance of the problem and the possible consequences of various solutions. Man does not view a problem in isolation but rather in the context of a larger system of wants and beliefs. A person searches for modes of action that will solve the problem in a way that will not jeopardize his other interests. Practitioners would hasten to add, "in a way that should not unduly jeopardize the interests of others."

Within this context, beliefs may be either functional or dysfunctional as guides to action. Beliefs are functional if they lead to action that alleviates the present difficulty without creating others; dysfunctional if they have opposite consequences. A father may believe that severe physical punishment is the way to make his unruly child more obedient. The belief may be dysfunctional in relation to the immediate problem, as the harsh treatment only makes the child more disobedient. Even if the punishment curbs the behavior, it may cause the child to run away (another problem for the father) or may result in physical injury to the child, a problem of concern to the community if not the father.

Points of Leverage

It is assumed that beliefs that guide problem-solving action can be modified, that is, made more functional, through dialogues between the practitioner and client or between the practitioner and others who interact with the client. If this is to happen, the practitioner needs to be aware of certain points of leverage in belief systems—elements that can be influenced by communication processes. Several that may be of particular use in clinical work will be discussed here.

Accuracy

The accuracy of a person's beliefs refers to the correspondence between them and some definition of reality. The match between one's cognitive map of the world and the world itself has been given a prominent place in various clinical theories. As Frank puts it: "For a person to be able to function successfully and enjoy life, his assumptive world must correspond to conditions as they actually are. For it is only to the extent that a person can successfully predict the results of his acts that he can behave in such a way to maximize chances for success and minimize those for failure" (1974, p. 30). Beck (1970) gives central importance to "idiosyncratic cognitions" as explanations of disturbed functions (p. 187). According to Beck, such cognitions "reflect a faulty appraisal, ranging from a mild distortion to a complete misinterpretation." He identifies various mechanisms that can produce distortions: *arbitrary inference* (the process of drawing a conclusion when evidence is lacking or actually contrary to the conclusion); *overgeneralization* (the process of making an unjustified generalization on the basis of a single incident); and *magnification* (the propensity to exaggerate the meaning or significance of a particular event).

Erroneous beliefs can misguide problem-solving action. A handicapped man does not apply for certain jobs, believing that he would not be hired because of his handicap, whereas in fact the firms in question would not regard his disability as disqualifying. Additionally, false conceptions can help create and maintain problems: the patient who believes he has a dread disease despite lack of physical symptoms or medical evidence; the wife who believes her husband "never does anything around the house" although there is tangible evidence to the contrary; the pretty teen-ager who thinks others find her unattractive.

Accuracy applies to factual rather than evaluative beliefs. In theory it is possible to obtain objective evidence on the validity of the client's beliefs. In practice, however, adequate evidence may be difficult to obtain. Use must be made of inferences, often those based on what the clients reveal about reality in their dialogues with the practitioner. And, of course, the practitioner must rely on his judgment about what constitutes "reality." Despite such limitations, it should be possible, in many instances, to gather sufficient evidence about salient current beliefs and to reach assessments that other observers would agree with. The practitioner can then proceed to make use of methods (to be presented in chapter 7) for correcting whatever cognitive distortions have been identified.

Although the accuracy criterion does not apply to evaluative beliefs, such beliefs may be supported by distorted perceptions of reality. In this sort of configuration, an analysis of the inaccuracies in the client's perceptions can provide the groundwork for altering, indirectly, the evaluative belief. A depressed person views himself as worthless. This self-evaluation is based, in part, on the assertion that he has accomplished nothing of merit. His belief about lack of accomplishment may be tested through an examination of what, in fact, he has accomplished. A mother's belief that her son, a fifth-grader, should spend at least two hours each night at his studies may be based on an erroneous perception of what the school expects of children in his particular grade.

Scope

A factual belief or system of factual beliefs may be thought of as informing a person about a given range of phenomena. His beliefs may be accurate in the sense that they can be empirically validated but still not reflect important aspects of reality. The distinction, perhaps, is analogous to the one made in law between the "truth" and the "whole truth."

In more operational terms, the accuracy criterion is applied to existing beliefs that can be supported, questioned, or refuted by evidence. The range or scope of a set of beliefs becomes a consideration if a belief that may be necessary or useful to solving a problem is simply not there, or not there when it matters. A mother may correctly perceive that her infant throws food on the floor but may not know that this behavior is normal.

I assume that possession of certain kinds of beliefs may be desirable if a person is to resolve certain kinds of difficulties. At this point, we have no system for identifying "missing" beliefs, but it is possible to identify some classes of belief deficits that contribute to problems. One class concerns the absence of accurate beliefs (knowledge) that might inform a person about the realities of his social or physical circumstances or of his own behavior. A client's lack of knowledge of the welfare system may be a barrier to his obtaining adequate financial assistance. Or a person with interpersonal difficulties may lack the knowledge that he engages in lengthy monologues in social conversation. It may be possible to demonstrate the fact through analysis of recordings of his conversations, but he may have no relevant belief, not even an inaccurate one, about this behavior. Deficits may occur in beliefs about future events. An important function of such beliefs is to guide future actions, a function identified by ego psychologists as foresight. We continually adjust our actions in relation to probable consequences. We restrain expressions of anger with superiors because of beliefs (usually well founded) that not to do so would have unfavorable consequences. When a person's actions repeatedly result in difficulty for him, it is quite possible he lacks a belief linking his actions to its probable consequences. This kind of lack is closely related to what Beck has identified as "cognitive deficiencies": "Patients with this deficit ignore, fail to integrate or do not utilize information derived from experience. Such a patient, consequently, behaves as though he had a deficit in his system of expectations. He consistently engages in behavior which he realizes in retrospect is self-defeating . . ." (1970, p. 191).

As the excerpt suggests, a person may hold a belief, but it does not occur at points when it might serve to guide his actions. Thus, the realization dawns, in retrospect, that certain behavior is "self-defeating." Or we may occasionally be aware that we have certain mannerisms, but this awareness does not occur when the mannerisms do. Thus the notion of a missing belief means, in effect, that the belief does not occur when it could influence action, if it exists at all. It is quite possible, of course, that a belief may be present without affecting what a person does. Some of the reasons why beliefs may not be active when needed or may have little impact will be explored in the next section.

Consistency

When a person becomes aware of a discrepancy among his beliefs, he may experience a sense of "dissonance" (Festinger 1957). In the process of trying to resolve this, his beliefs may be modified.

Depending on the nature of the inconsistency and the type of resolution effected, the process can either impede or facilitate the development of functional beliefs. Suppose I have a strong belief that I perform a particular job extremely well. If I make a gross error, I may, initially, be struck by the belief that I have made a mistake. To resolve this incongruity, I may distort the latter belief by attributing the error to factors beyond my control or may minimize it by not giving it serious attention or by putting it out of my mind altogether. The resolution may have negative consequences since I may not take steps to correct whatever produced the error.

Suppose, however, that a mother's actions are controlled by the belief that it is essential for her son, a poor student, to achieve good grades in school, and as a result she "helps" him with his homework to the point where she is practically doing it for him. While the boy enjoys some temporary advantage as a result of his mother's efforts, he is failing to achieve any mastery of his subjects. The mother may also hold an even stronger belief that it is important for people, her son included, to be able to do things on their own but may not associate this belief with the other. In this case, an awareness of the discrepancy between beliefs and resulting resolution may have positive consequences: the mother may be more willing to let her son do his own work. Most beliefs that influence problematic action do have "opposite numbers" that if identified and articulated would create at least some sense of dissonance.

Leverage for change can be obtained by noting inconsistencies among beliefs and bringing them to a person's awareness. In this way a more functional belief can be juxtaposed with one less functional. If the former is stronger, it can be expected to modify the latter in a positive direction. Efforts can be made to increase the attractiveness of the more functional belief (and to challenge the latter) through helping the person examine the consequences of each. This process leads to the development of a new belief representing some synthesis of the two beliefs that had previously been in opposition. A busy father could not find time to spend with his children because of his belief that it was essential for him to devote almost all of his waking hours to building up his business. Among his reasons for wanting his business to succeed was his desire to give his children some of the advantages he had not had. He then recognized that these advantages might be obtained at the sacrifice of one advantage he did have in his youth—a close relationship with his own father. The inconsistency was resolved through developing a more complex, discriminating belief: that it was important to achieve a balance between meeting both the material and emotional needs of his children.

The consistency theories have spawned a considerable amount of research that might inform a problem-oriented practice theory (Korman 1974). But there is particular need for work that can translate propositions and data on belief consistency into forms that can be applied to interpersonal helping processes. Some beginning efforts are discussed in Johnson and Matross (1975).

Emotion

Affective states may be viewed as a product of the interaction of beliefs and wants. An *emotion* is an expression of how the attainment of a want is evaluated. Different evaluations will lead to different affective reactions. A belief that something wanted may not be obtained or that something not wanted may occur will produce anxiety. A sense of despair or feelings of depression may result from the belief that something wanted has been lost. Anger may be the consequence if it is believed that unjust actions by others are the source of interference with want attainment. The perception that a want is about to be realized may bring a sense of pleasure or excitement. Various theorists have presented similar conceptions of cognitive influences on emotions (Beck 1976; Raimy 1975; Ellis 1962; Murray and Jacobson 1971).

As noted in chapter 3, all psychosocial problems have emotional aspects, whether the emotion is viewed as a concomitant of the problem ("I am doing poorly in my work and that makes me depressed") or as the problem itself ("I just feel depressed"). In either case, and in general, affects produce states in the person that are perceived as undesirable or desirable and hence augment or create wants. In some cases the affective state may be so dominant that no action occurs ("I was so scared I couldn't move"). Usually, however, some action occurs sooner or later. Whether it is functional or dysfunctional in respect to a given problem depends on the amount and character of the emotion and the relevant beliefs. I will attempt to illustrate the unfolding of these interconnected processes through the common example of test anxiety.

Let us assume a student very much wants to pass a particular examination. He believes, however, that he may not be adequately prepared. His belief that his want is in jeopardy produces anxiety. At the same time, he has the sense of having a problem since a want is threatened. That problem is something more than pure anxiety, however. It is not just that he is anxious, but that he is anxious about something—an impending event and its possible ramifications. But the anxiety can augment his want—if something wanted is threatened he may want it all the more—or may make him more alert to the threat to it. The anxiety can also create avoidance wants, causing him to do things just to reduce the unpleasant feelings, or may so preoccupy him that he does nothing. The anxiety may have then such diverse results as causing him to work harder at a higher state of alertness, propelling him into a round of parties to "take his mind off" his troubles, or just making him "sit and stew." More generally, emotions are always part of the problem, even if not its primary focus. In addition, they can serve to either mobilize or impede problem-solving action. In most interpersonal treatment approaches, the practitioner is likely to be concerned about the more distressful emotions—primarily anxiety, depression, and anger, and then chiefly as they present problems and obstacles.

Affective states can be altered through various means ranging from drugs to human interaction. Restricting our analysis to the interpersonal level, we can assume that emotions, like wants, are reached largely through the person's belief system. The use of beliefs to change emotions can be illustrated by examining the treatment process itself. The practitioner helps the client feel less anxious, depressed, or angry by affecting his beliefs about threats, losses, or transgressions. One means of doing this, as Murray and Jacobson (1971) point out, is through providing the client with disconfirming experiences. By being warm and accepting in the face of the client's emotional turmoil, for example, the practitioner disconfirms the anxious client's belief that other people are fearsome or the depressed patient's belief that he is unlikable. In addition, the practitioner structures more specific and forceful disconfirmations: the psychodynamic therapist may have the client "relive" in the treatment sessions experiences that once brought him emotional pain. An operant behaviorist might try to alter the reactions that others have when the client expresses certain emotions. Although their theories will differ, the response in either case will be designed to disconfirm the client's beliefs that certain experiences or behaviors will have certain consequences. Other means are used: beliefs that trigger emotions may be addressed through confronting, interpretative, reflective, or other verbal methods. As various studies (Frank 1974) have suggested, emotional distress can be reduced simply by giving the client the expectation that treatment is forthcoming or that it will be helpful.

Beliefs seem to play a major role in various methods of treatment that seem to rely primarily on other premises. For example, in systematic desensitization, the practitioner has the client imagine anxiety-arousing scenes in a progressive hierarchy of frightfulness while he is in a state of muscle relaxation. The procedures follow from a theory that posits that anxiety will be neutralized if anxiety-provoking stimuli are paired with an antagonistic state (muscle relaxation). Systematic desensitization appears to work, but experimental evidence (Valins and Ray 1967; Marcia, Rubin, and Efran 1969) suggests that it does so because the practitioner and procedure convey to clients the strong belief that the client is able to deal successfully with his fears. Murray and Jacobson

(1971) explain the effectiveness of the procedure as follows: "Neither muscular relaxation, nor a progressive hierarchy, nor imagined rehearsal seems essential. A variety of techniques aimed at influencing beliefs seem to be of central importance in successful desensitization" (p. 727). If beliefs provide the key to emotions, then it follows that efforts to alter affects must be directed at cognitive processes. It also follows that formulations presented earlier and elsewhere concerning the role of beliefs in psychosocial problems are germane to understanding and dealing with feelings.

Role of the Unconscious

Even before Freud, it was recognized that human beings may act for reasons outside their awareness. Freud developed this insight into a highly elaborate system of explanation of human conduct. His theory of unconscious motivation became one of the cornerstones of psychoanalytic thought and has profoundly influenced the practice of clinical social work.

The present framework has asserted the importance of wants, beliefs, and affects as determinants of action. These events have been assumed to be conscious. Do unconscious factors have any place in this scheme?

Since the present theory does not purport to explain totally human action or behavior, it is possible to posit the existence of influential psychological processes that may be outside the orbit of the individual's awareness; indeed, it seems quite sensible to do so. An understanding of these processes would then fall within the domain of a different theory—a theory of unconscious motivation.

If these processes are thought to be influential, why not include them as a part of the present theory? The main reason for not doing so is the inherent difficulty in operationalizing and studying unconscious factors, given current and foreseeable limitations in our research methodology. Individuals can scarcely give us direct reports on their unconscious processes, and it has been difficult to develop reliable objective indicators of such processes. Study of the unconscious must be, necessarily, indirect and inferential. Empirical investigation of the unconscious is possible, of course, and has been pursued through the use of projective tests and dream analysis, for example. Nevertheless, the theory of unconscious motivation, as Korman (1974) notes, is "basically untested in a research sense and perhaps is untestable in any experimental sense with human beings" (p. 23).

Not only are unconscious factors difficult to operationalize and measure, but their relevance to the daily practice of most clinical social workers may be rather tenuous. For example, Hollis (1972) has argued that "very few cases in casework agencies uncover unconscious material in the strict sense of that term" (p. 192). While she and other social work theorists in the psychoanalytic tradition give an important role to the "preconscious," the meaning of that concept is by no means clear in psychoanalytic writing, as Hollis herself acknowledges (p. 189). Moreover, a good part of the preconscious, such as "material that differs in no way from conscious material except that it is not the moment of conscious attention" (Hollis 1972, p. 192), would be considered to be conscious within the present framework.

A conviction that human action was predominantly motivated by unconscious forces—that a person's conscious wants and beliefs were largely epiphenomenal—would be incompatible with the present theory. But one could still ascribe a significant role to unconscious motives. For example, it is possible to see action being determined by self-perceived wants and beliefs, which in turn may have unconscious determinants. A woman may believe that her husband is domineering and may act in various ways upon that belief, such as accusing him of trying to boss her around. Her belief may strike us as strange since her husband's behavior does not seem to accord with her view. We have data, however, that her father was a very dominating individual. We might infer that her distorted belief that her husband is domineering results from an unconscious "transference" of her father's attributes to her husband. Even if this were correct, it could be argued that her current belief that her husband is domineering has an impact on her behavior. Furthermore, it may be possible to alter her belief and actions related to it without her gaining insight into these unconscious dynamics.

It is also possible to assume that certain reactions are produced more or less directly by unconscious mechanisms: slips of the tongue, tics, some speech disturbances, certain psychogenic illnesses. Such reactions, however, fall outside the problems of concern in the present theory and hence need not be explained by it.

Action

Although wants, beliefs, and emotions may determine actions, these constructs do not adequately account for the role of action itself in the dynamics of psychosocial problems. Action must be examined on its own terms, not only as it directly affects problem formation and resolution but as it interacts with other elements to exert powerful, though less obvious, influences on problems.

Action and Behavior

Since the concept of action is central to the present theory, it might be well to begin by defining action and differentiating it from a closely related concept: behavior. In so doing, we shall bypass the many definitional issues that have been of concern to philosophers and others over the ages (see, for example, Brand 1970; White 1973). We define action generally as what a person does to achieve a given effect. As White (1973) says, "An action is the bringing about of something" (p. 2). For there to be action, there must be an agent with a purpose or intent. If I stammer while trying to pronounce a word, my stammering may be considered a bit of behavior, but it is not an action, since I did not intend to stammer. In fact, the stammering interferes with carrying out the action; that is, with pronouncing the word.

For an observer to understand a person's actions he needs, then, to make a judgment about the person's intent. Such a judgment is not necessary if what the person does is viewed as simply behavior. For example, suppose Betty is talking about taking a trip by car and Allen, her husband, breaks in at some point to say that the car needs repair. The conversation then shifts to that topic. We can describe Allen's interruption as behavior by noting what Betty said prior to it, precisely when Allen broke in, and so on. Such a description would say little about Allen's *action* in making the interruption. Perhaps he interrupted because the conversation reminded him of the car repair or perhaps because he disliked the idea of a trip and wanted to divert his wife from that topic.

Thus, the concept of action casts events into a different perspective than the concept of behavior. With analysis of behavior, we are concerned with determining *what* happened and perhaps what preceded or followed the event. Analysis of action incorporates these foci but, in addition, draws our attention to the processes within the person that contributed to bringing about the events.

The concept of behavior has the advantage of permitting precise, objective analysis of events under study; for this reason it has proved attractive to those wishing to construct scientifically based models of practice. The concept of action is far more troublesome, since it deals with cognitive processes that are difficult to define and measure. It can be argued, however, that these processes must of necessity be dealt with, and hence understood, in a wide variety of clinical situations. Few psychosocial problems can be reduced completely to behavioral terms. Even if the problem is largely behavioral in nature, the practitioner must still be concerned with what the client wants to do, or intends to do, about his situation. The concept of action forces us to deal with such internal events in a formal, systematic (albeit imperfect) manner.

As Brand (1970) points out, action can be purely mental, although not all mental processes can be considered actions. What makes a cognitive event an action is again the bringing about of something. Thus, making a decision can be considered an action, since something has been accomplished; day dreaming, on the other hand, would not be. The concept of action, therefore, lends itself better than behavior to consideration of what the client might do about difficulties that may have largely cognitive solutions—a need to make a decision or formulate a plan, for example. It is possible to view such cognitive processes as behaviors, as some writers have done (Ullman 1970), but to do so sacrifices the more precise notion of behavior as referring only to events that can be recorded by external observers.

Action can be viewed at different levels of abstraction. An action can describe, in a summary manner, a sequence or a hierarchy of individual acts or can refer to any of the acts themselves. To divorce one's spouse is an action, which in turn is made up of a myriad of more specific actions, from contacting a lawyer down to signing a separation agreement. By contrast, behavior normally refers to more discrete events at lower levels of abstraction. Getting a divorce would not be referred to as a behavior, though the term might be used to describe a person's conduct at various points in the process. The concept of action is thus better suited for description and analysis of fairly complex, often nonrepetitive, undertakings—leaving or entering an institution, getting a job, and so on. With the concept of action it is possible, as we shall see, to break such undertakings down into discrete acts. At the latter level of description, the term "behavior" can be used when intent is not known or is not an issue.

Finally, the concept of action provides a better fit with the philosophy of task-centered treatment, which, to put it simply, is to help people do what they want. Although one can modify a person's behavior without his knowledge or even consent, one can scarcely help a person plan and execute problem-solving *actions* without securing his cooperation and without involving him in the process. We are not saying that behavior modification must be *necessarily* manipulative, only that it can be. The concept of behavior does nothing to preclude manipulation. The concept of action, however, can be used to place the intentions or will of the client in a central position. For these reasons perhaps the concept has become of increasing interest to social treatment theorists (Oxley 1971; Maluccio 1974).

Importance of Plans

As has been seen, a crucial element in understanding action is the intent of the actor. In fact, it might be said that wants and beliefs do not directly produce action but, rather, create intentions that, in turn, control what the person does. These intentions may be thought of as plans, following the formulations of Miller, Galanter, and Pribram (1960). A *plan,* in effect, is a description of intent. Since actions consist of hierarchies or sequences of operations, plans are needed, as these authors suggest, to provide cognitive maps of what operations are to be performed, in what order.

The element of intent distinguishes a belief from a plan. I may have the belief that if I quit my job I can find a better one but have no intention of acting on the belief. Should I have this intent, I would then have a plan. Plans are informed by beliefs, however, as the example shows.

It is probably true that the plans controlling most problem-solving action are derived without a great deal of forethought from preestablished modes of response and shaped on the spot to meet the exigencies of the immediate situation. A mother with a whining child says to herself, "The next time she opens her mouth I'll slap her." The mother has a plan, though perhaps not the best one available, for controlling her child's behavior. Planning becomes an effective tool in shaping problem-solving action to the extent that it can take advantage of human capacity for rational thought and foresight. Effective planning normally takes into account a range of alternative problem-solving actions and the possible consequences of each. Promising alternatives are "thought through" to determine specific steps that may be required to carry them out. Contingencies that may arise are considered, and ways of responding to them are devised. In planning action for complex problems, perhaps the ideal is a "flexible plan" (Miller, Galanter, and Pribram 1960, p. 67), one which is open to some modification or improvisation in the process of being implemented.

Planning of this kind is best done prior to and away from the problem situation that must be coped with. Successful planning also depends to a considerable extent on the range and accuracy of data available to the planner and on his capacity for devising and evaluating alternative strategies. An important function of practitioners in most models of interpersonal practices is to provide the client with structured opportunities for planning and to contribute to the process through their own knowledge of psychosocial problems and of the particulars of the client's situation.

Action as Feedback

As has been said, a person takes action guided by certain beliefs and plans to satisfy his wants. The results of his action provide feedback, which in turn directly affects his beliefs and, indirectly, his wants. Through this process, commonly called learning through experience, we test, correct, and expand our cognitive maps. Our beliefs that certain actions will get us what we want are confirmed or challenged depending on what those actions lead to. The resulting confirmation or modification of beliefs may then produce a similar or a different reaction. In this way, our evaluations of action maintain or alter our modes of response.

An action may be prompted by a currently experienced (occurrent) want, as in the case of a want that defines a psychosocial problem. Miss L, shy and isolated, wants to make friends at work. She finds that going to the coffee shop for a break at about the same time as other women her age enables her to engage in some informal conversation with her peers. Since this action is evaluated as a promising route to making friends, she repeats it. An action may also result in attainment of a standing want. David, who refuses to recite in class, happens one day to say something about a subject of great interest to him and receives a great deal of praise from his teacher. The teacher's reaction satisfies a standing want for positive attention from adults. This want now becomes occurent, and he begins to recite more.

The use of feedback from action is an important means of effecting change in most modes of treatment. By testing possible solutions through action, clients can try out tentative perceptions about what will work, discover new conceptions of effective response, or disconfirm beliefs that may constitute obstacles to problem resolution. Information acquired through action tends to have a particularly strong impact on a person's belief system and hence may lead to greater change in subsequent actions than information acquired through other means. Experience, as the proverb goes, is the best teacher—perhaps because experience gives us a lesson that is not only vivid but carries personal consequences. But what changes, if any, will occur depends on the operation of feedback processes—more specifically, on how we evaluate the consequences of our actions.

In the face of strongly entrenched beliefs, the action consequences may be ignored or distorted. For example, a man is convinced that any woman would reject his overtures because of his physical unattractiveness. He agrees to try to ask a particular female acquaintance for a date and receives what might be interpreted as an encouraging response, which he interprets as her "just trying to humor him" and proceeds no further. It is not the experience that counts but what is made of it.

As can be seen, this formulation amends the maxim of operant learning theory that asserts that behavior is controlled by its consequences. It is proposed instead that behavior or action is affected by the *assessment* of its consequences. To advance this view is not to deny the empirical evidence produced by operant research. Actions can be decisively altered by the systematic manipulation of consequences, through such means as providing (or withholding) reinforcements or punishments. The facts are not in contention. Rather, a different theoretical explanation of these facts is suggested, one that takes into account the cognitive and motivational antecedents of behavior. This position is reflected in a number of cognitive theories of behavior, of which Rotter's social learning theory is a prime example. According to Rotter, "The potential for a specific behavior directed toward a reinforcement to occur in a particular situation is a function of the *expectancy* of the occurrence of that reinforcement following the behavior in that situation and the *value* of the reinforcement in that situation'' (Rotter 1972, p. 338) (my italics). In our terms, action is likely to take place if the actor believes that something wanted will be obtained as a result.

Action Sequences

Often a problematic action is the end result of an action sequence. If this sequence is understood, it may be possible to locate prior actions that, if altered, might prevent the problem from occurring. Moreover, the prior actions are often more susceptible to change than those constituting the focus of the problem.

One of Miss T's problems was that she could not get to work on time. In tracing the sequence of prior actions leading up to this problem, it was found that she usually turned off her alarm clock and went back to sleep. When she did get up right away, she took a considerable time deciding what clothes to wear. Her problem was resolved not by making up her mind to get up on time, as she had often done to no avail, but rather by placing the alarm clock on a bureau so she would have to get up to turn it off and by deciding what to wear the previous night and laying her clothes out at that time.

Skill

A person may not be able to carry out a problem-solving action because of lack of skill. I use that phrase in a somewhat limited sense to denote competencies in action that one does not possess— he is unable to perform the action because he does not know how. Thus, the inability to say ''no'' in a literal sense to unreasonable requests would not necessarily be seen as lack of skill, since any-one can pronounce the word. The inability to refuse a request in a manner not to antagonize another might involve maneuvers that a person was ignorant of. He would not know what to say or would lack the verbal facility to say it effectively.

The concept of skill, as used here, requires a specification of the responses that would be considered skilled under a given set of circumstances. Thus, action is compared against some set of response expectancies. Although one hopes that these expectancies, if attained, would enable the person to achieve his immediate objectives more effectively, the question of whether they do or not need not be answered in defining what a skill is. It is possible to learn "wrong" skills as well as "right" ones.

In determining if a skill deficit is a remediable obstacle to a problem solution, one starts with a problematic or dysfunctional action. It is then necessary to ascertain if some presumably preferable mode of response is possible, if such a mode or response can be delineated, if the person lacks knowledge of what it is or facility to carry it out, and finally if he can learn to do it. It does little good or say that a client lacks certain skills if we have no idea of what the skills require or if the client can learn them.

This distinction between dysfunctional action in general and a skill deficit becomes important in determining the kind of treatment that may be required. Two men may make a poor impression in employment interviews. Their behavior may be similar—both may give monosyllabic answers to questions about themselves. One may know how to make a good impression but is operating under the belief that no one will hire him anyway because of his prison record. The other may not know what to say or how to say it in order to make a good impression on the interviewer. Clinical treatment of the first man might be directed at his beliefs (or to the social system if his beliefs were reasonably accurate). The second man might need training in skills of self-presentation.

We are particularly interested in skills that the practitioner can help the client learn. Skills in assertiveness (Rose 1975), in conflict negotiation (Kifer, et al. 1974), in expressing empathy (Guzetta 1976), in marital decision making (Thomas 1976), and in problem solving (D'Zurilla and Goldfried 1971) are among those that have been taught in clinical contexts.

So far, we have confined our attention to learning through one's own actions without considering the roles that others may play. These roles, which multiply the importance of this means of change, will be taken up at a later point within the context of the function of the social system in problem resolution.

Incremental Action

The acquisition of new modes of action may be greatly facilitated if a person proceeds through a series of small incremental steps leading progressively to the actions desired. Approach hierarchies (Sieveking 1972), reinforced practice (Leitenberg 1976a) and graded task assignments (Beck 1976) provide examples of intervention strategies based on this principle. A street-phobic woman brings herself to leave her apartment almost literally a step at a time (Brown 1977b); a child who has never spoken in class is able in a few weeks to read aloud by starting with one-word responses in a facsimile of a classroom (Rossi 1977).

Incremental change is most likely to work when the action to be performed can be broken down into a series of discrete steps with no large gaps in the "ladder of difficulty" and when the carrying out of each step results on balance in some degree of want satisfaction. Each additional step, which is presumably less difficult to perform than the action as a whole, can then be mastered with incentives to continue until the desired action is executed.

If large discontinuities in the progressive difficulty of the steps occur, forward progress may be stalled. For example, a shy man afraid of being rejected tries to work up to the point of asking a female coworker to have a drink with him after work by saying "hello" one day and engaging in small talk the next but cannot bring himself to ask the crucial question. The discontinuity or gap in difficulty between starting a casual office conversation and exposing himself to personal rejection is too great. He solves the problem in effect by introducing an intermediary step—he chats with her at a social gathering where they both happen to be and offers to drive her home. Having progressed that far, it is possible for him to suggest they stop along the way for a drink. He is encouraged by his previous success, and her refusal at this point could be taken less personally. Not all discontinuities can be bridged so easily, and many cannot be bridged at all.

In the example above, successful completion of each step brought the person closer to what he wanted. In some forms of incremental action, however, the individual must surrender something immediately wanted and each successive step may add to the frustration of the want. A graduated approach to overcoming an addiction offers a well-known example. Tapering off may lead to an increased desire for the substance to be avoided. The craving for a smoke, drink, or whatever may soon overwhelm the want to be rid of the addiction. Consequently graduated reductions of enjoyable activities are more apt to work if accompanied by some form of substitute gratification or self-reward.

The Social System

Although they can be thought of as properties of individuals, most psychosocial problems are a product of complex social interactions—among the person possessing the problem, other individuals, and often collectivities, such as organizations. Although nonsocial elements, such as material resources, are often essential to problem resolution, one finds that these resources are usually controlled by individuals or organizations. It is possible, of course, to view these interchanges as occurring between the client and his environment, but this construction becomes cumbersome and imprecise when the environment is made up of a large number of social elements interacting with the client and with one another, or when analysis is concerned with more than one client. When the client(s) along with relevant other persons and collectivities are viewed as constituting a social system, the analytic task is considerably facilitated (Meyer 1976). The notion of a *social system,* as used here, refers simply to a set of individuals and organizations that are considered relevant to the maintenance or resolution of target problems. It is not assumed that these systems have necessarily the elements of ideal systems as set forth in the literature of general systems theory.

A social-systems perspective focuses attention on the influ- ence of the client's interactions with others (individuals and collec- tivities) in processes of problem creation and resolution. Thus far we have emphasized one element of the social system—the client himself. Other elements of the system were referred to impli- citly—for example, as sources of feedback to the client in his eval- uations of the results of his actions. In this section, the remainder of the social system is brought to the foreground as we consider how these other elements affect the client and his problems.

Effects on Beliefs

A person's belief system is to a large extent the product of lifelong interactions with social systems. In our search for manipulatable factors, however, attention is directed at current influences on beliefs.

Perhaps the most obvious, but not necessarily the most pow- erful, mode of influence available to members of the social system is to tell the client, in effect, what to believe. This form of influ- ence can be specified in terms of the content of the com- munications from others to the client. What picture of himself and his world are they conveying to him? What do they tell him about actions he might undertake? What inaccuracies, circumscriptions, and inconsistencies are contained in their messages? What might they convey to the client that would help eliminate dysfunctional beliefs and strengthen or develop functional ones? A handicapped child may be led to believe by the cautions of overprotective parents that various activities (which he could readily perform) are dangerous or beyond his competence. A wife's inaccurate belief that she is stupid may be strengthened by her husband's verbal depreciation of her intelligence. A patient tortured with the inaccu- rate belief that he may have cancer might be helped by a detailed explanation from a physician of the actual nature of his illness. A mother benefits from the practitioner's advice about how to get her son to bed, advice that informs the client that a particular way of handling the problem might achieve her goals.

This form of influence is perhaps most effective when the client, for whatever reason, values the opinion of the other and when the information transmitted is specific, accurate, and discriminating. Simply to tell a person who thinks he cannot do anything right that he is really quite competent may have little effect, even if the statement is true. Pointing out specific things he can do well is more likely to affect his belief in himself.

Messages to the client may not always be expressed in words. Actions of others may convey information about their perception of the client, which may affect his beliefs. The husband in the example above might not explicitly tell his wife of his estimate of her intelligence, but he might get the message across by refusing to engage in intellectual discussions with her. Such ambiguous information may have strong effects because the person may "overinterpret" it and may not be able to get it clarified (or refute it), as in the case of verbal messages.

Another, often more powerful form of influence on beliefs occurs through processes of imitation or modeling, when the client observes that actions of others seem to lead to satisfaction of *their* wants. These apparently successful modes of response may then lead the client to believe that his own wants can be altered through similar action. The processes and potency of "vicarious learning" have been described and documented by Bandura (1971a).

Responses to Client Action

When the client moves from the role of observer to that of actor within the social system, additional forms of influence are brought to bear. Here we are concerned with the specific contribution of the system to the feedback processes that accompany action.

As previously discussed, a person evaluates the results of his actions against the criterion of want attainment. Thus, the response of the system to the client's action will influence the course of his future actions. In describing the variety of possible responses and their consequence, we shall, as before, extend the framework of the "operant paradigm" (Schwartz and Goldiamond 1975).

A member of the social system may respond in a way that enables the client to satisfy an occurrent or standing want. This may be accomplished by giving the person something he wants—attention, some tangible reward—or by removing something he does not want, such as criticism. In operant terminology the former type of response is called "positive reinforcement"; the latter, negative reinforcement (Risley and Baer 1973), although these equivalents are only approximate. The response may, on the other hand, frustrate a want. This may be accomplished through giving the client something he wants to avoid or depriving him of something he wants—"punishment" and "response cost" in operant vocabulary (Risley and Baer 1973). Finally, an action may elicit no response at all from the social system. The system neither satisfies nor frustrates but rather ignores the want behind the action. In operant terms, again roughly speaking, the action is being "extinguished."

Relating our formulations to the operant paradigm has the obvious advantage of connecting our work to the vast research base and technology encompassed by this paradigm. But why not use this paradigm as it is? The answer to that question is twofold. First, by translating operant theory, research, and methods into the terms of our framework, we can perhaps build a more comprehensive theory of problem-solving action. Second, we think that motivational and cognitive considerations add important dimensions to operant theory, particularly when that theory informs practice conducted in face-to-face encounters with clients. What the client wants from treatment, his conceptions of himself and his world, even what he might regard as reinforcers are obviously important and, as even cursory readings of most operant treatment approaches will show, are taken into account in one way or another. But usually motivational and cognitive concepts are not part of the formal theory underlying such models and hence are not systematically developed or defined.

Moreover, operant theory as such cannot explain the findings of certain experiments in which cognitive variables, such as the subjects' knowledge of reinforcement contingencies, have had marked effects on the behaviors studied. (See for example Resnick and Schwartz 1973.)

Responses to client action often have an impact beyond facilitating or impeding his wants. The impact occurs through providing evaluations or critiques of his action. If a young child does something reasonably well, we may simply express our approval through saying "good" (positive reinforcement). We may also give similar praise to an older child who does reasonably well but may add information that might help him improve his performance. His actions are not only positively reinforced but informed and corrected. Whether used by parents, coaches, supervisors, therapists, or antagonists, critiques of action are designed to modify in precise ways the cognitive maps that tell people what to do and how to do it.

The modes of response described thus far, plus others that might be thought of, can obviously serve to maintain problems as well as to resolve them. What is important is to be able to specify how responses, as feedback, affect beliefs and wants and how this feedback is likely to affect future action.

Interaction Sequences

We have already considered the role of action sequences in problem formation and change. When the social system is involved, these sequences become interactive: the actions of two or more persons become mutually influential. At one level such action-reaction cycles can be understood through the feedback processes described above. In response to a remark from Jimmy, Harold begins to tease him. Jimmy teases back; there is verbal interchange. Harold hits him; Jimmy returns the blow, and a fight ensues. Each is responding to feedback from the other in a series of mutually punishing actions. But the interactive processes can also be viewed in a more holistic way—as a temporary system. At this level they can be characterized as an "uninterrupted sequence

Stop 9/30

of interchanges'' (Watzlawick, Beavin, and Jackson 1967, p. 54) in which the point of origin (who started it) may not be a matter of great concern. Certain systemic feedback mechanisms are operating—in this case deviation-amplifying or positive feedback processes. The interaction has escalated into a fight. But the escalation might be reversed through negative feedback process—Jimmy starts to cry, Harold says he is sorry he pounded him so hard—until they become friendly again. Systemic concepts (discussed in greater detail in chapter 9 and in other works [Watzlawick, Beavin, and Jackson 1967; Buckley 1967]) not only provide additional perspectives on interaction but can guide analysis when data on the cognitive and motivational processes of the actors are not available. As in analysis of individual action sequences, it is particularly important to locate points in recurring sequences that are susceptible to change. Jimmy and Harold might not be able to restrain their aggressive actions after a certain point in the escalation but might be able to refrain from the kind of provocative teasing that leads to the fighting.

Not all interaction sequences are characterized by such a high degree of *reciprocal* influence as in the example cited. Consider a husband who periodically goes on drinking spells, returns home, and becomes abusive toward his wife. His behavior may not necessarily be responsive to his wife's actions; he might behave that way regardless of what she did. It might be tempting to say that the problem (if her complaint concerns his behavior) is simply his ''fault'' and to dismiss the relevance of any interactional formulations. But inasmuch as she is reacting in some fashion to his behavior, the problem may still be thought of as the product of interaction and fruitfully analyzed from that viewpoint. Analysis of the problem might suggest alternative actions on the wife's part that might mitigate the difficulty, even though it might be concluded that a change in the husband's behavior would be necessary for the problem to be altered in any substantial way. If none of the alternatives worked, then a radical change in the wife's social system—that is, leaving her husband—might be the only solution.

Clients frequently attribute the cause of their problems to the actions of others. In one study, for example, almost 80 percent of a sample of family agency clients identified the primary cause of their difficulties as the behavior or attitudes of their spouses and children (Reid and Shyne 1969). Nevertheless problems involving others are best analyzed in interactive terms. One can then assess the contribution the client actually makes to the problem (usually more than may first appear). Even if the client's actions toward another have not helped create the difficulty, usually the only route to solution is through affecting their patterns of interaction.

Role of Organizations

Formal organizations occupy a prominent position in the lives of most social work clients. The client is almost always related to a social work agency or department. His social system is likely to contain, in addition, a large number of organizations to which he is connected in one role or another—as a client, employee, patient, member, and so on. The interaction of clients and organizations plays a major part in the dynamics of psychosocial problems. An organization—the social agency—is expected to provide the client with a means of problem resolution through the actions of the social worker. Often organizations (including the helping agency itself) may have contributed, however, to the client's difficulty or to obstacles to its resolution.

In analyzying the role of organizations, it is essential to make a distinction between individuals and collectivities. We have already seen how individuals can influence the client through their interactions with him. Often these individuals are acting in organizational roles. Thus, we can analyze interactions of clients and teachers, physicians, foster parents, and so on. At this level one may take into account the motives, beliefs, and action patterns of the individual as these are shaped by a number of factors, including the requirements of his organizational role. The emphasis is still on the individual, even though knowledge of organizational influences on his actions may be important.

Frequently, however, we are concerned with the client's interaction with a collectivity—with an organization, or elements of it—that can be defined by particular functions, policies, rules, and roles. Even though the client's point of contact may be with an individual member, the interaction can be best understood in terms of collective or organizational factors. Thus, a public welfare department may rule that a client is ineligible for public assistance. While the rule may have been made by an individual caseworker, the point at issue may be the rule itself and how it is normally interpreted in that department. Any other caseworker would have made the same decision.

As idiosyncratic factors become known, our perspective may shift to organizational members as individuals. A couple's struggle to enroll their handicapped child in the public schools may be seen first as a conflict with the school system but eventually as a clash with a particular principal. Although at this level the personal characteristics of the organization member become important, they must be seen in relation to the organizational context. The principal's decision not to accept the child may represent a confluence of personal and organizational factors—his biases about handicapped children and rules governing their admission to the school system.

As is consistent with the general focus of the present theory, I am concerned with organizational influences on problems susceptible to modification by practitioner or client in the course of their work together. Problems may be greatly influenced by factors that neither can affect—for example, organizational goals, policies, and budgets. As a member of the social work profession, the practitioner may have an obligation to work for fundamental organizational changes that would improve the welfare of his clients, but probably cannot effect such change as a part of his problem-solving efforts with any particular client.

Certain aspects of the interface of clients and organizations have been selected for analysis. These aspects will be examined primarily from the perspective of how organizations may bring problems about or block their resolution.

Labels and Collective Beliefs

Organizations categorize people they wish to influence in a variety of ways—as clients, patients, inmates, status offenders, and the like. Such categorizations generally reflect a presumption that the person is not able to resolve difficulties or meet his needs through his own resources. In a limited way and for a limited time, this presumption may be correct. Still, the categorizations are made at a certain psychic cost to the person; the consequences of this cost need to be recognized and controlled. A person who becomes a client of a social agency, to take one of the more benign categorizations, usually does so at the expense of acknowledging some degree of insufficiency in his coping capacity or within his social system. In a society that extolls self-sufficiency and independent mastery of adversity, asking for (or agreeing to accept) help for personal troubles is often accompanied by a loss of self-esteem, a fact tacitly acknowledged when we credit clients for their "courage" in admitting their need for assistance. For many clients this loss may be the least of their problems; and one hopes that it will be usually more than recouped in the form of a change for the better in the client's life.

I would argue that the client's belief in his self-sufficiency is put in greater jeopardy when the helping organization defines his disability as involving his total functioning and when its engagement with him is prolonged. Under these conditions the client may come to believe that his capacity to manage his own affairs must be rather limited, and he may become increasingly dependent upon the agency for guidance. In some cases this sacrifice of autonomy may be the least of a variety of evils but, if so, the benefits should be great enough to make the sacrifice worthwhile. When the benefits resulting from pervasive and prolonged involvement with an agency cannot be established, as often seems to be the case (Reid and Shyne 1969), then the argument for an involvement limited to specific problems and brief periods of time is strengthened. Moreover, this involvement, whatever its scope and duration, should be designed to preserve, if not enhance, the client's belief in his own self-sufficiency. Otherwise, the social agency may help the client solve certain problems by creating others.

Further risks are added when the client is categorized in terms that denote types of social deviancy and is then dealt with according to *stereotypical* notions of what people so labeled are like. If staff members view a client as "schizophrenic" or "delinquent," they may convey to themselves and perhaps to the client a range of expectations that may interfere with remedial action. As labeling theorists (Lemert 1967; Scheff 1971; Waxler 1975) argue, persons who are officially defined as deviant may be treated in ways that may reinforce their deviance or deprived of treatment that may be beneficial.

Stereotypical descriptions of persons with such labels are not hard to find in the clinical literature. Thus, Wolberg (1967) describes the schizophrenic patient: "Like an infant the patient's emotional reactions to people are unstable and ambivalent. He is easily frustrated and feels rejection without ostensible cause. He is unreasonable and demanding. . . . Alone his ego is so weak that he is unable to tolerate complete responsibility" (p. 1009). Rosenberg and Short (1970) have the following to say about the "pseudo-neurotic client:" "These clients, still orphans in the storm of life, see people generally as the 'grown up giants' and have to defend themselves from destruction by turning to an earlier phase of development when the omnipotence was invested in self and they could—like the infants that they are—control the world" (p. 558). I am sure that even the authors quoted above would not claim that *all* persons with these labels are really like infants. Yet this is the message conveyed. To the extent that the staff of an organization believes it, clients so labeled may be treated as more helpless than they really are. The consequences may be a depreciation in their own self-concept and treatment that devalues their capacity for independent problem-solving action. I am not arguing that such categorizations have no value, although that argument has been made (Stuart 1970), but rather that they are often drawn with language that is imprecise and metaphoric—language that may caricature rather than delineate a person's attributes.

In general, categories of deviance, particularly psychiatric labels, are given more weight than they merit. Even qualified personnel find it difficult to agree on how a given individual should be categorized. The power to predict behavior from such categories is notoriously feeble. While their use may be inevitable, the misinformation they may convey should be given as much attention as whatever valid meanings they may contain. I am not arguing that labeling is a primary cause of deviance, even though it may be an aggravant under some circumstances. As Schur (1971) observes, the labeling process should be focal in our attention: the playing out of how a person's actions are defined and the consequences of these definitions. The process often works in subtle ways. A youngster enters a school system with a notation on his record from his previous school that he was a "discipline problem." The principal warns the teachers, who then watch his behavior more closely than they ordinarily would. As a result, he is sent to the principal for some minor wrongdoing that might otherwise pass unnoticed or be handled by the teacher. The principal "lays down the law"—to make sure this "troublemaker" does not think he can get away with anything. As a result, the youngster (who may have been trying to conform) feels resentful over being singled out. His resentment may aggravate his tendency toward mischief. Even if it does not, it is likely to contribute to whatever difficulties he may have with the school.

Breakdowns and Shortcomings in Service Delivery

If a service organization is to help people resolve problems, it needs to provide effective services in an efficient manner. Organizations not only often fall far short of this ideal but in trying to help may themselves add to the client's distress.

One set of impediments is an outgrowth of inherent strains between the client with his particular wants and large service bureaucracies with complex rules, procedures, and technologies that may not be readily responsive to the client on his own terms (Rosengren and Lefton 1970; Hasenfeld and English 1974). Service programs and goals are set up to meet the needs of *categories* of people, with the organization normally defining both the needs and the categories and establishing technical requirements for membership in the latter.

Over time, the operations of an organization become shaped to some extent to meet the interests and convenience of staff or to promote internal efficiency. As this happens, the gap between the workings of the organization and the client's self-perceived needs becomes wider; so does the gap between the client's and staff's mutual understanding of the rationale for these operations. The division of labor and the hierarchical structure that character- ize large organizations may make it difficult for the client to find the "right" person who can help him or to get prompt decisions on his request.

As a result, the client may find his attempts to secure services from welfare organizations both mystifying and frustrating. As part of the entry process he may need to complete intricate applica- tion forms or answer numerous questions, whose purposes are not readily apparent. The client may be shunted from one employee to another and then find that his requests must be acted on by still another official "up the line." Rules for determining eligibility for service or what services the client can receive may be narrowly applied without consideration of the particular circumstances of his situation. The technology—or the content of the service—may not be what he wants, or he may not be able to comprehend how it can help him.

Mr. and Mrs. Y, an elderly couple of modest means and in poor health, searched in vain in their small town for someone to help them with their housework and cooking. Unless help could be found, they doubted that they could remain in their home. A local agency provided such a service for the "elderly poor." Since the couple's retirement income was somewhat above the agency limit, they were ruled ineligible for the service. The agency refused their offer to pay for the service since its "domestic help was in short supply and needed to be conserved for those who could not afford to pay."

Their bureaucratic dysfunctions aside, many service organiza- tions lack sufficient resources (funds, qualified personnel, and so forth) to meet service goals at even a minimum level. This prob- lem compounds the one just discussed. Service staff who are swamped with cases and paperwork are even less likely to have time and energy to respond to the special needs and circumstances of clients. But the problem, of course, has far more serious ramifications, particularly for the poor, the stratum of society of greatest concern to social work. To a considerable extent service organizations control the survival resources of the poor in our nation—their money, jobs, and housing. They also control services to which the poor must turn for particular needs—for day care, homemakers, job training, counseling, to mention but a few. These resources and services are often delivered, if at all, in token amounts and with inferior quality—and in the public agencies, usually by hard-pressed and inadequately trained staff. For services in particular demand—such as training programs for desirable jobs—waiting lists, delays, and arbitrary rejection of applicants are too often the norm.

Multiorganizational Involvements

The resolution of the client's problems may require the inter-meshed efforts of more than one organization. The difficulties organizations have in coordinating their activities at the case level have provoked a considerable amount of professional self-examination. These difficulties have also stimulated some study and analysis and remedial efforts of uneven success (White and Vlasak 1970; Litwak 1970; Davidson 1976). The problem is complicated and to some extent made unsolvable by service bureaucracies' tendency to function as specialized, autonomous units, each with its own distinctive purposes, beliefs, and mode of operation, and each with its own definitions of its prerogatives and "turf." In most case situations, formal mechanisms do not exist, or are not used to ensure coordination, even when the units are part of some larger organization—a state department of welfare, for example. Coordination is generally carried on at an informal level without clear allocation of roles or any one organization or practitioner being charged with a coordinating function. Often contact among the agencies is minimal or at least not sufficient to promote knowledge of each other's activities. The result may be a crosshatch of discordant approaches that leaves the client confused, his problem unchanged.

After having been badly beaten up by his father, Dennis, 11, was removed from his home and placed in foster care. At the same time, his parents were advised by the court to take treatment at the mental health clinic as a condition for having their child returned. They did so, and Dennis himself was also seen there. As soon as the placement was effected, Dennis began to exhibit "aggressive behavior" toward his teachers and other children at school. The mental health clinic, the school, Dennis's foster parents, and his child welfare worker all responded promptly to the problem. Each had, however, a different diagnosis and treatment approach. The child welfare worker attempted with partial success to coordinate his efforts with the school's and foster parents'. The mental health clinic proceeded more or less on its own.

Modifiability
The foregoing analysis of organizational impediments to problem resolution has included factors that the practitioner will not be able to alter in a given case situation. For example, he usually cannot remove a label an organization has already attached to a client or create resources an organization does not have. Yet even in these cases he can intervene: he can modify the impact of labeling by emphasizing with the client and others specific actions instead of vague categorizations; he can guide the client through complex and confusing organizational requirements and can sometimes have them adjusted to the client's benefit; he can often steer the client to organizations that are better equipped to help him and can take steps to ensure that he is served more promptly and effectively. Finally, the practitioner can carry out coordinating functions when several organizations are involved.

In this chapter, I have tried to lay the groundwork for a testable theory designed to explain the formation and resolution of psychosocial problems. At its present state of development, the theory serves primarily to orient the practitioner to the spheres of influence that need to be taken into account in any attempt to understand how problems came into being and what can be done about them. Although ways of operationalizing central terms of the theory have been suggested, and evidence bearing upon certain of the formulations has been presented or cited, it does not yet qualify as a tested theory. The next step would be to derive and test (or accumulate evidence for) a network of explanatory propositions, which the theory suggests but does not articulate.

At present, however, we must settle for an accounting scheme. It is proposed that problems arise and change through the interaction of a confluence of dimensions: the person's wants, or motives; his beliefs, affects, actions; and the social system of which he is a part. The practitioner draws upon this constellation to find a provisional answer to the essential question: "What is the problem and what can be done about it?" To answer this question, he must identify both the obstacles and avenues to problem resolution.

Both avenues and obstacles can usually be found in transactions between the person and his social system. The social system shapes the individual's beliefs, which control his wants, emotions, and actions. Problem-solving action is generally directed at some part of the system which, through its individual and organizational elements, generally holds the key to what the person wants. His actions in turn affect the system, through the same processes by which the system affects him.

The theory so far presented is addressed primarily to problems in which the unit of attention is the individual client and his social system. This focus fits well to a wide range of problems. Even in multiple-client situations, attention can be fruitfully centered at any given time on a single client and his particular problem without losing sight of the importance of his interactions with others. For some problems, however, such as difficulties in family relations, the unit of attention may be the interaction between clients. For these problems, additional theoretical perspectives are needed. An effort to supply them will be found in chapter 9.

Chapter 5
Intervention Strategy

The strategy of the task-centered model flows from two purposes: (1) to help the client alleviate problems that concern him; (2) to provide him with a constructive problem-solving experience that will enhance his willingness to use help in the future and will strengthen his own problem-solving capacities. After outlining this twofold strategy, I shall consider its range of application, with particular attention to situations in which it may not be the treatment of choice. Finally, I shall discuss the relation between the present strategy and other types of practice.

Alleviating Target Problems

Utilizing formulations in the preceding chapters, the practitioner helps the client identify specific problems that arise from unrealized wants, and that are defined in terms of specific conditions to be changed. Work proceeds within the structure of contracts in which the client's problems, goals, and the nature and duration of service are explicitly stated and agreed on by both practitioner and client. Analysis of a problem leads to consideration of the kinds of actions needed to solve it, what might facilitate those actions, and obstacles standing in the way of their implementation.

Change is effected primarily through problem-solving actions or tasks the client and practitioner undertake outside the interview. The practitioner helps the client select tasks to realize his wants. He facilitates task work through assisting the client in planning task implementation and establishing his motivation for carrying out the plan. He helps him rehearse and practice the task and analyze obstacles to its achievement. Reviews of the client's accomplishments on each task allow the practitioner to provide corrective feedback on the client's actions and serve as the basis for developing new tasks.

To supplement the client's problem-solving efforts, the practitioner may carry out tasks within the client's social system. These tasks are usually designed to assist others in facilitating the client's task or to secure resources from the system that the client cannot readily obtain on his own. Although a client's problem may be resolved exclusively through practitioner tasks, the theory and methodology of the system are obviously oriented toward problems in which at least some client initiative is indicated and will be of most value when such problems are at issue.

The central and distinctive strategy of the present system is found in its reliance upon tasks as a means of problem resolution. The client's and practitioner's efforts are devoted primarily to the construction, implementation, and review of tasks. The success of these tasks largely determines whatever benefit results from application of the model.

The stress on tasks is an attempt to build upon the considerable capacity of human beings to take constructive action in response to difficulty. In effect we have modeled our intervention strategy after the way most people resolve most of their problems—by doing something about them.

To be sure the problems brought to the attention of social workers have usually not yielded to the client's problem-solving initiatives. Nevertheless, we assume that a capacity for problem-solving action is present. It is the social worker's responsibility to help the client put this capacity to work.

The strategy we advocate leads to a parsimonious form of intervention that respects the client's right to manage his own affairs. If the client is clear about what is troubling him and has a reasonable plan for resolving the difficulty, the practitioner's role may be limited largely to providing encouragement and structure for the client's problem-solving efforts. If more is needed, more is supplied, to the extent necessary to help the client resolve his difficulties. Even when the practitioner's involvement is great, his purpose is to develop and augment the client's own actions. Thus the practitioner may need to help the client determine what he wants and in the process may need to challenge wants that are unrealizable. He may need to help the client identify and modify action and interaction sequences contributing to the difficulty, to provide corrective feedback on the client's action, to teach him necessary skills, to work with him to alter beliefs that are interfering with problem-solving, to bring about changes in the social system and to secure resources from it, and even to suggest specific tasks for the client to carry out. But whatever is done is done collaboratively and leads to actions that must be agreed to by the client. The decisive actions in most cases are those that the client himself performs in his own way and on his own behalf.

Enabling the client to take constructive and responsible action in his own interest has an important corollary: the action so taken is likely to be incorporated as part of his problem-solving strategy for continued coping with the problem. Since he has participated in its planning, has an understanding of its rationale, agreed to carry it out, actually implemented it and reviewed its results, one can assume that the action is more a part of him and, if successful, is more likely to be used again with appropriate variations, than if he were simply following the practitioner's instructions or unwittingly responding to contingencies arranged by others.

Aspects of strategy just presented—building upon the client's problem-solving capacity and promoting incorporation of successful coping strategies—can also be achieved although perhaps in a less straightforward manner, through traditional treatment approaches, that is, those that stress helping the client develop an understanding of himself, others, and his situation as a means of problem-resolution. These modalities are perhaps most effective, however, with clients who are able to use verbal and reflective processes to good advantage and who find this mode of problem-solving to their liking. While such clients are found in all social strata they are more likely to be middle than lower class. A good deal of evidence (Goldstein, 1973) suggests that lower-class clients can better utilize and prefer a different mode of helping; one that is more structured, more directive, and places more emphasis on action. This orientation is a result not only of their educational limitations and cognitive styles but also, as Goldstein observes, of the "harsh environmental realities of lower-class living" (p. 18). That is, the problems of greatest concern to poor people often reflect deficits in tangible resources and require action on their part or someone's part to secure them. As noted earlier, considerable effort in clinical social work is devoted to lower-class clients. It is probably fair to say that lower-class clients, as compared to those in the middle class, offer a greater challenge to the profession and are more in need of its help.

Our focus on client and practitioner action is in large part the result of our interest in developing a system of practice well suited to the needs and orientation of lower-class clients. While reflective methods can be used to advantage within the task-centered framework to help clients examine beliefs about themselves and their situation, these methods are not essential to the model and, when used, are always a part of a larger action-focused strategy. Although the task structure, as we employ it, emphasizes a collaborative effort with the client rather than a unilateral use of practitioner authority, the task-centered practitioner is expected to make use of direct suggestions about task possibilities and about means of task achievement. In fact there is evidence (chapter 10) that considerably more advice-giving occurs in task-centered practice than in conventional social treatment approaches. We have not conducted studies comparing the task-centered model to other approaches with lower-class clients but have had considerable experience in using the task-centered model with such clients, who have in fact vastly outnumbered middle-class clients in our work to date. Evaluations by lower-class consumers of task-centered treatment have been quite positive, particularly in respect to such critical considerations as getting the kind of help they wanted and understanding the nature of service (Reid and Epstein, 1972; also chapter 10).

We assume that the task structure of the model can also be used effectively with clients more inclined toward introspection, although adaptations may need to be made (Ewalt, 1977), and it may not be suited for all such clients, as discussed below. The tradition in social work has been to reshape treatment approaches devised for the middle class for use with lower-class clients. In view of social work's long-standing commitment to serving the poor, we are not unduly troubled by having to move in the opposite direction.

While the distinctive strategy of the model flows from its task structure, other elements are needed if the approach is to work successfully. Two merit discussion at this point: the practitioner-client relationship and the social agency.

The relationship between the practitioner and client provides a means of stimulating and promoting problem-solving action. Their sessions together do not provide the essential ingredients of change; they rather serve to set in motion and guide subsequent actions through which change will be effected.

It is assumed, nevertheless, that this purpose will be facilitated through a relationship in which the client feels accepted, respected, liked, and understood. This kind of relationship is considered fundamental in most forms of interpersonal practice, although it has been difficult to define and measure the various qualities it is supposed to contain. Perhaps the most promising work in this regard has consisted of efforts to isolate and study what have been called the "core conditions" of an optimal therapeutic relationship: empathy, nonpossessive warmth, and genuineness. These qualities have been defined by Truax and Mitchell (1971, p. 302). In their terms, the communication of accurate empathy refers to the practitioner's ability to convey his ability to understand, "be with," what the client is experiencing "on a moment-to-moment basis." "Nonpossessive warmth" refers to his ability to provide "a nonthreatening, safe, trusting or secure atmo-

sphere through his own acceptance, positive regard, love, valu-
ing.'' A practitioner is ''genuine'' if he is ''nonphony, nondefen-
sive, and realistic'' in his encounter with the client. While research
on the core conditions has usually lacked adequate controls and
has produced mixed results, the evidence on the whole suggests
that these conditions do contribute to successful treatment outcomes. (Mitchell, Bozarth, and Krauft 1977). Moreover, as a
product of this research, ways of measuring these elusive qualities
have been developed (Truax 1967) and testable methods of training practitioners in their use have been devised (Calkhuff 1972; Fischer 1978).

The strategy of the task-centered model calls for the actualiza-
tion of these conditions within the context of a treatment relationship that is problem-focused, task-centered, and highly structured. This means that the expression of these conditions must be
fitted to the requirements of the model. It is assumed that this fit
can be made without unduly sacrificing either these relationship
qualities or the essential structure of the treatment program (Reid
and Epstein 1972, pp. 121–38). But in so doing it may not be
feasible, or desirable, to push the core conditions to the limits possible in less structured forms of treatment. Thus, the task-centered
practitioner may bring a client back to focus on an agreed-upon
problem rather than simply responding at a high level of empathy
to a tangential communication. Nevertheless, ways can be found, I
think, to maintain a reasonably high level of the core conditions
and keep at the business of the contract. The practitioner can let
the client know that he understands and appreciates his feelings
about a tangential issue but also remind him of the need to address
the problem at hand. The model may in fact lend itself to the
expression of genuineness. The emphasis placed on sharing of information and evaluation with the client pushes the practitioner
toward an open, honest, and hence genuine posture. That structured approaches are not necessarily incompatible with these relationship qualities is suggested by a study comparing psychotherapy
and behavior therapy (Sloane et al. 1975). Analysis of taped inter-

view samples in that study revealed that behavior therapists either equaled or exceeded psychotherapists in expressions of these qualities, despite the greater importance attached to them by the latter. Fischer (1978) provides additional justification for the use of structured approaches in combination with the core conditions.

Perlman (1957) has described a good treatment relationship as containing both support and expectancy. Its supportive elements, which assume specific expression in the core conditions, have perhaps been given the greater weight in social work practice theory. Within the task-centered system, the expectations the practitioner conveys to the client are viewed as a therapeutic force of at least equal importance. The practitioner expects the client to work on agreed-upon problems and tasks and communicates these expectations to the client both explicitly and implicitly. While he respects the client's decision to reject his services, he also holds the client accountable for following through once a contract has been established. These positions are not inconsistent: they both reflect an acceptance of the client as a person who can make responsible decisions. Expectations, if clearly communicated, serve to influence the client's actions, since the client is likely to regard the practitioner as an authority who can be trusted to advance his interest and whose approval is important. The practitioner's reaction, which is likely to be more approving if the client makes an effort to resolve his problem than if he does not, serves to strengthen the force of these expectations. This is as it should be if the practitioner-client relationship is to be used to full advantage on the client's behalf. But if clients are to be helped to resolve problems, qualities of the relationship must be fused with specific problem-solving methods. The relationship provides the raw material but not the finished product.

Behind any social work practice model stands a social agency. The intervention strategy of a model can be seen, in fact, as an expression of the agency's purposes. One often gets the impression from the social treatment literature that the main function of the agency is to provide office space and salary for the practitioner and a sanction for his clinical work. Too little attention has been paid to the agency's contribution to the potency of a treatment approach.

The agency's role in the task-centered approach is twofold. First, it provides a variety of resources, including supervision (particularly for inexperienced workers), staff training programs, and tangible services. Second, the agency confers on the practitioner an "authority of office" critical to the helping process. In order to be helped a client must be willing to place himself under the influence of a helper. The client must then perceive the practitioner as someone who has the capacity to help him and is worthy of his trust. In well-established professions, like law or medicine, the practitioner relies on the image of his profession to provide this aura of authority and competence. The social worker whose profession still lacks a clear-cut image must usually rely on the agency to perform this function. The client is likely to see him as qualified to help, not because he is a social worker, but because he is an employee of an agency. Similarly, the practitioner's agency status exerts more influence than his professional identification with other persons and with organizations in the client's social system.

A Constructive Problem-solving Experience

The immediate purpose of the model is to help the client resolve problems through enabling him to plan and execute necessary problem-solving actions. This objective should be attained in such a way as to provide the client with what might be called a constructive problem-solving experience, that is, an experience that, regardless of the specific problem worked on and the amount of resolution achieved, should hold the client in good stead in his future problem-solving activities.

The experience should benefit the client in two ways. First, his attitude toward potential helpers should be enhanced, so that he will be receptive to using another if the need arises. This result is most likely to be obtained if the practitioner respects what the client himself wants. Should the practitioner think the client is misguided, then he should so inform the client and tell him why he thinks so, rather than trying to impose his own goals in a devious way. In general, the practitioner should present himself as the client's agent. In this role he may counsel the client about his problems, but in the final analysis he should be subservient to the client's informed wishes. In addition, the practitioner needs to demonstrate competence in helping the client define his problem and take action to solve it. It is crucial that he follow through with his part of whatever plans he and the client have developed.

[handwritten margin note: What would Haley say?]

If the social worker can act in this manner, he has, perhaps, done more than help the client with his immediate problem. He has given him the sense that turning to another for help can be a rewarding (or at least not degrading) experience, one that he may wish to repeat in the future.

The second kind of extra benefit should consist in enhancement of the client's ability to alleviate psychosocial problems on his own. I assume that skills in solving personal problems can be learned. Although learning problem-solving skills per se is not the major objective of our model, we expect that the client will be able to apply to other situations what he has learned from his problem-solving experience. In particular, this application should take place with problems similar to those he has dealt with in treatment. The practitioner does certain things to help this process along. During the course of treatment, he makes the various problem-solving steps explicit so that the client can comprehend the logic and process of the approach. He tries to stimulate and utilize the client's own strategies for working on the problem, thus giving him practice in independent problem solving. At the close of treatment, as we shall see, he goes over the client's problem-solving experience in a systematic manner. The client is helped to see how he might apply the methods he has used to problems that may remain or arise after treatment.

The provision of a constructive problem-solving experience is then a constant feature of the model, though not its central purpose. In one sense, it defines the way treatment is conducted. Even if the experience yields only a modest amount of added benefit for the client, it will, at least, give him a benign and facilitative context for work on the target problems of immediate concern to him.

Assessment and Planning

In carrying out this twofold strategy, the practitioner utilizes modes of thinking that serve to guide the activities that will be detailed in chapters to follow. These mental processes are directed primarily toward understanding the client's problems and toward developing possible routes to their alleviation.

The terms "diagnosis" and "treatment planning" have been used in the treatment literature to describe the practitioner's efforts to grapple with the questions of what is wrong and what can be done about it. In some systems of practice (Hollis 1972), diagnosis or assessment may be the culmination of an elaborate process of study and is seen as taking place in large part before treatment goals are planned. In the task-centered system, this process is viewed rather differently. Once basic data on the client's personal-situational characteristics have been obtained and target problems identified, the first question to be asked is, "What can be done to alleviate the client's difficulties?" This question then serves to direct further assessment. The practitioner's thinking is guided by both general and case-specific knowledge of the action that may prove useful for the problem at hand and of factors that may facilitate or impede the implementation of such action (chapter 4). In this analysis, attention is centered on three aspects: (1) *action requirements*—what action is needed and how can it be produced; (2) *obstacles*—what barriers susceptible to alteration by practitioner or client are preventing such action from occurring; (3) *constraints*—what unmodifiable factors in the client's capacity or social situation might limit action alternatives.

In the usual case, attention is first given to action requirements. The definition of the problem normally suggests certain courses of action to obtain what the client wants. Miss L, a shy, isolated young woman with a hearing loss, has been unable to make friends at her new job as a file clerk—in fact, she is not even able to initiate informal conversations or to respond when others talk to her. To alleviate the difficulty, she might start up friendly conversations or respond in an amicable manner when others try to chat with her. Drawing on his knowledge of problem-solving action and of Miss L, the practitioner thinks of different action possibilities. It might be useful if she began incrementally by smiling and saying hello to one person in the office—a person thoughtfully selected and approached in a planned way. Since she had complained that she did not know "how to talk to people," possibly some effort to enhance her skill in making small talk would be helpful. She might be more willing to take the first difficult step of initiating a conversation if she could reward herself by buying something she liked if she did so.

Certain obstacles to her carrying out required actions are observed. Obstacles here (and generally) refer to active agents whose presence impedes action. By definition, obstacles are barriers to be removed and, as noted, must be modifiable if not entirely removable. In Miss L's case, the practitioner is able to identify two possible obstacles: her distorted belief that others will not be interested in talking to her or being friendly to her once they learn of her hearing difficulties; a particular interaction sequence that hampers her efforts to sustain conversations. He noticed during their own dialogue that Miss L tended to look down and away from him and to mumble, which made the practitioner slightly uncomfortable and made it sometimes difficult to understand what Miss L was saying. He surmised that others might react the same way, and if so, might withdraw from her conversational forays. The first obstacle might be addressed through helping her to examine critically her beliefs about others' reaction to her hearing loss. The second might be dealt with in the course of helping her develop better conversational skills.

Throughout this assessment and planning process, the practitioner takes into account constraints imposed by her hearing loss and by her being young and single in an office populated largely by older, married women. With her consent, he will look further into the possibility, which she alluded to, that her hearing might be improved with a better hearing aid—any presumed fixed factor needs to be assessed to determine if, in fact, it may be modifiable. As can be seen, assessment and planning provide the practitioner with ideas about how to proceed. The formulations in themselves do not provide the basis for the task plan—rather, they are introduced as input into a process of collaboration with the client. The initial plan will emerge from that process and will be modified in the light of new data as service proceeds. Although they may receive more stress at the beginning of treatment, planning and assessment are processes that continue throughout the life of the case.

In some cases, task plans may be developed in a straightforward way with minimal recourse to knowledge of obstacles and constraints. An unemployed person may need help only in filling out job application forms, or the practitioner's action in securing a homemaker may be all that is required for a father with a temporary child-care problem.

In other cases, obstacles to problem solution must be located and deciphered before appropriate courses of action can be identified. Although Mrs. H had a number of worries, none, she thought, was great enough to explain her increasing "nervousness" over the past several months. In examining her situation, it was found that she was particularly upset by a tentative plan that her aged mother-in-law, whom she disliked, would come to live with her and her husband. Although this source of concern did not seem sufficient to account for her general anxiety, it seemed to be a likely contributing factor—and thus could be identified as an obstacle to her resolving her problem as she perceived it ("being nervous"). Tasks addressed to this obstacle were then devised. They included Mrs. H's expressing to her husband her reservations about his mother's living with them and involving him in an examination of alternate care arrangements. As is shown by the example, obstacles can be thought of as problems in themselves that maintain the target problem and can be worked on through appropriate tasks. In fact, it may happen that the client's concerns may prove to be centered more on the obstacle than the original problem, in which case the former can become the target problem. Thus, Mrs. H might have decided that her mother-in-law's moving in and not her general "nervousness" was the primary difficulty. If so, her reluctance to express the full range of her objections to her husband about the move would become an obstacle to the solution of the redefined problem.

Finally, constraints may prove to be the overriding consideration. In fact, they may be so limiting that the problem as originally defined is unsolvable, as in the case of the rejected suitor who conceives of his problem as getting back his girl friend who is now happily married to another man. With a redefinition of the problem, say to one of his depression over the loss of his girl friend, the original constraint would no longer apply.

The distinction between obstacles and constraints may be difficult to draw, but the effort is worth making since it is useful for the practitioner to focus his attention on factors that can be modified (obstacles) rather than on more or less fixed elements in a situation. As we have seen from examples given, the distinction is provisional. Apparent constraints may prove to have manipulatable aspects or may be altered by a redefinition of the problem.

The two most common types of constraints—those relating to the client's behavior patterns and his social system—merit some additional comment. Well-established characteristics of the client's functioning may be considered constraints if they would limit his ability for problem-solving action and if they appear to be relatively unmodifiable. A practitioner might decide with reasonable justification that a father's pattern of drinking heavily on the weekends is a constraint that limits his ability to engage in constructive activities with his son. Often, however, seemingly entrenched and unmodifiable patterns of behavior can be altered in limited ways and hence can be viewed as obstacles. An anxious, overprotective mother can perhaps be helped to allow her child a greater amount of freedom under particular circumstances, even though her anxiety and overprotectiveness are not altered in any fundamental way.

Constraints within the social system may take many forms, including characteristics of particular members, patterns of interaction, organizational roles and policies. One of the most common and troublesome constraints occurs when the solution to the client's problem as defined is blocked by unmodifiable characteristics or actions of others. There seem to be two ways out of this difficulty: the client moves out of the system; or the problem is reformulated. When the first option is foreclosed, as it often is, by limits on the client's mobility or the other disruptions that might ensue if such a change is made, then the second must be considered. Suppose we have a husband who is dissatisfied with his marriage because of his wife's extramarital affairs. If the wife expresses no interest in changing, and the husband is unwilling to consider leaving her, then the problem of his dissatisfaction with the marital relation must be considered intractable. Other kinds of problem definition would then need to be considered, perhaps concerned with the husband's inability to cope with his wife's behavior or with his inability to leave her.

Range of Application

A question inevitably asked of any treatment system, in one form or another, is, "For what kind of case is, and is not, the system applicable?" It is never an easy question to answer for reasons that will become immediately clear.

A practical answer, in fact, has already been given in the attempt (chapter 3) to define the types of problem that are considered legitimate targets of the model. On this basis, we could say that if one can define with a client a specific, acknowledged, psychosocial problem that he can alleviate through independent action, then task-centered methods are appropriate. Applying this principle, one could appropriately use the model with any problem that meets these criteria, regardless of other characteristics of the client or his situation, or I might add, regardless of the form of treatment that might precede or follow its use. At the level of specific problems, a practitioner could use the core methods of the model in a case that might be treated on the whole within another framework of practice.

An illustration of this partial use of the model was provided by work with Cheryl, an adolescent girl in a residential treatment center. The youngster had been under long-term care for problems of extreme aggressive behavior. The treatment program consisted of a combination of milieu therapy and psychoanalytically oriented casework. One of the issues in her individual treatment was her relationship with her mother. Their visits at the institution had become increasingly upsetting to Cheryl because her mother dwelt on problems at home, particularly her difficulties with Cheryl's father. Matters came to a head when Cheryl refused either to see her mother or to talk to her on the phone. Since her caseworker thought it was essential for Cheryl to resume contact with the mother, she identified the breakdown in communication as a specific problem that Cheryl and her mother needed to work on. Somewhat reluctantly, Cheryl agreed; she would give her mother another chance. A plan of action was devised. Cheryl's task was to call her mother and have a five-minute phone conversation about her own recent activities. Her mother's task (worked out with her by another caseworker) was to participate in the conversation without making any reference to problems at home. Both tasks were planned in detail, rehearsed with mother and daughter in separate sessions, and carried out. Problem-task sequences of this kind have been used in a variety of contexts ranging from very brief (one or two sessions) crisis-oriented intervention to long-term psychodynamic approaches.

The use of full, time-limited sequences of task-centered treatment within the context of long-term, personal-care arrangements has been previously described (Reid and Epstein 1972). In brief, the model is employed to work on specific problems that arise in the course of cases for which the practitioner may have legally mandated responsibilities that may extend beyond the limits of a brief service design. Thus, in a child-welfare setting, a practitioner may be responsible for investigating a situation in which the removal of a child from the home may be required, locating a foster home for the child (if removal is indicated), working with the court, natural and foster parents, and the child to effect the placement, and developing and carrying out a service plan that may involve long-term foster care for the child, return to his parents, or other options. The model in full can be used at strategic points in this process to help foster parents, natural parents, or foster children resolve particular problems. Practitioners can either apply the model selectively in their own caseloads or make a "limited-purpose" referral to another practitioner specially trained in the method.

In one recent application of this strategy (Rooney 1977b), cases accepted for foster placement were referred to a unit of task-centered practitioners who worked with natural and foster parents and children on a range of specific problems, including aspects of the child's adjustment to foster care and obstacles preventing return to natural parents. In some cases, it was possible to effect a return of the child to his natural parents at the conclusion of the brief treatment program. When this outcome was not possible, an effort was made to work out visiting arrangements with natural parents, set a plan for them to follow in order to have the child returned, and to resolve problems the child might be having in foster care. These cases were then transferred to other staff for continued supervision.

When the task-centered system is used in full as the sole or primary method of treatment, its range of application is of course narrower. Nevertheless, the range is broad enough, I think, to serve as a basic approach for the *majority* of clients served by clinical social workers. This conclusion has received support from a large number of demonstrations of the model in most settings in which social workers practice (Reid and Epstein 1977).

But the majority is not all. It is possible to identify certain types of case situations for which the model in full may not provide the optimal mode of practice. For these situations, more appropriate approaches will be suggested. At the outset, it should be recognized that the effectiveness of any method of interpersonal treatment, including the task-centered model, will be limited by deficits in the client's motivation, capacity, and opportunity, to use Ripple's (1964) paradigm. There are obviously cases that might be expected to do poorly regardless of the method of treatment employed. Little would be gained by a shift in approach. My interest here is rather in those cases for which some modality other than task-centered would be indicated or in which an issue of choice of treatment might arise.

I shall not consider cases for which open-ended or long-term treatment as such might be more suitable than brief service. While there are cases of this type, they can be best identified, in my judgment, *after* short-term methods have been tried. Accordingly, this question will be taken up in relation to possible options following termination of the model (chapter 8).

Existential Issues

Some clients want a form of treatment not directed at helping them resolve specific problems in living but instead designed to help them explore issues concerning their life goals, identity, self-concept, mental processes, psychic history, and the like. These clients are troubled by questions of who they are, why they are that way, where they have been, and where they should be going. Even when there are focal concerns, such as a decision about marriage or career, they are seen in relation to these more fundamental questions. Typically well-educated and articulate, the client is interested in a searching and freeranging self-examination. While mental tasks (Ewalt 1977) can be used for purposes of introspection, the structure of the model would probably be too confining in such cases. Modes of treatment that encourage a good deal of client self-expression (such as psychoanalytic, existential, and rogerian approaches) would be more appropriate.

Expressive Needs

Certain clients are motivated by needs to share stressful experiences with an accepting, empathic person. People who have lost loved ones; victims of accidents, rape, and disasters; and fatally ill patients are among those who may be receptive to a social worker's help during the emotional crises precipitated by their traumatic experiences. They have a need to "talk about it" to someone who can understand what they are going through and perhaps help them achieve some perspective about their experiences. While tasks may prove useful in some cases to enable such clients to take action that might relieve their emotional distress or to deal with other problems resulting from the traumatic event, primary attention is given to facilitating their self-expression (see, for example, Grossman 1973).

Resistance to Structured Treatment

It is possible within the task-centered framework to make assertive efforts to engage reluctant persons in treatment (chapters 3, 5). But to preserve the client's autonomy and right to refuse intervention, the practitioner must present his case for treatment in an explicit manner at the beginning of contact and should not proceed either with additional efforts to engage the client in treatment or with a program of intervention without the client's consent. If this principle is judiciously followed, the practitioner should be able to form treatment contracts with most clients who are amenable to help and to avoid fruitless meddling in the lives of those who are not. I have noted that this principle does not apply to persons who lack cognitive capacity to participate in decisions about what needs to be done on their behalf. An alternative mode of helping might be considered for another class of individuals—those who do not want to work in a systematic way on defined problems but who may be willing to accept a less structured, quasi-helping relationship.

Sandra, 15, was referred to a school social worker by the principal because of her class cutting and because she seemed to be "angry, isolated, and unhappy." Her home situation was described as chaotic. She was in a "constant battle" with her parents, and she had run away twice. Suspicious of anyone in a position of authority, Sandra told the social worker on her first visit that the only reason she had come was to get out of class. While she talked freely about her dislike of school, she rejected the practitioner's offer to try to help her identify and work on specific problems. Just as she was leaving the office, Sandra did say that the practitioner might do one thing for her—find out what happened to a request she had made for a course change. The practitioner did this, and they met again. Sandra talked about her difficulties with her teachers, and perhaps in response to the practitioner's friendly interest and concern, about some of her problems at home. But she still did not want to commit herself to any systematic effort to work on them. The practitioner accepted Sandra's invitation to attend a basketball game in which she would be playing. She dropped by the next day to talk about the game and abruptly asked the worker to "check out" a group home she had heard about. Anything would be better than living with her parents.

During the remainder of her stay in high school, Sandra continued to see the worker, mostly dropping in about specific requests, for advice on a range of school and family problems, and "to get things off her chest." With the practitioner's encouragement, she successfully tried out for a part in the school play, and for a time the practitioner worked with her in a role of "assistant drama coach." Her adjustment to school improved significantly, and her situation at home, though remaining problematic, seemed to stabilize somewhat. It is difficult, of course, to evaluate the practitioner's contribution to these gains, but one might assume that it made some difference. Sandra certainly thought so. While some task-centered methods might have been used during the course of their encounters, the model as a whole did not seem to meet her needs.

Unstructured, informal, "mixed-role" relationships of this kind can be developed most readily in settings like schools and residential institutions in which there are opportunities for frequent, casual contact between the social worker and client. But they can also be formed in contexts, such as probation work, in which a certain amount of such contact is required. In some cases, this approach may lead to more deliberate forms of treatment. It perhaps can be best viewed as a second-choice modality that may be tried after an effort has been made to engage the client in a more systematic, and presumably more effective, form of treatment. Potential ethical problems, such as pursuing a treatment agenda without the ''client's'' consent, need to be resolved by making clear the general purposes of the practitioner's involvement and by clarifying more specific change objectives that might arise along the way.

Lack of Stable Problem Focus

One of the assumptions underlying the task-centered model is that a psychosocial problem, once identified, will remain a focus of attention long enough for problem-solving actions to be planned and carried out. This assumption may not hold when the client lacks ability to maintain focus on any particular issue for very long or is in the midst of a highly turbulent situation in which rapid problem change is occurring. Both factors may be present and feed into one another. A client who, for whatever reason, cannot concentrate on one problem at a time may need a less structured approach (in fact, will probably move any approach in this direction).

A good illustrative case has been supplied by a state department of welfare. An unemployed man walked into a local office to apply for assistance. He had just driven into town with his wife and two teen-age daughters and had no funds to buy food. An emergency grant was given, and he was referred to a service worker in the department for his unemployment problem. As work on this problem was getting under way, his two daughters were arrested for shoplifting. This event was followed in quick succession by the family's eviction from the mobile home they had moved into, the disappearance of one of his daughters, and by his own arrest for reckless driving (while looking for his daughter). Although no model of practice has yet been invented for a situation of this kind, the literature of crisis intervention (Specter and Claiborn

1973; Parad 1965) would provide a more fruitful source of ideas than anything in the present volume.

Purely Protective Situations

As has been noted (chapter 3) and will be further discussed (chapter 6), the task-centered approach can be used with many persons who may not have sought the social worker's help or who may be initially reluctant to accept it. There are situations, however, in which the practitioner's efforts to engage the person in collaborative problem solving are unequivocally rejected, but for "protective" reasons the practitioner must remain on the scene. His role is, then, not to provide "help" for the person on his terms, as prescribed by the task-centered model, but rather to "protect" others such as children; the interests of society, as in the case of offenders; or the person himself, as may be required with some mentally retarded or impaired individuals. While elements of helping approaches, including the present model, can be employed in such situations, there is need for alternative models of practice clearly based on the social worker's protective or social-control function. Efforts to develop such approaches have perhaps been retarded by the narrow view that social workers must always be helpful or therapeutic in their work with deviant persons.

Conditions Not Responsive to Client Action

As has been stated, the client must be able to take independent action to alleviate his difficulties if the principal methods of the model are to be applied. The ramifications of this criterion in respect to certain common types of case situations will be examined.

This criterion needs to be considered in cases in which the principal target is a condition for which no remediable action on the client's part can be identified. Psychogenic or psychosomatic difficulties may fall into this category. In the case of such disorders, however, it may be possible to locate problems that seem to aggravate the difficulty and that may be responsive to client action. In such cases, these problems become the agreed-upon focus of treatment on the assumption that their alleviation will help the physical complaint. Task-centered work in these cases should be carried out with medical or psychiatric consultation, or may be used as an adjunct to medical or psychiatric therapy.

In some cases, a potential course of remedial action can be identified, but the client lacks sufficient self-control to carry it out. For example, a chronic alcoholic can presumably solve his problem by eliminating or reducing his intake of alcohol but may not be able to accomplish tasks to this end. He may need stronger supports for his self-control, such as might be provided through a self-help group. Task-centered methods might be used, however, to enable the client to make use of other forms of help.

Task-centered and Behavioral Treatment

Since the problem-solving strategy of the task-centered model now makes use of many behavioral methods, it is important to consider the relationship between the model and what is generally referred to as behavior modification. It might be well to consider first why and how we began to incorporate behavioral technology.

Originally the methods of the task-centered model were essentially a highly focused variation of traditional casework techniques. They were employed not because of their known effectiveness, but rather because they seemed to be the best available at the time. They were seen not as having intrinsic value but only as a means to task achievement. We intended to supplement or replace them with more demonstrably effective methods that might emerge in our testing or from the work of others.

In our own efforts to develop effective task-centered methods, we began to break global or "general" tasks down into more specific "operational" tasks. If the client's general task was to make new friends, then such specific tasks as initiating a conversation with a coworker were developed. This strategy not only seemed to increase the effectiveness of the model but also provided us with better means of assessing its outcomes. At this level of specificity, our work began to resemble behavioral research and treatment. As it did, we were able to draw upon the many advances produced by the behavioral movement, particularly an array of tested and apparently effective methods that could be applied to helping clients achieve tasks.

As attractive and useful as behavioral methods appeared to be, they did not appear to offer a sufficient base for a general system of social work practice. These methods are designed to alter specific problem behaviors. Many of the problems dealt with by social workers cannot be readily reduced to behaviors to be modified. Thus, in problems involving lack of resources, difficulties with organizations, troublesome environments, decision making, novel situations, and crisis events, it may not be possible (or feasible) to single out particular behaviors on the part of the client or others to be changed. A man needs a job; a family wants to get out of an overcrowded, rat-infested apartment; an indebted couple is being badgered by creditors; a child, because of his race, is being bullied by other children; a wife must decide whether to stay with her husband; a child wants help in making it in a new foster-home placement; a young woman has attempted suicide because her boyfriend has broken their engagement. The solution to such problems may not require modification of specific patterns of client behavior but rather a unique configuration of actions taken by a variety of persons—the client, the practitioner, and others. Moreover, behavioral methods do not address the range of mental processes that are a part of the origins and resolution of human problems. To be sure, some forms of behavioral treatment are concerned with cognitive factors, but to the extent they are, they no longer can be said to be behavioral in the strict sense of the term.

Techniques of behavior change can often be effectively applied to many problems dealt with by social workers, but overall treatment strategy often requires more than those techniques can supply. The question is: How can this new and powerful behavioral technology be used to best advantage in social work practice?

One answer is to build systems of social work practice that can handle the complexities of the problems dealt with by social workers while incorporating behavioral methods for use when appropriate. In general, the need is to design models of service that first meet the requirements of problems brought to social workers, rather than to adapt the problems we see to treatment systems borrowed from other fields.

In developing the task-centered model, we have attempted to incorporate behavioral methods into a system of social work practice. These methods, translated into our own terms, provide an essential part of the structure used to help clients carry out specific tasks. In general, if the best route to problem alleviation is a change in client behavior, then the course of treatment followed may resemble behavior modification. If this kind of change is not demanded by the problem, then our treatment, as we shall see, may take on a different character.

The concept of task provides a way of integrating a technology for behavior change, on the one hand, with strategies for effecting other kinds of action often required to resolve problems faced by social work clients. Thus, an unmarried mother overwhelmed with the burden of caring for several young children may undertake the task of approaching a relative to provide temporary care for one of the children; at the same time, the practitioner might assume the task of locating a day-care facility for another child. In addition, the mother might work on very specific tasks designed to bring about changes in her parenting behavior; to help her in carrying out these tasks, self-administered incentives (or reinforcers) might be used following a certain type of behavioral program. These various strategies can be organized within one frame of reference and through one set of terms, which may facilitate the practitioner's thinking and the client's understanding of the treatment process.

It can still be argued, of course, that the model in its present form, particularly the developments stressed in this book, represents "another form of behavior modification." That argument is difficult to answer since the term "behavior modification" (or "behavior therapy") is used loosely to refer to an increasing variety of often rather diverse approaches, many of which contain "nonbehavioral" components. If one wishes to make a distinction between the present system and at least most approaches labeled "behavioral," ample basis for so doing may be found in our acceptance of complex, client-perceived problems that may involve more than behavioral difficulties and in our theories of human problems and problem-solving action; in our use of client tasks to denote more than specific behavior; in the role accorded practitioner tasks; in the stress placed on such cognitive activities as task planning and analysis of obstacles; and in the limits placed on the amount and duration of service. Since the boundaries of "behavioral" treatment cannot be adequately defined, the argument over whether or not a given approach is "behavioral" does not seem to be very productive. Fundamentally, our interest is not behavioral methods as such but in methods that are scientifically testable.

Task-Centered Treatment as a Part of Social Work

Some time ago the methods of social work, like Caesar's Gaul, were divided into three parts: casework, group work, and community organization. During the 1960s, a new realignment emerged: individual and group treatment methods began to be viewed holistically as social treatment or clinical social work. On the other side of the profession, the renaming of old approaches and the addition of new ones produced a configuration of methods (community organization, community development, social planning, social action, etc.) to which the terms "macro social work" (Schwartz 1977) and "social development" have been applied. At the same time, efforts to bridge this new division began to emerge. Systems of generic social work practice incorporating elements of both "micro" and "macro" practice appeared (Pincus and Minahan 1973; Goldstein 1973; Siporin 1975), accompanied by a growing emphasis in schools of social work on generic social work training and on social problem and other concentrations that bring together methods of social treatment and social development. New forms of cross-methods practice began to appear. To provide a rationale and an impetus for these developments, the search for unifying conceptions of social work has been intensified (National Association of Social Workers 1977).

Although these bridging and unifying efforts have their limitations (Schwartz 1977), they are forging useful links between different elements of the profession. Moreover, they are producing a new breed of social worker, versatile in, or at least knowledgeable about, the diverse methods of social work intervention.

While these developments by no means obviate the need for systems of social treatment, they do suggest that the intervention strategies of such systems be linked to other types of social work intervention. To the extent that it is so linked, a social treatment system can be used with greater facility by practitioners with generic social work training and can contribute to unifying conceptions of the profession. At the very least, how a social treatment system relates to the rest of social work should be articulated.

The change strategies of the task-centered system find a connection with the profession as a whole through three central concepts: problem, task, and obstacle.

Problem

As has been argued (chapter 1), a central purpose of social work as a whole is the alleviation of psychosocial problems. The objective is pursued at different levels: the level of individuals and families expressing the problem, and at the neighborhood, community, state, and national levels. A multilevel attack on psychosocial problems can perhaps be carried out more systematically if it is organized around a common problem typology. Thus, work with individual clients on lack of child-care resources can be better related to the efforts of community planners to resolve the same difficulty if the target is thought of in the same terms at both levels. Exchanges of information on problem type and frequency between levels would facilitate work at each. The problem categories addressed by the task-centered approach (chapter 3) might facilitate such a coordinated effort.

We must remember, however, that the present model is concerned with client-acknowledged problems. Problems may not always be defined in this way, particularly problems reflecting deviations from societal norms—delinquency, child abuse, and the like. This lack of fit may create difficulties but can also be used to advantage. Since social treatment seems to work best when addressed to problems clients want to alleviate, there may be value in making explicit the probably limited contribution of individualized treatment to the remediation of problems of social deviance and the like. Thus, one could determine for a given number of "abusing" parents how many were engaged in working on acknowledged problems and of what kind. It is quite likely that only a small proportion would be so engaged and that in many of these instances the problems worked on would be only indirectly related to parental aggression toward children.

In addition, identification of client-perceived concerns would help specify the social problems clients themselves want help with. Social problems may be defined in rather gross ways at such societal levels as the community or state; moreover, their definitions are often based on untested or rather crudely tested assumptions of social planners. Thus "lack of adequate housing" may be seen as a major problem for a particular community, and this lack may be interpreted to mean insufficient new housing. If people in the community view their housing inadequacies in terms of need for certain kinds of repairs, then the housing problem in general may be cast in a different light.

Task

The concept of task has been used by various writers as a means of integrating diverse types of social work activity (Bartlett 1970; Siporin 1975). If a task is seen as a type of problem-solving action, the concept becomes particularly relevant to social work as a whole. As Pincus and Minahan argue (1973), social work intervention, regardless of the particular form it takes, can be viewed as being carried out by "action systems" consisting of clients, workers, and others.

Promoting problem-solving action seems to be at the heart of much social work activity, whether it occurs with individual clients, community groups, or agency representatives. Elements of task planning and implementation with individual clients or families in the present model certainly have much in common with efforts to devise and carry out courses of action in other social work contexts. Suppose, for example, that a worker was attempting to help a group of parents of mentally handicapped children take action to obtain more resources for their children from the local school system. In developing strategies and tactics to achieve this goal, the practitioner might well plan with the group specific actions (or tasks) to be carried out and how they might be best implemented. Methods used in the present model for task planning, establishing incentives, rehearsing proposed actions, and the like, could be applied.

Obstacle

Finally, the model can be linked to other forms of social work through the notion of obstacles to problem resolution and task accomplishment. Of particular relevance here are such external obstacles as lack of resources or dysfunctional organizational policies and practices. External obstacles that typically prevent people from achieving their goals are of central interest to community organizers and social planners, who may have the capacity to resolve them on a large scale if they are properly identified.

Thus, in one state in which the task-centered approach has been used, one recurring obstacle to task achievement was lack of transportation facilities. There was little public transportation; clients without automobiles found it difficult to carry out tasks requiring movement from one place to another. Agencies usually lacked the resources to help. By pinpointing this kind of obstacle in various contexts, workers were able to develop specific recommendations, such as provision of funds to reimburse costs incurred by volunteer drivers who might be willing to donate their time and vehicles to provide transportation for clients.

Task-Centered Treatment
as a Part of the Social Services

In addition to such links to other parts of the profession, a general model of social work practice, such as the task-centered approach, needs to be related to other forms of human service in the field of social welfare. The need to articulate this relationship has been accentuated by the growth of the "personal social services" during recent years (Kahn 1976). The problem is illustrated by a recent compilation of data on social services provided by public welfare agencies throughout the nation as a whole (U.S. Department of Health, Education, and Welfare 1975). Some 40 services were listed, only one of which ("counseling") could be readily related to social treatment models as these are customarily defined. Of those remaining, a good number were tangible services (such as chore, homemaker, and day-care services), which would be clearly differentiated from task-centered or other forms of interpersonal helping, but others (such as foster care, protective, unmarried mother, and employment services) might be expected to contain at least elements of such methods of helping. How does a model like the present one fit into this array of services?

I assume that for large numbers of clients problems of greatest concern can be best resolved through approaches, like the task-centered model, that can help the client through a systematic problem-solving process. Problems in human relations provide the most obvious case in point. In such cases, other forms of service have a subsidiary role.

For another large group of clients, a more complex mix of different forms of service seems to be required. A client may have one problem for which problem solving is needed to effect a resolution; he may have another difficulty that can be resolved through a tangible service. Or both "counseling" and "noncounseling" services may be required to alleviate a particular problem or interrelated set of problems: an isolated, elderly person may benefit from help to become more active in making social contacts and the services of a volunteer visiting program; a neglectful parent may need a combination of a homemaker and help in altering her functioning as a parent; a child might use counseling to work through difficulties in adjusting to foster-care placement; a problem-solving approach may be used by a disabled person to reach a decision about what rehabilitative services he would like to have. As these examples suggest, a social treatment model may need to be closely coordinated with other services or be instrumental in helping the client obtain and make use of them.

Tangible services alone may be quite sufficient for still another large group of clients, those who are not interested in a problem-solving approach or who do not need it in order to make use of the service. For this group, the social worker may provide information, determine eligibility, assist with application forms, arrange for referral, or even take action to obtain the service for the client. A therapeutic approach serves little purpose when routinely built in or added on to the tangible service.

From the foregoing, one can demonstrate the need for an individualized model of social work practice in which clients are helped to identify and resolve complex personal problems. It is also apparent that such a model of practice needs to be designed with connections to other services that clients may utilize. More than a model of in-session counseling is required since the practitioner may need to work collaboratively with the client and other service providers. The present approach attempts to meet this requirement through treatment of problems involving lack of services or lack of utilization of them; and provision for client and practitioner actions (tasks) that can be used to help the client secure other services or to increase their usefulness.

Chapter 6

Problem Specification
and the Service Contract

The theoretical and strategic considerations that guide the task-centered model have been set forth in preceding chapters. This chapter and the two following will be devoted to the activities of the model—the collaborative efforts of practitioner and client to identify and resolve target problems.

Specifying the problem and forming the service contract are the basic activities during the initial phase of contact, which normally consists of from one to four interviews with clients and collaterals over a one- to two-week period. It is desirable to specify at least one problem and reach a contract by the end of the initial interview, even if the session needs to be extended beyond the usual hour limit. This ideal cannot always be realized, however. Clients' uncertainties about what their problems are and the kind of help they want, the complexities of some problem situations, the need in certain cases to involve several clients (or collaterals) in problem specification or contracting activities are among the reasons why the one-interview ideal is often exceeded.

When problem specification extends beyond the first contact, it is important to be clear with the client about next steps, so that each session during this phase ends with an understanding (a precontract, one might say) about what is to be done next. Usually no advantages are to be gained by spreading out these activities over time. While the practitioner may need to see the client more than once or to involve others, he is well advised to compress this effort within the shortest period feasible. Until his problems have been specified, the client is not able to use time to the best advantage to attempt remedial action.

If it is difficult for the client to engage himself with the worker because of shyness, lack of trust, or other reasons, the problem specification and contracting processes may need to proceed at a slower pace, though they should not be protracted or diverted simply in order to "allow time to develop a relationship." The best way for a social worker to begin to secure the trust and confidence of his client is to move ahead in a businesslike but humane manner toward the goal of finding out what is troubling the client and what can be done about it—in other words, to act like a professional with a job to do. The practitioner who steps out of this role may well exacerbate the client's anxiety and create confusion, if not suspicion.

Before taking up problem specification and contracting in detail, we need to make a final, general point. While these activities may, as we shall see, be continued throughout the life of a case, it is essential that they produce agreement on specified target problems before the client is engaged in problem-solving efforts. That is, to the extent that he follows the model, the practitioner does not offer advice, provide explanations of the client's or others' behavior, or indulge in other forms of change-oriented efforts before a contract is reached. Both the effectiveness and propriety of such premature "therapizing" are open to question. At this point the practitioner's understanding of the client's problems is still nebulous, and the client has not yet assented to be subject to the practitioner's influence. As much of the so-called treatment of respondents (involuntary clients) illustrates, it is possible to "counsel" persons for prolonged periods and to little avail in the absence of any agreement on what the problem is or any acceptance on the person's part of the worker's "helping" role. Thus, our admonition is not only against jumping the gun but also against running indefinitely in the wrong direction.

Problem Specification

The purpose of problem specification is to enable the practitioner and client to achieve an understanding of the problem adequate for the development of tasks and for an analysis of obstacles to their accomplishment. While the bulk of problem specification may be completed prior to the introduction of subsequent steps, the activity almost always continues throughout the course of work on a problem. Problems are seldom *completely* specified at the outset. New information invariably comes to light as work proceeds and, in addition, changes in the problem itself require continual examination. Problem specification can be broken down into a set of subactivities, presented below.

Identification of Potential Problems

Usually the first step in problem specification is to identify problem areas from which may be fashioned specific target problems that the practitioner and client will work on. The course of this activity will be determined to a large extent by whether or not the person comes to the practitioner for help with a problem. Because of the importance of this distinction, we shall consider the two types of situation separately, beginning with the person who has requested to see a social worker because he wants help.

Applicants
The help-seeking person, or applicant, may have sought out the worker on his own or, as is more common, may have been referred by someone. In any event, he comes because of a want that he hopes the social worker can help him satisfy.

In these cases the practitioner "begins with the request," to use Hamilton's phrase (1951, p. 55). Some applicants will initially focus on one or more problems that, with further refinement, would fit the requirements of the model. If so, the practitioner usually proceeds by eliciting the applicant's concerns and by maintaining focus on what is troubling him. Within this general focus he permits the applicant to unfold his difficulties in his own way. Through facilitating questions, the practitioner attempts to help him draw a general picture of his problem areas. If the applicant is reluctant to express himself, or seems uncomfortable about revealing himself, the practitioner may need to acknowledge his hesitancy or distress and provide reassurance and encouragement. As this process unfolds, a number of possible problems may be generally described, perhaps without clear lines of demarcation between them or a sense as to which is the most troublesome. After presenting a brief summary of what has been revealed, the practitioner may then attempt to identify the problem areas that seem to be of greatest concern to the applicant. These impressions are then checked out with the applicant and modified accordingly. In this process the practitioner begins to help the person formulate his problems—at this point to put into ideas and words what up to now may have been an unarticulated sense of discomfort or a jumble of unsorted complaints. With a tentative agreement reached on problems of greatest concern, the practitioner and applicant are then ready to consider each in greater detail.

Often (if not usually) things do not go so smoothly. The applicant may be unclear about the nature of his dissatisfaction; he may settle on an issue that appears trivial in relation to other issues he has revealed; or he may formulate a problem whose solution appears unfeasible to the practitioner. In the ensuing exploration, the practitioner may ask questions which may probe possible areas of dissatisfaction, or may make comments to help the applicant sharpen his perception of his difficulties. In this phase, the practitioner's role is still primarily that of clarifier of the applicant's concerns—what it is he wants that he is not getting.

The applicant's definition of the problem that emerges from this clarification process is accepted unless there are specific grounds to challenge it. Grounds for challenge arise most often when the problem, as the applicant defines it, appears to the practitioner to require a solution that would be unfeasible, illegal, or would have negative consequences for the applicant or others. A

mother about to be released from a state hospital had lost custody
of her children on a child-neglect petition. She presented her problem as "wanting the immediate return of her children." Given the
circumstances of the case, the practitioner regarded the stated
problem as impossible to resolve and considered the proposed
solution as entailing too great a risk for the children. He stated his
position and the reasons for it, in a forthright manner, avoiding the
temptation to try to "talk her out of" her wish. Recognizing the
legitimacy of her desire to have her children returned and her frustration at not being able to get them back immediately, he nevertheless attempted to point out the reasons why her present request
could not be realized. Inaccurate beliefs shaping the mother's want
were taken up; for example, she believed that she was legally entitled to have her children back upon her release from the hospital.
He then proposed a more realistic definition of the problem—her
lack of understanding of what might be required to have them returned and her lack of a feasible plan for getting them back.

As the example illustrates, the practitioner tries to help the
applicant reformulate intractable or ethically unacceptable problems, yet still attempts to respond, to the extent possible, to what
the applicant wants. In rejecting an applicant's definition of the
problem, the "burden of proof" is clearly on the practitioner. He
should have a clear reason for his decision. He should be reluctant
to write off an applicant-stated problem as unsolvable simply because the means of solution may not be clear or because of his
doubts about the applicant's capacity to solve it.

Certain other contingencies need to be considered. The applicant may present as his only problem an issue that appears trivial
in relation to other problems that appear to be bothering him. In
handling this contingency the practitioner normally accepts the
problem presented but asks that the other issues be considered, following the approach suggested below for persons who do not acknowledge problems. Or the applicant's problem may be one that
can be more effectively dealt with by another agency or practitioner, in which case referral possibilities are discussed.

Finally, the involvement of others may be indicated before

the applicant's problems can be properly formulated or even before the question of who may be the clients in a case can be settled. This circumstance usually arises when one member of a social system is initially seen concerning problems relating to other members of the system. The system in question is normally a family but may take other forms, such as a peer group or a student-teacher dyad. Typically the problem presented by the applicant who is initially seen involves some complaint about the behavior of another member of the system. In these situations the initial definition of the problem may be altered considerably when other members are brought in. For example, the applicant's initial complaint may be modified in the light of reactions of other members; the others may have problems that are interdependent with the applicant's, or a definition of the problem at a system level (interpersonal conflict) may emerge. Moreover, there are usually strategic advantages in work with any client who has system-related problems if other members can be involved; normally it is better if this involvement with other members is made before closure is reached on the target problem. (Approaches to problem specification in simultaneous work with different family members are taken up in greater detail in chapter 9.) For various reasons, the applicant initially seen may not wish to have others involved. Although such reasons may be legitimately examined and the advantages of including others, at least for purposes of problem specification, may be pointed out, ultimately the applicant's wishes need to be respected.

Respondents

Problem specification proceeds on a different premise when the person has no presenting request, that is, when he is a respondent. He may have been sent to a social worker by a referral source in a position of authority who has attributed a problem to him. The respondent complies with the referral and sees the social worker, not because he wants help with a problem but because of his fear of possible consequences if he does not comply. Or he may acquiesce because he is reluctant to go against the wishes of someone he regards as having considerable power. Thus judges, school officials, physicians, and welfare and protective agencies send to social workers streams of reluctant persons who come with the message, "——— told me to see you." The respondent may not even be the one to initiate contact. Prompted by referral information or a complaint from the community, a social worker may seek out the respondent.

Regardless of who has initiated contact, the practitioner attempts to review with the respondent why he was referred and to determine whether or not problems attributed to him by others, or other aspects in his life situation, are presenting difficulties for him. In this process the social worker usually reveals, at least in general terms, information he has about the person's situation as perceived by referral sources and others.

In this review, emphasis is placed upon what is troubling the respondent, even though such difficulties may not be quite what the referral source, or other problem attributors, had in mind. Often the respondent-perceived difficulties will be in the same area, although cast in a different perspective. Thus, a child referred for fighting may acknowledge a problem of being picked on by other children (which he may see as a cause of his fighting). The practitioner may challenge the person's definition of the problem in the light of what he knows or can reasonably infer about his situation and, in the process, may present evidence that might help the person define the problem in more "realistic" terms. The practitioner then accepts, at least tentatively, the modified conception of the problem as the person now presents it. It is assumed that more can be accomplished in working with the respondent's definition of the problem than with a definition imposed by the social worker. Not only will the person achieve greater benefit but usually others will profit more in the long run. To use the previous example, a resolution of the problem of being picked on may also alleviate the problem of fighting, whereas nothing at all might be accomplished if the worker had attempted to "help" a recalcitrant child with the fighting problem.

The person may, of course, acknowledge that he has a problem but may not see the social worker as the person to help him with it. The typical response is, "I can work it out on my own." The practitioner then needs to explain how he might be of help. While this kind of orientation is normally taken up as a part of contracting (see below), it may be necessary to begin the process during this initial stage of problem specification; otherwise the contracting stage may never be reached.

Suppose the person comes up with no problem he wants to work on or one that bears no relation to some difficulty of great concern to others, including the practitioner. How far should the practitioner go in trying to influence him to acknowledge the attributed problem, and how should he go about it.?

We see nothing wrong with the practitioner's presenting as convincing a case as he can for a problem he thinks is important for the respondent to work on. Since any problem-solving experience in the model should be constructive, the practitioner should not try to press the issue in a way that the person would find upsetting or offensive. Such an approach would do little good in any event. Both ethical and practical considerations dictate that the practitioner's case should be made in an explicit, forthright, and expeditious manner. The issue of whether or not agreement on the problem can be reached should be settled before subsequent activities are attempted.

If the respondent does not acknowledge a problem in the first interview, the practitioner has certain options. He can simply terminate contact at that point. He can offer a stipulated number of additional sessions, usually one or two, to continue the search for a possible problem the respondent might want to work on. If others are involved in the problem or have information about it, the practitioner may suggest that he see them and then get together with the respondent again. If the practitioner thinks the respondent might be more amenable to accepting help elsewhere, referral possibilities can be discussed. In some cases, the social worker may be required or feel obligated to continue contact with the person, to discharge supervisory, protective, or investigatory responsibilities. This kind of contingency is most likely to occur in work with offenders, the mentally ill, the retarded, and parents suspected of child abuse or neglect. In these situations, the social worker should make it clear why further contact is necessary; he need not—and should not—pretend he is going to help with difficulties perceived by the respondent, unless the respondent indicates his desire for this kind of help.

In attempting to bring about acknowledgement of a problem, the practitioner must, obviously, proceed with caution. He is faced with a person who is likely to be defensive about his supposed difficulties and likely to deny or minimize their importance. Moreover, he is apt to regard the social worker with suspicion, as another representative of an oppressive officialdom.

The usual focal point is the difficulty that occasioned the person's contact with the social worker. How this difficulty may be affecting the person is explored. An effort is made to involve the person in discussion of the possible adverse consequences for him if the problem continues, what he might be able to do, and how the social worker might help him do it. The practitioner attempts to elicit the respondent's thinking about adverse consequences and possible actions to avoid them. From his own information of the person's situation or his general knowledge, he tries to expand on, or offer possible corrections to, the person's perceptions.

P.:   What do you think might happen if you go out and leave your children alone at night?
Mrs. T: Nothing. They can take care of themselves. I don't leave matches or anything around.
P.:   Maybe so. But still a lot of people in this town don't think that children this age should be left alone. Someone may call the police. It happened to you once.
Mrs. T: It's none of their damn business!
P.:   Perhaps not, but it can cause you difficulty. The court might want to find another home for your children. Would you want that?
Mrs. T: Are you kidding?

This dialogue may or may not result in Mrs. T's recognizing that she has a problem providing adequate care for her young children or at least a potential problem of conflict with the court, but it illustrates the approach we are suggesting. The practitioner's appeal is to the respondent's self-interest. He avoids threats and moralizing while still presenting, in a clear-cut but tactful way, the adverse realities that might result if the person's behavior is not modified—and the benefits that might ensue if it is.

In such cases the referral source often assumes an important role. Usually the referring agent expects that the social worker will "do something" about the "obvious" difficulties the respondent is having. A teacher wants a child to be better behaved in class, the manager of a housing project wants a family to stop throwing debris out of the window, and so on. In the eyes of the referral source the problem may be clear-cut; what is needed is a solution. The practitioner then finds himself in a quandary: a referral source expecting results, on one side; an "uncooperative" respondent on the other. This quandary is not unique to the task-centered model. In the present approach, however, the conflict is brought to a head more quickly and more clearly. A practitioner operating within a task-centered framework cannot do what is often done: to see the person over a period of time in a series of inconclusive and unproductive contacts with the hope that whatever crisis occasioned the referral will eventually abate. While such a tactic may appear to "work" in those cases in which the referral problem does subside, it is an ineffectual form of practice that in the long run helps no one.

It is better, we think, to inform the referral source without delay that the person, in spite of the practitioner's efforts, is not willing to work on problems for which he was referred. With the status of the case thus clarified, the worker and referral source can reassess the situation and consider available options. From this discussion may emerge additional information about the respondent's problems as the referring person sees them, or the practitioner can present aspects of the respondent's situation that may cast these problems in a new light. This process can sometimes provide the practitioner with the basis for developing a problem acceptable to the respondent. Even if it does not, the referral source is at least clear about where things stand and does not proceed on the erroneous assumption that the problems of concern to him are being taken care of by the social worker.

Detailed Exploration

Once acknowledged problems have been identified, they are explored in detail. The exploration is designed to obtain a picture of the events leading up to, characterizing, and following the problem. In most cases these events consist of a complex scenario of actions and interactions involving the client and members of his social system. From this scenario the practitioner hopes to construct a statement of the target problem and conditions to be changed, to gain a perspective on the effects the problem is having on the client's life, to locate obstacles to solution, and to identify the basis of possible change strategies.

Although the scenario can be constructed from any point of departure, it can be most easily presented and understood if it is thought of as moving forward in time. Thus, one will consider first the point of origin of the problem—when it started. If we know when a problem began, we may then be able to identify causative factors that may still be operative. When a practitioner hears a mother say, "Daniel began to act up just after I gave birth to Susan," he may then suspect that Daniel's reaction to his new sibling may be contributing to his current behavior difficulties and guide further inquiry accordingly. Often, determining the point of origin gives us little more than an estimate of how long the problem has been in existence, a useful piece of information perhaps, but one that provides little guidance about what to do next. The client may not be able to offer clues about what brought the problem into being, and it may be impossible to identify and sort out historical factors that may have been present some time past.

Knowledge of the history of the problem is only important in the present system to the extent it can shed light on immediate modifiable factors. The client who says she has always been afraid of being rejected by people in authority because her father abandoned her when she was a child suggests that she may have developed the inaccurate belief that those in authority will reject her. The practitioner is more interested in exploring the current belief and its present consequences than her early filial relationship.

In any case, attention soon becomes focused on events that are currently influencing and characterizing the problem. How can the problem be defined, and what is preventing its resolution? These are the master questions that guide specific inquiry at this point.

A useful procedure is to trace the development of the problem from its point of origin to the present, with emphasis on recent developments bearing on the problem, the actions of the client, his interactions with others, relevant beliefs of the client and others, and the role of organizations when pertinent. Inquiry then proceeds to apparent consequences of the problem. How does it affect the client and others? When problems are recurring in nature—interactional difficulties, for example—it is helpful to select a recent occurrence, or, as Taylor (1977) has put it, a "critical incident," that typifies the problem. An analysis of the incident may reveal details that might go unnoticed in a more general review. One can then inquire about ways in which the incident may be atypical.

However it is conducted, the exploration attempts to capture precise details. This is done in large part by getting the client to spell out vague and general terms that most people use to describe events. A husband may complain that his wife "nags." We would want to know what his wife says that he interprets as nagging and how often it occurs. Being "in debt" needs to be translated into approximate dollar amounts; "drinking" into how much alcohol (ethanol) is actually consumed during specified periods, and so on. Sequences of action and interaction need to be carefully traced, again in concrete terms. Who says or does what to whom in what order?

Particular emphasis is given to what the client has done (or is doing) to alleviate the problem. Such data not only add to understanding of causation but provide leads to the kinds of tasks that might be the most effective. Thus, if the practitioner learns that certain actions have alleviated (or aggravated) the problem, he has a better understanding of what is causing it. These actions can then be used as a base in task planning. If the client is not able to recall his previous efforts to cope with the problem, the practitioner's inquiries are guided by the range of possible actions that the client might have undertaken given the nature of the problem and the circumstances of the case. If the client's problem is depression, the worker might ask if there is any special kind of activity that helps him snap out of it. Or the practitioner may ask for instances when an occurrence of the problem threatened but did not materialize. Suppose a husband has difficulty in controlling his temper with his spouse. Can he recall any instances when he reached a "boiling point" but did not explode? What happened to avoid a flare-up? Negative as well as positive consequences of the client's problem-solving efforts need to be explored. Actions that alleviate one problem may aggravate others. A husband who avoids certain topics of conversation with his wife to avoid quarrels may be perpetuating misunderstandings between them and adding to the tension in their relationship.

The following scenario will give some idea of the scope and detail of the inquiry process. Mrs. S's chief complaint was that her husband (who refused to see the social worker) often came home drunk and was both "physically and verbally abusive" to her and their daughter. The practitioner explored events during the preceding week, which Mrs. S said was typical and, upon further inquiry, appeared to be. Mr. S had come home about 2 A.M. Saturday morning, intoxicated, and had started to cook a steak. Mrs. S, awakened by the noise, came down to the kitchen. Mrs. S, angered by being awakened and seeing the next day's meal ready to be put into a frying pan, grabbed the steak. At this point, Mr. S grabbed her wrist, and she let the steak go. A quarrel then ensued in which Mr. S accused his wife of nagging and interference. She berated him for his drunkenness and brutality. The following night he "drank himself to sleep" while watching TV, but nothing else happened. Another incident occurred later in the week. Again Mr. S came home drunk, this time not so late. He started to watch TV. Their nine-year-old daughter, Bessie, wanted to watch a different program. Mr. S became angered and pushed her away, causing Bessie to run to her room crying. This incident again led to a quarrel between Mr. and Mrs. S. He accused her of being sexually cold. What could he expect, she responded, if he behaved the way he did.

Between incidents there was "little talk but no fighting." As a result of these incidents, however, Mrs. S felt bitter toward her husband, a feeling she expressed by communicating with him as little as possible. Her daughter was upset, she thought, by her father's behavior and the quarreling; her schoolwork was suffering as a result.

In this instance, the details of the scenario serve to clarify the problem and to lay the groundwork for planning remedial action. Thus, it can be seen that the husband's physically abusive behavior, while naturally disturbing to Mrs. S, was limited to grabbing and pushing and that it was in response to some provocation. It is a different picture than one of a father coming home drunk and committing wanton acts of aggression on members of his family. Although the actions of mother and daughter that provoked Mr. S might be considered justified, it may be possible that if they left him alone during these periods the destructive interactions might not occur. Moreover, one notes that much, if not most, of their meaningful talk about their problems seems to occur when he is drunk and belligerent, and that as an aftermath of their quarrels they withdraw from one another. Perhaps some headway could be made if they discussed their concerns when he was sober. Since Mrs. S did not want to leave her husband, and he could not be involved in treatment, some actions on her part, possibly along lines suggested, might make a difficult situation more tolerable.

Problem Definition and Explication

After the problem has been explored and laid out in this fashion, the next step is to develop an explicit definition of the problem, including a general statement of the difficulty and a specification of conditions the practitioner and client will attempt to change (see chapter 3). The practitioner usually begins the step by formulating a problem statement and describing the conditions it refers to. His formulation is an attempt to distill and reflect back the problem that the client has expressed. If the practitioner's formulation is somewhat different in scope or focus from the client's apparent conception of the difficulty, the practitioner needs to point this out, state his reasons for the difference, and elicit the client's reaction. The practitioner and client then work over the problem definition until it is acceptable to both. In this process more precise data describing the nature and occurrence of the problem may need to be obtained.

In the example just discussed, the following definition was developed:

Problem Statement:
Mrs. S does not know how to cope with her husband's behavior when he is drunk.
Specification:
Mr. S frequently comes home drunk or gets drunk in the evening while at home. When he does, he becomes belligerent and loses his temper with her or their daughter, Bessie, if he doesn't get his own way. Quarrels between Mr. and Mrs. S are likely to occur, and Mr. S may use physical force, usually in the form of grabbing or pushing Mrs. S or Bessie. His physical and verbal behavior are very upsetting to both mother and daughter. There have been two such incidents during the past week.

From prior discussion, it was clear that little could be done directly to effect a change in Mr. S's behavior. What Mrs. S. could do about his behavior or the siutation became the focus for work.

The definition of the problem needs to be made with some care, since it will provide the direction for the collaborative efforts of practitioner and client. Both need to make sure they are not only aiming at the right target but at the same target.

Thus, in the case just presented, the problem was defined in terms of Mrs. S's *coping* with her husband's behavior. It would have been not only imprecise but misleading to have defined the problem in terms of her husband's behavior. One hopes it will change, but it is not the immediate target.

The explicit, shared definition of a target problem may be formed earlier or later in the process. Usually it is necessary to develop at least a rough scenario of what appears to be the problem before either the practitioner or client can order the complexities of the problem situation sufficiently to arrive at a meaningful definition. Once a definition has been reached, the scenario may need to be fleshed out in greater detail or perhaps revised in the light of how the problem has actually been defined. Here (and elsewhere) in the model, collaboration between worker and client does not necessarily proceed in a straightforward step-wise fashion, but rather in a back-and-forth manner between different activities.

If possible, the frequency of problem behavior or events is determined for a period of time preceding the interview. Such retrospective baseline information adds to precision in specifying the problem. It also provides a base for assessing the client's progress in treatment. Typically a seven-day period is used (as in the example above), although the length of the period varies according to the frequency of the problem: the less frequently the problem occurs, the longer the baseline period.

Some problems, of course, do not lend themselves to this kind of baselining. For certain difficulties, variation over time is not applicable: an adolescent runaway wants a place to stay; a child has been expelled from school and wants to be reinstated; a wife wants to come to a decision about whether or not to leave her husband. If variation in a problem state is a possibility, then some exploration of frequency of occurrence is warranted. For example, a client may report that he is "depressed all the time," but further investigation may reveal significant variation in the occurrence of his depressive spells.

Additional data on the current characteristics and frequency of the problem can be obtained from tests or self-report instruments designed by the practitioner and client. For example, a child experiencing difficulty in academic skills can do some work for the practitioner, giving him firsthand data on the problem. Clients can record instances of problem behavior on charts or logs. A person who has difficulty being assertive can record instances in which he thought he was not sufficiently assertive, noting when the instance occurred, with whom, and so on. A variety of approaches and procedures that can be used for client recording has been described (Thoreson and Mahoney 1974). In some situations, the practitioner's direct observation of the client's problem behavior can be used, particularly in work with children in school and residential settings and with problems of marital or family interaction (chapter 9). A considerable literature on observational methods for this purpose is available (see, for example, Bijou, Peterson, and Ault 1968; Hersen and Barlow 1976).

Whenever feasible, supplementary and corroborative data should be obtained from others (family members, teachers, etc.) with firsthand knowledge of manifestations of the client's problem or who can supply contextual information about it (see below). The client's knowledge and consent is normally obtained for this type of data collection.

The sources of data described above are used to monitor changes in the problem once treatment has begun. In the present model, treatment is normally not delayed while ongoing baseline data are obtained. Retrospective data are admittedly less precise but have the advantage of enabling active treatment measures to be undertaken immediately, an advantage that may be telling when the client's motivation for help may be uncertain or short-lived, or when the problem at hand requires immediate action. In some cases a delay in intervention may be worth the added precision gained in collecting current data free of treatment effects. This step may be warranted when the problem occurs with a relatively high rate of frequency, when immediate corrective action is not demanded, and when there is opportunity to gain precise data through direct observation.

Determining Desired Changes

In specifying conditions to be changed, the practitioner and client generally assume that certain changes are desirable, but what the client wants exactly may need more explicit delineation. This activity may be interwoven with, or even precede, determination of target conditions.

The question is, "What kind of change will need to occur in order for the client to regard the problem as solved to his satisfaction?" A high school student's problem may be summarized as doing poorly in his studies and may be specified in terms of test scores, grades, and so forth. But what does he want to achieve? He may wish to avoid a failing grade, or he may wish to do well enough to get into a particular college. Or, he may not have any particular objective in mind—he just wants to do better than he has been doing.

Clarifying what the client wants is the first step toward establishing a treatment goal, although the client's wants and a goal for treatment are by no means synonymous. The client may aspire to certain things that cannot be realistically achieved through his efforts with the practitioner: a treatment goal reflects what can be.

The practitioner's role is to elicit what the client would like to obtain. In this process he attempts to help the client clarify what he wants and to distinguish, if need be, what he might attain in treatment and what might represent longer-range goals.

Person-situation Context

Any psychosocial problem may be thought of as the product of the interplay of psychological and social factors. In the present system the nature of the data to be collected about such factors is primarily determined by the target problems. From these focal concerns the practitioner branches out into areas of the client's functioning and situation. The intent is not, as in some models of practice, to gather and sift a large body of information about these areas to serve as a basis for determining what the client's difficulties are. Rather, the purpose is to secure information that will provide guidance in work with problems whose essential outlines have already been determined, not on the basis of what is "wrong" from a theoretical perspective but on the basis of what is troubling the client.

A good deal of data about the person and his situation will have been collected and analyzed in the course of problem exploration, definition, and assessment. The present category comprises additional information of this kind that serves two functions: to provide further elaboration of factors that may be a part of the defined problems or contribute to them; to identify important features of a case that may become pertinent to these problems or other problems that may be likely to arise in the course of treatment. Thus in work with a mentally retarded man concerning difficulties on the job, we might want to have data (that might not be contained in statements about the problem) on the extent of his retardation. It also might be important to know that his brother (with whom he lives) has a serious heart problem, even though that fact has no immediate bearing on the problem at hand.

With these considerations in mind, the general areas of usual concern may be briefly enumerated. Moving from inside out, we are interested in problem-relevant data about the client's wants, beliefs, action patterns, and affective states; his physical condition and mental capacities; his identification with ethnic and other reference groups; his performance and interactions within his social system and the characteristics of that system—particularly his family and work situations and his involvements with other organizations; and his tangible resources and physical environment, such as income and housing. The same areas apply to client systems, such as couples and families, with particular attention paid to patterns of interaction of the clients making up the system.

The extent to which any of these areas are investigated depends entirely on the problem. Unfortunately, no effective system has been developed to enable us to specify precisely what data may be relevant to what problem, largely because we lack good theories to inform us about which factors impinge upon what kinds of problems with what consequences. Guided by the requirements of the problem assessment (chapter 5), the practitioner must rely largely on his own judgment. Time constraints, always a factor in any service model, and the need to maintain momentum in carrying treatment forward pose additional limitations.

If a problem is relatively well encapsulated, that is, confined to a particular sphere of the client's life, the amount of personal and situational data that are needed is correspondingly limited. Anne, age seven, had a problem getting along with her teacher, who reprimanded her "without good reason" for getting out of her seat and talking. The teacher thought Anne had a problem controlling her behavior. For this problem it is useful to know that Anne is a bright, vivacious, talkative girl, sensitive to criticism, who believes, in common with some other children in her class, that the teacher treats children unfairly. It is also important to be aware of the teacher's rather strict standards and her frustrations in struggling with a class of active, noisy children. Some would consider Anne's home situation even more of a "problem." She sees little of her parents, both of whom work and are seldom home until late evening. Teen-age siblings prepare supper and look after her. She spends weekends at her grandparents. She enjoys being with her mother and wishes she could see more of her. Although these factors may be related to the school problem, it is difficult to establish clear connections. One might, of course, speculate that Anne's sensitivity to criticism might be a consequence of feelings of being "rejected" by her parents, but there was no corroborating evidence that Anne felt that way and, even if this were so, this factor may well be unmodifiable—a constraint in the situation. Though the family situation of any child with a problem, no matter how well defined the problem is, needs to be explored for factors that might affect it, detailed data about the family in this case would probably not contribute a great deal to the practitioner's pool of *useful* information. If the parents had indicated they wanted help with family problems (in response to the practitioner's routine offer made during her initial visit with them), then problems more related to family functioning might have been developed, and more detailed data about this area would have been obviously needed.

Some situations require a fairly wide-ranging review of the client's life situation. Mrs. F's problems concerned lack of meaningful activity and interpersonal difficulties with her 18-year-old son. Widowed the previous year and beset with functional diarrhea, Mrs. F had been housebound for several months, periodically depressed about her husband's death and quarreling with her son about issues of independence and control. In order to understand her problems it was necessary to gather information about most of the general areas listed earlier. Nevertheless, the problem focus still limited inquiry. Since her depressive episodes were not a target of treatment, material relating to the episodes and to the context of her ruminations about her husband and their relationship was not explored in any detail.

Initial data on person and situation characteristics are obtained, often in the form of rough approximations, as needed in order to proceed with problem exploration, analysis, and assessment. Additional data are accumulated as the case proceeds depending on what the practitioner needs to know to further his work on the client's problems.

Forming the Contract

Contracts between practitioner and client are being used increasingly in social treatment (Maluccio and Marlow 1974; Seabury 1976). Although they may vary in form and detail, contracts have one essential purpose: to set forth explicit agreements between practitioner and client on what is to be done and how. In our approach, an initial contract is developed after tentative accord has been reached on the target problems. It is then modified and added to as treatment proceeds.

The initial contract specifies at least one explicitly stated, acknowledged problem the social worker and client agree to work on. If more than one target problem has been identified, the problems are ranked (and numbered) in order of their importance to the client. The sequence in which they are to be dealt with in treatment is established. Usually attention shifts back and forth among problems as the case proceeds; and it may be that a less important problem is dealt with first because it is more pressing at the moment or because an opportunity for solution seems at hand.

Formulation of goals of treatment is the next logical step in the contracting process. The function of this step is to make explicit what the practitioner and client expect to accomplish through their joint efforts. A treatment goal sets forth the desired end state the practitioner and client agree to work toward. Since any problem is an expression of an unsatisfied want, a treatment goal can be thought of as a statement of what the client wants adjusted to the reality of what he can realistically expect to attain with the social worker's help. In keeping with this formulation the goal can be best stated in a phrase consisting of a noun and modifiers that describe what the client hopes to acquire as a result of service: a new pair of reading glasses; fewer absences from work; ability to talk to girls without getting nervous; better control over temper when disciplining children.

As can be seen from the examples, goal statements can vary considerably with respect to level of abstraction and degree of precision. Specific and precise statements of goals are desirable, but may not always be feasible. Clients may be clear that they want a change but may not be clear about the kind or amount of change to aim for. A husband and wife know they do not like to quarrel about money but would be hard put to say how much of a reduction in quarreling would be regarded as a legitimate goal. Efforts to further specify the goal, particularly at the beginning of service, may in fact be futile, if not counterproductive. A goal of "less quarreling about money" may be the best that can be fashioned.

Even though it may lack delineation and offer little guidance for problem-solving activity, the goal statement does provide a necessary shift in frame of reference: from what is wrong to what is needed. In most cases the goal statement will also specify an end state that offers a direction for work beyond what is implied by the definition of the problem. A mother may state her problem as "missing her children placed in foster care" but possible goals might range from "a reduction in feelings of longing for children" to "return of children from foster care." Ideally then a goal stipulates which of a variety of possible solutions will be pursued.

The point of departure in goal formulation is what the client has revealed earlier concerning desired changes in his problems. It may be only necessary to review and record the goals the client has previously stated. Usually, however, further clarification is necessary, and in some cases, considerable discussion may be needed in order to decide among possible alternative goals. Like all parts of the initial contract goal statements should be open to revision as work proceeds, although the practitioner should feel obligated to help the client attain goals originally agreed on unless the client himself wishes to change them.

Formulation of goals sets the stage for the development of tasks, which then becomes the means of goal achievement (see chapter 7). The first round of tasks may also be incorporated as a part of the initial contract.

Orienting the client to the purposes and nature of treatment is an essential activity that should be completed during formation of the initial contract, though some preliminary orientation often is begun earlier. How the practitioner and client are to go about working on the target problems needs to be made clear. In particular, the client needs to understand that movement toward problem resolution will be provided in large measure through his work on specific tasks that the practitioner will help him develop and carry out. As certain studies have suggested, efforts to help the client achieve clarity on what his role in treatment will be may contribute to positive outcome (Hoehn-Saric et al. 1964; Goldstein 1973).

Orientation to treatment can be probably best accomplished after the practitioner has some conception of the target problems and goals. He can then particularize the operation of the approach in relation to what the client wants to work on. However, it may not be possible to wait until this point. Some explanation of the purpose and nature of treatment may be needed at the beginning of contact if the practitioner is trying to engage a reluctant client or if the client is skeptical about the practitioner's ability to be helpful. Whenever it is given, an orientation to treatment should be brief, nontechnical, and related as much as possible to the client's circumstances. The client is, of course, concerned about what may be in store for him, not how the approach works in general.

Finally, the contract incorporates an agreement about the expected amount and duration of service, usually expressed in terms of numbers of interviews over some span of time. In current practice there is considerable variation in number of interviews and time span, depending on the nature of the problem and on the frequency and duration of the interviews. Most contracts call for a specific number of interviews, usually six to twelve, within a range from two to four months; extensions are provided when indicated (chapter 8).

As observed in chapter 1, the short-term, time-limited features of the model were based on a good deal of research evidence that suggested that such an approach was as least as effective as open-ended treatment of relatively lengthy duration (Reid and Shyne, 1969; Reid and Epstein, 1972). If so, then planned, brief service would be generally preferable on grounds of its greater efficiency. Similar conclusions may be found in several recent reviews of research on interpersonal treatment that have taken into account studies appearing since the original formulation of the model (Luborsky, Singer and Luborsky, 1975; Bergin (in press); Butcher and Koss (in press); Gurman and Kniskern (in press).

Formulation of the initial contract establishes the principle that the purposes and nature of the worker-client relationship will be controlled by explicit agreements rather than by the practitioner's hidden agenda. It is normally the first in a series of contractual arrangements which may include modifications in the initial contract and agreements on additional problems to be dealt with, on subsequent client and practitioner tasks. In this way the contracting process continues during the life of the case.

The essence of the contract is an explicit agreement between practitioner and client. In formulating the initial contract the practitioner and client normally go over what has been discussed. The practitioner determines if tentative agreements or other features of the proposed contract are acceptable to the client. If not, there is further discussion until they arrive at agreement. When this point has been reached, the practitioner elicits the client's express approval of the contract and indicates to him his own commitment to it.

We have preferred oral over written contracts, since the former are less formidable and time-consuming and run less risk of premature closure. Written contracts may be indicated, however, when agreements involve several goals or tasks or several participants. In such instances the written form may avoid misunderstandings. Moreover, when the contract calls for actions to be undertaken by the practitioner, the client may find a written agreement reassuring.

Chapter 7
Task Planning and Implementation

The core of our intervention strategy consists in helping the client plan and execute problem-solving actions. Sessions with the client are used to determine what he should do and how and why he should do it; to help him rehearse and practice agreed-upon actions; to analyze obstacles that might prevent him from carrying them out, and to review what he has been able to accomplish. These activities usually take place in weekly (or twice-weekly) sessions which vary in length, usually from 30 minutes to an hour, depending on the length of time required to complete the activities that may be indicated. In addition, after prior planning with the client, the practitioner undertakes tasks to supplement and facilitate the client's problem-solving efforts.

Task Planning

Plans are conceptions of intended action. Deliberate problem-solving efforts, such as those that occur in task-centered practice, inevitably involve the construction of plans. In fact, task-centered treatment may be thought of largely as the joint efforts of practitioner and client to design and execute constructive plans for problem-solving action. Plans spell out the actions both are to undertake following their sessions together and suggest how these actions are to be carried out.

Tasks

Tasks describe the central problem-solving actions the client or practitioner agree to undertake. They are the heart of the action plan. Tasks are stated in a sentence, with the client or practitioner as subject and the intended action the verb (Mrs. C. will bring Debbie to the dental clinic on Thursday. The worker will determine if client is eligible for legal aid services). To simplify presentation the simple term "task" will be used to refer to actions to be carried out by the client; actions to be carried out by the worker will be designated as "practitioner tasks." The discussion that follows will concentrate on the former; the latter will be taken up subsequently.

A task undertaken by a client is a particular kind of problem-solving action. In order to qualify as a task in the present framework, the action must be: (1) planned and agreed on with the practitioner; (2) capable of being worked on by the client outside of the treatment session. The first criterion insists that tasks are part of an explicit contract between worker and client. Thus, incidental suggestions or advice that the client try this or that would not be considered tasks. At a minimum, the client must agree to try to carry out the action. It is hoped that the client may carry out problem-solving actions not called for in the agreement or in some cases may come up with better ones, but such additional or substitute actions would not be considered tasks. The second criterion restricts tasks to actions the client can work on without the practitioner's being present. Tasks stress the client's autonomous problem-solving actions. Activities the client might be asked to engage in as part of the treatment process ("Tell me about your fears") would not be considered tasks.

Tasks may be formulated at various levels of abstraction, as we have seen. *General tasks* give the client a direction for action but do not spell out what exactly is to be done—for example, Mrs. B is to develop a firmer, more consistent approach to handling her child's behavior. *Operational tasks* call for specific action the client is to undertake—Mr. A is to apply for a job at Manpower, Inc., within the week.

A general task may be used to provide an initial focus for the client's activity and direction for the construction of operational tasks. A general task need not be developed if the formulation of the problem and goals suggests the necessary operational tasks. Operational tasks, whether derived from general tasks or directly from the problem, provide the basic structure for the practitioner and client activities to be described in subsequent sections.

Tasks, by definition, involve action, but action may involve either mental or physical effort. All tasks require mental activity since planning is essential to their conception and execution. Tasks may consist only of cognitive activity, such as making a decision. Such tasks normally require, however, specific, well-defined effort that can be monitored at least through the client's own reports.

Additional distinctions among tasks have proved useful. Some tasks call for one-time, *unique* actions: Mrs. L will contact the Legal Aid Bureau to initiate divorce proceedings. Others specify actions that are to recur: Lisa is to spend an hour each evening on her math homework.

Tasks may be unitary or complex. A unitary task can be described as a single action, even though its execution may require a number of steps: Mary will join a swimming class. Complex tasks consist of two or more discrete actions, closely enough related to be regarded as part of the same task, but still requiring separate descriptions: Jimmy will read eight pages of a book at home and ask mother for help with words he does not understand. More complex tasks may set forth programs of activities, such as a daily schedule for the client to follow.

Finally, tasks may be *individual, reciprocal,* or *shared.* An individual task is carried out independently by a single client. Reciprocal tasks are separate but interrelated tasks worked on by different individuals, usually members of the same family. They tend to assume a *quid pro quo* form: Mr. F will not reprimand Suzy if she is less than 15 minutes late in coming home. Suzy will try to come home on time but will be no more than 15 minutes late. A shared task is a single task worked on together by two or more persons: Mr. and Mrs. C will go to the movies together.

Although the difference between a task and a plan have been outlined, further clarification of this distinction may be helpful. A task essentially describes a future course of action that, as noted, can be expressed in a single sentence. A task states what is to be done but not how it is to be done. A plan is a more inclusive concept. It incorporates all tasks that are to be worked on and whatever means of implementation have been developed. Since they are based on tasks, plans may be more precisely described as "task plans."

The Planning Process

After the problem has been specified and the treatment contract formed, the social worker and client attempt to develop a plan of action. This process consists in generating alternative actions that might be taken, agreeing on one or more actions or tasks to be carried out, developing strategies and tactics for their implementation, summarizing the task plan, and, if indicated, devising a means for the client's recording of task progress.

Generating Alternatives

A natural point of departure for generating alternatives is the client's unsatisfied want and its related goal. The question then becomes, "What can the client do to obtain what he wants?" It makes sense to begin with whatever plan the client himself has in mind or has begun to work on. While the plan may not be adequate to resolve the problem (otherwise he probably would not be seeing a social worker), there may be elements of it that can be built upon. The practitioner can also make use of prior data on what actions the client has tried in the past to overcome his difficulty. Past actions that seemed to work, if only for brief periods or in small ways, may give clues as to what might work at present.

In some cases the nature of the problem and the client's circumstances may point to a particular course of action which can then be developed. In others, alternative actions need to be considered and appraised. The process works best if both the practitioner and client can freely suggest alternatives as they come to mind, without too much consideration initially as to their appropriateness. Research on problem-solving indicates that this kind of "brainstorming" is an effective means of devising solutions, perhaps because it stimulates imaginative thinking about a wide range of approaches to a difficulty (Osborn 1963). The best alternatives can then be selected for more serious consideration.

Jerry, an eight-year-old boy, was being teased and bullied on his way home from school by an older girl. She would call his mother names, push him down, and kick him. Jerry walked home each night in terror of an attack. When asked by the social worker to think of ways he could handle the problem, he first proposed that he could "run real fast" when he saw her and maybe get away but noted that she was a pretty fast runner. When encouraged to come up with other suggestions, he mentioned that perhaps he could disguise himself in some way. Then he remembered an older boy that he knew. Perhaps he could ask him to walk home with him as his bodyguard. The social worker and Jerry decided that the last alternative might be the best to try. He executed the plan and it worked well.

While attempting to carry out tasks, the client may come up with other ways of attacking the problem. Promising efforts can then be converted into new tasks or can serve as the raw material for further task construction. Practitioners should not only be alert to these possibilities and try to build on them when they occur but should encourage client experimentation with problem-solving. The tasks generated are often quite successful since the client has an investment in them and has already done some "pilot" testing; moreover, one of the standard goals of task-centered intervention is to bring about this kind of independent problem-solving activity.

Florence, age nine and black, had become quite unpopular because of her aggressive, bothersome behavior. Other girls avoided her or teased her about her physical appearance (she was tall, thin, and not pretty). She wanted desperately to make friends at school but was having only limited success with a task directed at getting a particular girl to have lunch with her. She then started on her own to make a list of people she could either count as friends or with whom she wanted to be friends. She used her own definition of a friend ("someone who would talk with you, eat with you, and take your side in a fight"). On the list were both peers and adults (including the worker and several members of a black family in a popular television comedy series!). Although the "friendship list," as Florence called it, could have been seen as a retreat to fantasy, the practitioner wisely interpreted it as a valid effort to cope with the problem and praised her for what she had done. Since Florence did not know how to spell some of her classmates' names, the practitioner suggested that her task be to ask them. Florence enthusiastically agreed. As she and the worker were leaving the interviewing room, Florence encountered a girl whose name was on the list. She showed the girl the lengthy list and asked her how to spell her name. The girl, naturally enough, asked what the list was all about. Florence casually told her it was just a list of her friends. The girl (perhaps not wanting to be left off the bandwagon) nodded and said, "Okay, I be your friend," and spelled her name.

Often the practitioner is the primary generator of alternatives. The client may not be able to produce much on his own. Moreover, the practitioner may have special knowledge about kinds of tasks that generally work well for particular problems, as subsequent chapters will demonstrate.

Our research does not indicate a strong relationship between the source of the task and task accomplishment (chapter 10). Tasks initially proposed by practitioners tend to show about the same amount of progress as those suggested by clients. It should be kept in mind, however, that the practitioner proposes *ideas* for tasks which are then gone over with the client. The client's contributions normally become a part of the task plan. He does not "assign" the task to the client.

Regardless of who first suggested the task, it is important that it be one that the client expresses willingness to carry out. A judgment about the client's willingness to attempt the task (*task commitment*) can be made on the basis of the client's reactions during the process of task formulation. Does he seem eager or reluctant to take on the task? As our research suggests (chapter 10), task commitment may be a good predictor of task progress. Thus, if a client shows signs of disinclination to work on the task, the practitioner and client should try to reshape it or search for another.

Task Agreement

An agreement between practitioner and client on the client's task may occur after alternatives have been sorted out and the best selected. Generally an agreement at this point concerns the global nature of the client's proposed action, and not the detail, which is developed later. In some cases the practitioner may prefer to explore in some depth the strategies and tactics of carrying out a possible task before reaching agreement on it with the client. This option may be used when extensive planning of a possible task may be necessary before a judgment can be made about its usefulness. In any event, a final agreement on the task is made at the end of the planning process after it is determined what the execution of the task will involve.

Planning Details of Implementation

Once an action alternative has been selected for consideration as a task, the practitioner and client work on the plan for its execution. Most tasks involve hierarchies or sequences of operations, or subtasks. A task can be carried out in an endless variety of ways depending on which operations are selected and how they are ordered and executed.

Generally, planning proceeds by breaking the task down into sequences of operations that may be required to carry it out. Suppose the client's proposed task is to look for a job. The question then becomes, "How can he proceed to do this?" As this question is answered, a number of immediate steps become apparent. He may need to decide what kind of work he wants to look for; he may want to consult the want ads, contact friends or acquaintances who might be able to inform him about job openings, look up employment agencies, make arrangements to visit one, and so on. The question of how to proceed may be meaningful for some of these steps as well. For example, the client may have a friend who might be able to give him a job. He may want to approach the friend but may be uncertain about how to do so without jeopardizing the friendship.

Even tasks that are specific to begin with can profitably be broken down in this manner. A client's task may be to initiate a conversation with a coworker. Whom should he select? What might he say? How? When?

Whatever the level of client action under consideration, the process proceeds until a plan is developed that the client can begin to execute prior to his next visit with the social worker. The plan may consist chiefly of a general task (to look for a job) together with one or more operational tasks that can be carried out in the interim (to contact an employment agency). Or it may be built around one or more operational tasks. The plan always contains at least one operational task. In addition, it generally includes some guidelines for the execution of the operational task(s).

Regardless of the form of the plan, the practitioner attempts to make sure that it calls for initial actions the client will be able to carry out. We have found that it is better to err on the side of having the first task be too easy rather than too difficult, since it is important that the client experience initial success in his work on the problem. There is empirical evidence to support this position. It has been found, for example, that subjects in laboratory experiments will do better on a second task if advised that their completion of the first was successful (Stotland 1969). The impression that one has performed successfully can create a sense of mastery and self-confidence that can augment problem-solving efforts. The actual experience of success is perhaps the best way to acquire this impression.

Summarization

For a task plan to work, it is essential that the client emerge with a clear notion of what he is to do. To ensure that he does, the practitioner and client go over the plan in summary fashion, normally at the end of the interview. This final wrap-up may be preceded by summarizations of parts of the plan during the process of its formulation. An important part of this procedure is to elicit from the client the essentials of the plan. The client is asked to present the plan as he sees it. The practitioner can then underscore the essential elements or add parts the client has left out. Summarizing the plan gives the practitioner the opportunity to convey to the client his expectations that it will be carried out and that his efforts will be reviewed. "So you will try to do———. We'll see how it worked out next time we meet."

Task Recording

If the practitioner and client have developed a task to be carried out with frequent repetitions or if several tasks have been devised, the practitioner may ask the client to keep a record of his progress on a chart, which can be constructed during the session (Example 7.1). Such recording of task progress gives both practitioner and client a detailed picture of what has been accomplished and serves as a basis both for crediting the client with successful performance and for pinpointing obstacles. (It also reminds the client what he has agreed to do!) A form for this purpose has been found to work well with client systems, such as families, in which several interrelated tasks may be undertaken by different members. Copies of the form are given to different members of the system so they can keep track of (and review) their own and one another's tasks. Tasks are filled in on a form (Example 7.2).*

*These forms were developed by Ronald H. Rooney when he was a doctoral student at the School of Social Service Administration.

Example 7.1

Task	Circle Each Day Task Is Carried Out
	Mon. Tues. Weds. Thurs. Fri.

Paul will be no more
than five minutes late
for school each day

Example 7.2

Form completed by ___Mrs. K___

Who Does It?	What Will be Done?	When?	How Did It Go?
Jim	clear table	every night	did every night but had to be reminded
Laurie	wash dishes	every night	did every night
Jim	take out trash	every night	every night except Tues.
Laurie	vacuum house	Sat. a.m.	did downstairs only
Mrs. K.	buy Jim a pair of sneakers and Laurie a new coat	by end of week	bought sneakers and looked for new coat with Laurie but didn't find one

Task Strategies

In the process of task planning the practitioner may draw upon strategies in which certain types of tasks and task plans are used in relation to particular characteristics of the client's problem or circumstances. Some of these strategies will be briefly discussed and illustrated.

When the client's goal consists of carrying out some action he is unable to perform, an incremental strategy based on principles presented earlier (chapter 4) is usually employed. A series of tasks of progressive difficulty are developed to help the client gradually achieve his performance goal. Suppose a person's fear of riding a bus prevents his attending a clinic to obtain medical treatment. His goal might be to attend the clinic. It could be approached through a graduated series of tasks, starting with waiting for a bus, then taking a bus until the first stop, and so on.

Successful accomplishment of each step is rewarded by praise, from the worker or significant others, or by some tangible compensation. Failure to complete a task may mean that the gap between steps was too much for the client to master and that finer gradations are necessary. Gradations may be achieved not only by cutting the client's progression toward the goal into smaller units but also by altering the context of his task. Thus, a program of graded tasks was used to help a woman enter a bedroom in her home in which her mother had died. The client had experienced a frightening vision of her mother when she had gone into the room and had since avoided it—at a considerable personal cost, since it was now her children's room. Tasks calling for her to spend increasing amounts of time each day were set up, but she could not proceed further than spending a few moments near the doorway. Several ways of trying to lessen the difficulty of this step (including having the client play relaxing music while entering the room) were tried without success. Through trial and error it was discovered that the client could tolerate staying in the room for short periods if her children were there and if an interesting television show was playing. She was able to remain in the room for progressively longer periods of time when these contextual supports were present. It was then possible gradually to eliminate the supports until she could move comfortably in and out of the room without either the children present or the TV on.

The difficulty of an incremental step may also be lessened by placing an upper limit on the task. In this way, the client is helped to control anxiety-creating impulses to do more than he is prepared to cope with. Thus, in one case an initial task for a woman who feared leaving her apartment was "to open the door completely but under no circumstances to step over the threshold'' (Brown 1977b).

When the problem results from an action or interaction sequence, the most appropriate strategy may be one in which tasks are directed at modifying some point in the sequence. When the chain of actions or interactions has been described, the practitioner and client attempt to identify a "weak link," normally an early action over which the client has greater control than the actions that make up the problem. In our efforts to help aggressive children avoid physical fights, we have found that the fights are often preceded by elaborate verbal interplay that may start out as friendly teasing. A child may resort to his fist (or to some other weapon) when his verbal retorts can no longer provide the punishment he thinks his antagonist deserves. Task plans designed to help youngsters become more skillful at verbal riposting and to stimulate this form of response have enabled some to achieve purely verbal conquests.

One of the tasks revealed in an earlier example—the woman with fears of leaving her house—contained a two-sided payoff. If the client accepted the injunction against proceeding too far, she was carrying out the task as directed and could credit herself with following the treatment program; if she failed to obey the injunction and went farther than the prescribed distance, she could credit herself with having made further progress on her problem. Either way, the client gained. The obvious therapeutic advantages of tasks that can cut two ways for the client merit further consideration.

As Haley (1976) points out, one problem can be used to resolve another. Two-sided tasks can be used as the means. In one case, a father ''couldn't shake'' the persistent and troubling belief that he was responsible for his daughter's partial deafness because he had not seen that she had adequate medical attention for an illness that may have caused it. At the same time, he had a related problem in being harsh and impatient with her when she made demands on his time. He seemed unable to make progress with either difficulty through usual task-centered procedures. The two problems were "paired" through the following task: whenever he was troubled by feelings of guilt over his daughter's handicap, he was to initiate, as soon as possible, some kind of activity with her that she would enjoy. He would not need to make this effort if he did not experience the guilt feelings. Since he could see the task as making up for a past wrong, it made sense to him to have it connected to his guilt. Although the task could be described as utilizing a defense mechanism ("undoing"), what is of interest here is its two-sided aspects: if he is troubled by obsessive thoughts, then he has motivation to improve his relationship with his daughter and at the same time relieve his guilt feelings; if the guilt feelings abate, not only is *that* problem alleviated but he may then be less irritable with the girl. Interestingly enough, he began to do things with his daughter as a means of *warding off* the disturbing thoughts.

Ingenious practitioners sometimes invent two-sided tasks that are difficult to categorize but are nonetheless effective. Allen, a six-year-old, had night terrors about a "bogeyman" in his bedroom closet. The practitioner worked out a simple two-sided task with the boy and his mother. They were to place a cookie in the closet before he went to bed. The next morning they were to check to see if the cookie was still there. If it was, then that might suggest that the bogeyman no longer lurked in the closet at night. If the cookie was gone, then Allen could be reassured that he was "winning him over" and thus did not have to be so afraid of him.

As can be seen from these examples, two-sided tasks may exploit paradoxical elements in the client's situation. The therapeutic leverage afforded by paradoxes has been discussed extensively by Watzlawick, Weakland, and Fisch (1974) and by Haley (1976). In Haley's "paradoxical tasks," the practitioner may, for example, direct an overprotective mother to increase her hovering over her child on the expectation that people are likely to discontinue dysfunctional behavior they are *required* to perform in ways prescribed by the practitioner.

The theory underlying paradoxical tasks is too complex and subtle to be summed up in a few words. While neither the theory nor procedures has been adequately tested, the latter at least seems readily testable. The testing, however, would need to be done with caution. As Haley recognizes, and as should be apparent from the nature of the technique, paradoxical tasks might have adverse effects if improperly used.

A strategy may make use of mental or cognitive tasks. Such tasks are most frequently used when the problem itself requires a cognitive solution, such as a problem in not being able to decide whether to remain in a particular situation or to leave it. While the client's task work is essentially cognitive, planning is necessary to provide structure and direction for his efforts and to avoid unproductive ruminating. Normally, the client is to think through some aspect of his difficulty or possible solutions and to write them out. For example, a young woman who cannot decide whether or not to continue living with her parents might undertake the task of thinking through and recording the advantages and disadvantages of the move or what she foresees happening if she did decide to move. In a case reported by Ewalt (1977), a 29-year-old married woman who was preoccupied with the question of whether or not her mother loved her assumed the task of identifying "why the extent of her mother's love for her was now of major importance." Frequently, cognitive tasks are followed by tasks requiring overt behavior. In the case just cited, the client subsequently undertook a task in which she was to involve her mother in some mutually enjoyable activity (rather than to call or visit with the intent of reassuring herself of her mother's affection). A cognitive task, once planned, can be worked on in the treatment session, as can any task involving actions that can be performed with the practitioner.

Some situations call for a number of different client and practitioner activities to be initiated, more or less concurrently, once the problem has been formulated. The initial plan may then set out an array of tasks representing a division of labor between client and practitioner. Thus, in the case of Lilly, a mildly retarded woman who wanted help in finding a job, the initial task plan took the following shape.

Tasks for Lilly:
1. To draw up a simple résumé to be typed at Hill House (where Lilly is a resident)
2. To read the want ads in Hamston newspaper and follow up on any interesting job possibilities
3. To go to employment service and have interview with Harold Thompson, employment counselor

Tasks for worker:
1. To look through want ads in Foureville newspaper (neighboring town) and follow up on any interesting job possibilities
2. To arrange transportation for Lilly to go to employment service on job interviews
3. To contact vocational rehabilitation to see if Lilly is eligible for services there

Concurrent task strategies become more complex when they involve several clients or members of the social system. The plan may then include not only tasks for the practitioner and clients but also "tasks" for personnel of cooperating organizations. The latter tasks may be thought as contractual arrangements between the practitioner and representatives of other agencies (Ewalt 1977). The practitioner does not become a "taskmaster" for workers from other organizations but rather a collaborator in an action plan in which all participants agree to do their part. With the agreement of his coparticipants, the practitioner may, however, serve as coordinator of the efforts of the different agencies.

Case management

Mrs. Harrow, elderly and in poor health, requested help from a state department of social services for problems concerning the care of her three-year-old niece, Ellie, whom she was raising. Ellie had been recently diagnosed at a mental health center as "developmentally delayed." The child had only rudimentary speech and was not yet toilet-trained; she had frequent temper tantrums and attacked others without apparent reason. Her mother had been in a state mental hospital for some time. The whereabouts of the father were unknown. After sessions with the grandmother and contacts with other agencies, the task plan took the following form.

Tasks for worker:
1. To arrange for home-care worker to help Mrs. H learn to teach Ellie self-care routines
2. To arrange for Ellie to enter a half-day nursery school for developmentally disabled children
3. To take Ellie and Mrs. Harrow to the mental health center for periodic evaluations (because of Mrs. H's apprehension about going there)
4. To provide Mrs. H each month with a schedule of Ellie's appointments and other activities

Tasks for Mrs. H:
1. To get Ellie ready for scheduled appointments and activities
2. To take Ellie to speech therapist once a week
3. To learn ways of teaching Ellie self-care routines from home-care worker

Tasks agreed to by others:
1. Mrs. Rollins, special education consultant, will arrange for Ellie to be given speech therapy.
2. Miss Rall, public health nurse, will visit Ellie every other week to give her allergy shot.
3. Mrs. Janow, director of nursery school, will provide periodic reports on Ellie's progress.

The task plan in this example may not necessarily require regular or lengthy sessions between the practitioner and Mrs. H. The worker's function may be largely to develop and orchestrate a complex action system. This is, of course, a time-honored role for a social worker and certainly not unique to the present system. The task-centered approach does force, however, clear understanding of who is to do what and when and provides methods for facilitating and following up the actions that have been agreed upon.

The last strategy to be considered is an outgrowth of the eclectic posture of the model. The practitioner can fashion a plan by adapting methods or programs from the treatment literature.

Normally a task-centered practitioner would be interested in interventions that had been tested with the problem at hand and that could be used within the framework of the model.

For example, if the practitioner were attempting to help a child overcome a problem of social withdrawal, he could make use of a variety of approaches described in the literature. In building a task plan, he might draw specifically on a treatment package tested by Ross, Ross, and Evans (1971). In their study an extremely withdrawn boy was treated with the help of a model (a young adult male). In the first phase of treatment, the child learned to imitate the model's behavior in various situations. Once an imitative pattern had been established, the model, under the practitioner's direction, began in graduated steps to interact with a group of children. Within a short period of time the child was able to join the model in these interactions and finally was able to approach children on his own. This imaginative intervention program (which included other procedures) could be conceptualized in terms of helping the child carry out a series of specific tasks aimed at bringing about his interaction with other children.

The literature on behavioral methods, from which this example was drawn, provides a rich source of interventions and programs that can be fitted into the framework of the task-centered model. Works that the task-centered practitioner would find particularly useful for this purpose include Gambrill (1977); Leitenberg (1976b); Fischer and Gochros (1975); Kanfer and Goldstein (1975); Schwartz and Goldiamond (1975); and Shelton and Ackerman (1974). Additional literature can be located through bibliographies of behavioral approaches (Klein 1973; Shorkey 1977).

In utilizing the treatment literature as a source of task plans, the practitioner does not abandon the task-centered model but rather augments it. In fact, a major purpose of the model is to provide an organizing framework for a variety of methods for helping clients take constructive action.

Establishing Incentives and Rationale

In order for the client to carry out the plan of action, he needs to believe that its accomplishment will result in a benefit sufficient to make the effort worthwhile. He needs both an incentive and a rationale. His incentive refers to the gain he anticipates in carrying out the task. His rationale is his anticipation that the gain will provide adequate justification for completing the task.

Perhaps the most compelling incentive is the belief that accomplishing the task will effect some degree of alleviation in his problem, that is, will help him attain a want that is currently unsatisfied. In some cases, the presence of this kind of incentive will become clear in task planning. It may only be necessary for the practitioner to underscore the benefit that will accrue to the client.

When it is not obvious that the client has a strong incentive, the practitioner may need to determine what payoff the client sees in executing the task and to take steps to strengthen it. This approach is particularly indicated when the client's motivation to work on the problem is questionable, when the connection between task achievement and problem alleviation is not clear, or when the proposed action may have negative, as well as positive, consequences for the client. He may then ask the client what benefits he sees coming to him if he can achieve the task. The practitioner emphasizes the positive consequences the client might reveal and explores for others. Possible negative consequences are examined and their impact considered. The client is helped to see the risks within the perspective of the gains that may result from his proposed actions. If the risks still loom larger than the gains in the client's mind, the task may have to be modified or another found. For example, suppose the client's task is to ask her boss for a raise. She may fear that her request will be refused and, further, that it will anger her employer. What might the consequences lead to? Would her unsuccessful bid for a salary increase be held against her? How likely is any of this to occur? Might it not be worth the risk? Through such inquiries, together with his own observations about what might be likely to occur, the practitioner would try to help the client develop an "eyes-open" rationale for proceeding with the task.

In establishing incentives, the practitioner may also wish to direct the client's attention to the consequences of not doing the task, that is, of allowing the problem to continue. While the client is presumably motivated to avoid discomfort created by the problem, he may not have sufficiently taken into account the various short- and long-term costs of inaction. A young person whose task is to get immediate attention for a venereal disease may not have really thought about the consequences of allowing the disease to go untreated. The practitioner attempts to draw from the client whatever awareness he may already have and attempts to reinforce or expand upon it. While he may point out negative consequences the client might not have perceived, he avoids "lecturing" or painting a grim picture. The point can often be effectively made with a light touch or a little humor. The principle is to reinforce awareness of the incentives for task accomplishment and to create an awareness of the costs of ignoring the task.

In helping the client see the consequences of doing or not doing the task, the practitioner in effect is enabling the client to develop *reasons* for taking action. The efficacy of this approach, at least with children, has been demonstrated in several studies reviewed by Taffel, O'Leary, and Armel (1974) and in one these authors themselves conducted. In their controlled investigation, children were asked to complete arithmetical tasks. Providing the children with reasons for so doing, such as some of the practical advantages of learning arithmetic, proved to be an effective means for promoting task completion, equal to or surpassing the effects of praise of the student's work. The best effects were achieved when giving reasons and praise were combined. The study not only underscores the importance of helping the client develop a sense of why the task is important but provides support for our assumption that a combination of different approaches to enhancing incentives and rationale may be particularly effective.

Other kinds of incentives for executing the task include praise or approval (as noted), the sense of accomplishment or mastery the client might receive from task completion, praise or approval from others, including the worker, or tangible rewards provided by the worker, others, or the client himself. These kinds of incentives can serve to supplement incentives derived from anticipation that achieving the task will bring about relief of the problem.

The practitioner can enhance anticipatory mastery by pointing out both the difficulty of the task and the client's capacity to achieve it. The worker conveys his expectation and hope that the client will succeed, thereby implying that his approval will be forthcoming if the client does. Once the worker has given praise for work on tasks, the client will be even more likely to anticipate it. The practitioner can also arrange with others to provide tangible or intangible rewards to the client contingent upon task achievement. This approach requires a prior agreement with the client and the worker's involvement with others (see "Implementing Practitioner Tasks" below). Incentives can also take the form of a tangible self-reinforcement—a reward that the client gives himself upon successful execution of task behavior. The reward may be in the form of a "treat," such as eating a special food, making a purchase of some desired object, or engaging in a recreational activity. Or the client can give himself points for actions that further the task and "cash" them in for a major indulgence after a certain number have been accumulated.

Tangible incentives, whether self- or other-administered, may be particularly indicated if the execution of the task results in some immediate deprivation for the client, such as restricting intake of food or alcohol. A substitute form of gratification may make him forgo something he finds highly pleasurable.

Usually, tangible incentives serve a temporary function: to help initiate action. After a point, they either tend to lose their incentive value or it becomes impractical to continue them. For example, gold stars may help a child stay in his seat, but sooner or later one would expect the child to remain there without this particular inducement. One usually assumes that other incentives, such as approval from significant others, will take over the function served by the concrete rewards. It is wise not to rest on this assumption but rather to try to help the client develop other incentives as soon as possible. The client can be told that the tangible incentives are a device to get him started; then other, more enduring, incentives can be discussed.

The incentives and rationale for a task need to be evaluated in the light of the client's success in carrying it out. If the task is successfully completed, the practitioner has evidence that the kind of incentives and rationale used might be used as the basis for another task. If the task is failed or only partly accomplished, then the adequacy of these elements needs to be examined.

It should be apparent from the discussion thus far that attempts to motivate the client to work on a specific task involve his motivation for work on the problem in general. The client's willingness to work on the problem has presumably been established during the problem specification and contracting phases, but his willingness does not guarantee a high degree of investment or the absence of mixed feelings. Moreover, the client's initial determination to tackle a problem may weaken when he is faced with the prospect of carrying out the possibly difficult tasks necessary to resolve it. The client's motivation for work on the problem needs to be sustained, if not built, through a continuing effort to help him see how the achievement of particular tasks will make things better for him.

Simulation

The essence of simulation is trying out elements of the action plan under simulated conditions in the interview. It enables the client to perfect and carry out task behavior under controlled and nonthreatening conditions. Such tryouts capitalize on the advantages of learning by doing. They also graphically demonstrate the extent of the client's knowledge of the task.

Usually the plan is rehearsed by means of role-play, a technique that is used for this and other purposes in a variety of treatment approaches (Corsini 1966; Boies 1972). In the form of role-play most frequently used, the client plays himself and acts out the task behavior called for in the plan. The practitioner takes the role of a person with whom the client will need to interact in executing the task—family member, teacher, employer, friend. The client is asked to try out the task in response to the role-played actions of the practitioner. The practitioner asks the client how the other person is likely to act and performs accordingly. He may repeat the role-play to introduce possible behaviors of the person that the client might find difficult to cope with. Thus, if the client's task is to say no in a nice way to a demanding, domineering relative, the worker might make a demand in a mild manner. If the client responds successfully to this, the practitioner might then make a demand in a more aggressive manner. Each role-play is discussed. The client may be asked to criticize his own performance. The worker approves successful execution of task behavior and suggests how the client's responses might be improved.

If the task involves behavior that may be unfamiliar to the client, or if he is unable to act out the task, the practitioner may take the client's role and model the appropriate behavior while the client takes the role of the other. It has been well demonstrated that clients can learn new modes of problem-solving behavior from observation of models (Bandura 1971b). Various uses of the technique have been reported in the social work literature (McBroom 1970; Rose 1975). In our work, modeling is used largely to assist the client in task rehearsals. After the woker has modeled the task, the client is then asked to rehearse it in another role-play.

We have found that this activity is easier to use with children than adults. Children (and many adolescents) like its make-believe, gamelike quality. Adults may find it difficult to "let themselves go" sufficiently to enter into the spirit of the activity. Consequently, the adult may need somewhat more preparation, including a statement of its rationale. The practitioner can often achieve the equivalent of a role-played rehearsal through task planning. The client can be asked how he would respond to different hypothetical situations presented by the practitioner (Perlman 1975).

Rehearsal through role-play is not appropriate for certain tasks—for example, those in which the kind of action to be carried out is relatively simple and familiar to the client. Thus, this activity would not be used for such tasks as handing in an assignment to the teacher.

The following example illustrates an effective and interesting use of simulation, as well as some of the specific processes that occur in this activity. The client is Hazel, age nine, a bright, vivacious youngster. One of four children in a mother-headed family on public assistance, she was referred to a school social worker by her teacher for problems in academic performance, peer relations, and classroom behavior. The example concerns work on the latter problem. To quote from the worker's summary, "Either she tells them to put down their hands or ridicules their answers. She will also shout out her answers once the other children have given theirs." Because of such behavior, she was excluded from the classroom on two occasions, reprimanded by the teacher numerous times, and socially ostracized by a number of her classmates. The practitioner and Hazel developed a straightforward task: "I will let other children say the answer." In planning the task, it was made clear that it meant that Hazel was not to interrupt other children's recitations, and that she would raise her hand and wait to be called on before speaking. After this discussion Hazel was asked to say what she would do; she responded with a realistic description of the task. Incentives for task accomplishment, which were gone over with Hazel, included, in her words, "getting a star on my chart" and "good grades on my report card." (As part of the plan the teacher would reward Hazel by giving her a star on a chart, which Hazel had constructed, for each day of appropriate classroom behavior.) Simulation was the next step, as this excerpt from a tape recording of the fourth session shows.

P: Let's practice some of this. Let's practice what you're going to do in the class.

H: I'm going to let the other people say the answers.

P: Unhuh.

H: Like, if somebody else raise their hands up I'll let them go up to the board and . . .

P: Let's practice. Now, I'll pretend I'm Miss Lovell [the teacher].

H: Okay.

P: And, I'm going to put some math problems on the board. Okay? And then she's going to say, . . . "Here are some problems, okay class, now raise your hands if you want to come up to the board and do these problems."

    Now, I'll pretend I'm Nellie [one of Hazel's classmates]. . . . Okay, now you show me what you used to do. I'll say [as Nellie], "I know the answer."

H: I used to say, . . . "No you don't! Let me go!"

P: [Amused] That's what you used to say?

H: Yeah.

P: Now we'll do it again, the new way.

H: Now the new way . . .

P: [As teacher] "Okay class, raise your hands if you know the answer. Nellie?" [Now as Nellie] "2 + 1 is 3."

H: [Breaking in with great verve] "2 + 1 is 4 . . . 'cause 2 . . . I don't understand . . ."

P: [As herself] Is that something else you do if someone gives the wrong answer? Do you say what you just did?

H: Sometimes . . . it be wrong and then I say, play like . . .

P: Just a minute . . . let's do . . .

H: . . . Play like you're Jenny . . . sometimes she don't even know what 2 + 2 is. She say it's 5. And I say, "2 + 2 is 4."

P: And what does Hazel's job say?

H: I will let the other children say the answer. . . . I will not interrupt.

P: But that also means, Hazel, that if they say the wrong answer you don't say anything 'til teacher calls on you. Then you just did that when Nellie said the wrong answer. Okay?

H: Now let's do it the right way.

P: All right. [As teacher] "Okay class, who knows the answers to these problems? Nellie?" [As Nellie] "2 + 1 is 4." "Does anybody else know the answer? Hazel?"

H: "2 + 1 is 3."

P: [Warmly] Good. You see how you're supposed to do it?

    Despite her verbal grasp of the task, Hazel immediately reproduces her problem behavior in the role-play situation by interrupting the dialogue between "teacher" and "Nellie" and giving the wrong answer to boot! The child thus experienced the problem in a vivid way. The practitioner then had the opportunity to engage the child in an on-the-spot critique of her behavior more or less as it actually occurred and to suggest specific elaborations of the task. The simulation ended, as it should have, with an appropriate implementation of the task and the practitioner's approving response. The practitioner might have made verbally a point implicit in the last trial—that it was good that Hazel was able to supply the correct answer and that she was so willing to recite when called on. A comment to this effect would have provided additional insurance against a risk (slight as it may be) that Hazel's spontaneity and eagerness to participate in the class would be impaired by carrying the task "too far." According to the teacher's report, Hazel's classroom behavior did improve noticeably during the following week, and Hazel herself was quite proud of her accomplishment. It is questionable whether this change would have taken place without the simulation, given Hazel's initial failure even to role-play the task successfully.

Guided Practice

Guided practice involves actual, as opposed to simulated, work on the task. For example, if the child's task involves work on an academic subject, he may be able to work on the task in the session with the practitioner serving as a tutor or coach. The client is not rehearsing task behavior—rather, he is carrying it out. Guided practice can be used, of course, only with tasks that can be carried out in the worker's presence, but the variety of such tasks is considerable, particularly in work on marital or family communication problems and in work with clients in natural, as opposed to office, settings. As will be discussed in chapter 9, marital or other family pairs can work on communication problems through tasks carried on in the treatment session. Work with clients in natural settings opens up an even greater range of possibilities. For example, in one study (Callahan and Leitenberg 1970), acrophobics were successfully treated by having them climb fire escapes, in graduated stages, under the supervision of a therapist. The general strategy in such efforts has been to help the client approach the feared object or situation through incremental steps with the practitioner at his elbow. Training parents in the handling of behavior problems of young children, helping children control aggressive behavior with peers, or enabling disabled persons to develop self-care routines are additional examples of areas of application of guided practice.

The worker's role in guided practice approximates that of a teacher or coach. He provides initial instruction, encouragement, approval for work well done and corrective feedback to improve performance. He may also model appropriate behavior.

Analysis of Obstacles

As we have seen, identification of an obstacle to problem resolution may lead to tasks designed to remove the obstacle. But tasks themselves may encounter obstacles. In the present activity, the practitioner and client take up specific obstacles that are interfering with attempts at task achievement or that might be expected to interfere with a planned task.

Many obstacles have their origins in the client's belief system. If dysfunctional beliefs can be identified, and if they appear open to change, the practitioner may attempt to help the client modify them through verbal interchange. In general, the practitioner makes use of methods of rational-emotive and cognitive treatment (Beck 1976; Raimy 1975; Snyder 1975; Mahoney 1974; Werner 1974; Ellis 1962). In our approach, in contrast to those cited, methods to bring about cognitive change are usually directed at obstacles to particular tasks.

Once beliefs are identified as an obstacle, the practitioner may engage the client in an examination of their accuracy, scope, and consistency (see chapter 4). In carrying out this examination, the practitioner stresses challenging questions rather than giving his own opinions. As Mahoney (1974) has observed, "When individuals are allowed to examine and evaluate the rationality or coherence of their own beliefs, resulting cognitive changes are often more effective and enduring than when a didactic strategy is applied. . . . It may be more therapeutic to be 'gently directive' in self-discovery exercises than to beat the client over the head with the salience of his own irrationality.''

Miss F was a young, black, divorced woman who had been hospitalized with a diagnosis of paranoid schizophrenia. She lived an isolated existence, supported by public assistance. She was unable to carry out the task of accepting a standing invitation to go to the movies with a man, despite her wish to have male companionship and some interest in the man in question. She refused, she said, because if she accepted the invitation, ''he would want to have sex with me afterwards.'' She would not want to but would probably yield anyway. She would find the whole experience upsetting. Some exploration revealed that her refusing the invitation was based on a certain system of beliefs. Her conviction that her male acquaintance would want to have sex was based on the belief that the only thing men really wanted from her was sex. This belief in turn seemed rooted in her feeling that she had little else to give them. Her fear that she would yield to his advances reflected a belief that if she did not, he would not want to have anything further to do with her.

The accuracy of her notion that all men wanted from her was sex was examined against her prior experiences with men. It was agreed that, while most men she had gone out with did seem to want to go to bed with her fairly soon, they might have been interested in other things about her. Moreover, perhaps she had more to interest them than sex. The scope of her belief was addressed. She was viewing men entirely in terms of their sexual interest—as sex machines rather than human beings. The inconsistency in beliefs also became apparent: to keep a man interested in her, she would have to do something that ruled out getting involved with him in the first place!

Some progress was made in the interview toward helping her see men as creatures with an interest or two besides sex, and herself as contributing more than a body to an evening out. Since she wanted a man with more than sexual interest in her, perhaps she needed to say no to whatever advances her acquaintance might make, to see if he would want to take her out again. She was able to complete these tasks quite successfully.

This example involved a more extended and complex analysis of beliefs than is usually undertaken in respect to a single task. It was chosen because it illustrates various possibilities that may occur in dealing with beliefs as obstacles. The example also illustrates how altering beliefs can bring about related changes in motives, affects, and actions. As the client sees men in a more realistic light and herself as better able to handle their advances, her encounters with them are likely to be less anxiety-provoking and her motivation to seek out relationships is likely to increase.

It should not be assumed, however, that inaccurate beliefs yield readily to such methods. As Raimy (1975) argues, a person's misconceptions tend to be self-perpetuating, perhaps in part because they serve a protective function. Miss F's belief that all men wanted from her was sex quite likely shielded her from feelings of inadequacy in encounters with men, which also may have been based on inaccurate beliefs. In his attempts to alter beliefs the practitioner must exercise patience and persistence in presenting disconfirming evidence and must often deal with intricate webs of faulty conceptions. He must also be prepared to accept frequent thwarting if not defeat of his efforts.

When problematic beliefs do not respond to in-session analysis, other methods may be tried to work through the obstacles they pose. One approach is to develop tasks that will help the client come to terms with deficits in his belief system. Thus, a mother who believes (inaccurately) that her children "never listen to her" might take on the task of recording their responses to her requests for a period of time. If it is difficult to engage the client in dialogue about his beliefs, tasks may be used to provide the necessary leverage. If the mother in the example above had been reluctant to discuss her perceptions of her children's reactions to her, the task suggested might have increased her readiness to do so. Tasks may also be used for unwanted beliefs that do not yield to verbal methods. Common obstacles in our work with actively psychotic patients are dereistic beliefs that they hear voices telling them what to do, that people are laughing at them, that the FBI or syndicate is on their trail, and so on. Rational dialogue may accomplish little. Usually, more is gained if the practitioner, rather than questioning the validity of the beliefs, helps the client set up tasks to treat them as annoying, alien thoughts to be gotten rid of. Thus, the client's task may be to tell his "voices" to "bug out." Additional procedures can be found in Thoresen and Mahoney (1974).

When the obstacle is located in the social system, then analysis is directed at understanding how elements in that system are blocking the client's task work. This process leads to revising current tasks, or devising new ones, in an effort to remove the obstacle. The practitioner follows the same procedure he would use in task planning and implementation for a target problem. In addition, he may undertake tasks of his own (see below) to modify obstacles in the social system.

Other In-session Activities

With the exception of task review the major activities that take place in sessions with the client up to the terminal interview have been described. We shall review, in a more summarized fashion, activities that generally occupy a less prominent place in these sessions or in the model. Planning for practitioner tasks outside the treatment session is, perhaps, the most important of these. In some cases the practitioner is in a better position to act on the problem than the client; for example, if the solution is a service or resource that the practitioner can arrange to provide. In others, the practitioner will act with collaterals to facilitate the client's task progress. Here again the practitioner needs to plan with the client. How such practitioner tasks are carried out will be discussed below. Another activity consists of planning how time in the session will be spent and of determining priorities respecting work on different problems and tasks. Sometimes clients wish to talk about immedi-

ate concerns that would not be considered part of an actual or potential target problem—a serious illness of a family member, for
example. The practitioner normally lets the client say what is on
his mind (as would any humane professional under the circumstances), then leads the discussion back to the problems at hand.

Finally, in work with children and younger adolescents particularly, a certain amount of time in the session may be devoted to
"recreational" activities—drawing, listening to the client's voice
on the tape recorder, or small talk. With children such diversions
may be used to add a needed element of fun and informality to the
relationship and as rewards for periods of productive effort.

Implementing Practitioner Tasks

Practitioner tasks are undertaken outside the session either to help
the client achieve his own task or to bring about changes in the
problem independent of the client's actions. As indicated above,
such tasks are discussed with the client in the session; the worker's
agreement to carry them out becomes a part of the contract, and he
is responsible for reporting back to the client on his efforts. Not all
the environmental work undertaken by the practitioner needs to be
formalized as tasks. Unforeseen opportunities and contingencies
may arise: the practitioner needs some degree of flexibility in
responding to them. Similarly, we do not expect clients to restrict
their problem-solving activity to agreed-on tasks. Nevertheless,
practitioner tasks provide a means of ensuring that critical efforts
to influence the social system will be planned in a collaborative
manner with the client; moreover, they place the worker under the
kind of accountability requirements demanded of the client.

Some guidelines for carrying out practitioner tasks have already been suggested by previous formulations concerning the role
of the social system (chapter 4) and in the discussion of strategies
earlier in this chapter. In general, the practitioner tries to obtain
from the social system whatever would help the client resolve his
problem. In so doing, he serves as the client's guide and advocate

in the complex world of people and organizations that makes up the system. He presents the client as he really is—in terms of his specific problems and actions—rather than in terms of vaguely defined labels. To the extent possible, he structures his work with others in the form of explicit agreements about their responsibilities and actions. With these considerations in mind, we shall take up the principal forms of practitioner task.

Facilitating Tasks

Certain practitioner tasks are designed to enlist and structure the assistance of others in helping the client carry out problem-solving action. The others may be clients or individuals who have some relationship with the client but are not themselves receiving service. The term "facilitator" will be employed to describe any person in the client's social system used to assist the client in the accomplishment of his task (except when two or more clients are being treated as a system, chapter 9). Two major types of work with facilitators can be distinguished.

The first type consists of efforts to influence incentives that might affect the client's actions. As has been demonstrated by innumerable studies within the operant framework, clinicians can bring about significant changes in a person's behavior through manipulating rewards and punishments dispensed by those in his environment. To carry out this strategy, the clinician needs to have access to potential facilitators and to be able to enlist their cooperation; the facilitators, in addition, must control incentives of sufficient interest to the client and be able to observe the performance or the results of the task. These conditions can be more easily met in certain practice situations, such as work with children or family systems, than in others, such as treatment of single adults in open settings.

If these conditions are met, then one needs to determine the kinds of incentive for the client that might be under the control of a person in his social system. The client may be asked to indicate what he would like to obtain from the facilitator or to respond to the practitioner's suggestions about possible incentives. The practitioner may also ask others, use his powers of observation, and draw upon his general knowledge. In the case of children, typical incentives are food, symbols (such as gold stars), small amounts of money, special treats or privileges, and expressions of approval. Typical adult incentives include approval and reciprocal actions undertaken by others. Although the practitioner may proceed provisionally on the basis of assumptions about what may be an incentive for the client, he will soon need to determine from the client himself whether or not these assumptions are correct.

Discussions with the client of incentives that may be provided by others may be considered a part of an activity mentioned earlier—establishing incentives and rationale with the client. Such discussions need to be synchronized with efforts to enlist the cooperation of the person controlling the incentive. How this is done will vary according to the circumstances of each case. A preliminary plan may be worked out with the client and taken up with his facilitator, or vice versa. Regardless of how it is developed, the plan must be understood and agreed to by the client.

In planning with the facilitator, it is important to be clear as to what incentive will be provided following which actions on the client's part. It should be agreed that the facilitator should provide the incentive promptly upon the client's completion of the stipulated actions and should not provide it if the client does not carry them out. An incentive may be provided upon accomplishment of the entire task, if it is one-time or unique, or upon execution of specific actions, if it is a recurring task. Incentives provided by facilitators are more commonly used for tasks of the latter kind. For example, in our school program, teachers award children with tangible incentives (gold stars, cookies, etc.) if they complete each day (or each half-day) such tasks as staying in their seats, raising their hands for permission to leave their seats or to speak, and not hitting or kicking other children.

How the facilitator responds to actions that are *contrary* to those called for in the task needs also to be taken into account. Facilitators inadvertently may be providing incentives for such actions by giving them attention, showing approval for them in subtle ways, and the like (chapter 4). Incentives of this kind, which would obviously work against the task, need to be identified and, to the extent possible, eliminated. Thus, the facilitator should provide incentives only for actions furthering a task and should avoid rewarding those that are contrary to it.

The second type of activity in this category is using others to facilitate the client's *actual execution* of the task. A task for a non-talkative child may be to read out loud in class; his teacher can ask him to read a short, simple passage, perhaps one already read aloud by his best friend. Parents may be asked to provide an adequate place to study for a child whose task is to work an hour each night on her math. An escort can be provided to help a client carry out an anxiety-laden task—attending a clinic to obtain needed medical care. As these examples suggest, the facilitator does not increase the gain the client will realize from task execution; rather, he makes it easier, or possible, for the client to achieve the task.

The practitioner carries out the activity in a manner similar to working with others to increase task incentives. Again, planning proceeds with the involvement and consent of the client. The practitioner must first identify a facilitator in a position to help the client with his task. In addition to more obvious possibilities, such as teachers, caretakers, and family members, one can also make use of peers and paid or volunteer assistants. The practitioner attempts to enlist the cooperation of the facilitator and to structure his role with the client. At a minimal level, the facilitator may be requested not to interfere with the client's task performance. More involvement is required if the facilitator's role is to maximize the client's opportunity for success with the task—for example, a teacher may be asked to call on a child when he raises his hand. In still more extensive levels of involvement, facilitators may serve as models or coaches in activities similar to rehearsal or guided practice. For example, peers can be used to model appropriate behavior, a technique that has been used with apparent success with children. Peers can also be used in a more active way to help clients execute tasks. Thus, in work with adolescents expelled from classes, we have found that the adolescents are better able to carry out tasks of going to the teacher and asking to be reinstated if they are accompanied by a peer.

This activity can be used with any task on which another person can be, and is willing to be, of help. Its use may be particularly indicated for tasks the client is unable to perform to any degree on his own, for one-time tasks whose achievement is critical for the client's well-being, and for working through environmental obstacles to task achievement. If the task involves actions the client will need to do on his own at some point, one needs to be careful that the facilitator does not provide an excessive amount of assistance and make the task too easy.

Independent Tasks

Independent practitioner tasks are designed to affect the target problems directly rather than to facilitate the client's tasks. They are intended to complement rather than to assist particular client actions. For example, if a client's goal is to obtain employment, the practitioner's task might be to check out certain job possibilities; the client's task might be to look into others. Or the practitioner's task may involve work on a problem quite separate from the client's own activities. Thus a practitioner may attempt to secure financial assistance for a client whose tasks are confined to her relationship with her children.

When are such tasks called for? While the model is centered on helping the client define and carry out problem-solving actions, there are certain situations in which the practitioner is in a better position to effect changes than the client. The most frequent occasion of this kind arises when the client lacks needed resources or is having difficulty in his dealings with an organization. In either case, he must usually cope with complex and unfamiliar bureaucracies. With his special knowledge of the workings of relevant organizations and with his status as representative of a social agency, the practitioner may be able to move with greater efficiency; what is more, his intervention may be necessary if the client is to obtain what is needed. For the sake of promoting the client's own problem-solving capacities and of helping him learn to deal with complex organizations, the practitioner may correctly decide to assist the client in developing the necessary tasks and to facilitate his carrying them out. To proceed in this fashion, however, we must be reasonably sure that the client can, with the worker's assistance, obtain the needed resource, or whatever, without excessive difficulty or risk of failure. In the present model, problem resolution takes priority over learning problem-solving skills, even though the latter is seen as an important dividend. Another consideration has to do with the client's task load. Thus, the worker would normally assume more responsibility for obtaining resources with a client at work on other problems than he would for a client whose only problem was the lack of the resource. Finally, time pressure on the worker is a factor: practitioners with heavy caseloads may be limited in their capacity to carry out tasks for clients.

As previously indicated, most independent practitioner tasks involve dealings with organizations with which the client is already involved or that may be of help to him. The range of possible tasks is broad. A task may call for the practitioner simply to secure information about possible resources for the client's consideration. The practitioner may determine if the client is eligible for a particular service offered by an agency and refer the client for the service. He may negotiate with an agency to bring about an improvement in a service the client is already receiving. In some cases, the practitioner may try to convince an organization not to take or to postpone certain action that may be detrimental to the client, such as initiating garnishment or eviction proceedings. In others, the practitioner may attempt to alter the behavior or attitudes of a particular member of an organization toward the client.

To carry out such tasks effectively the practitioner needs to know how organizations contribute to psychosocial problems (chapter 4). In addition he needs knowledge that will guide his interventions with organizations. The three R's of this intervention knowledge might be thought of as resources, rules, and roles.

The *resources* provided by organizations include services, material benefits, personal-care arrangements, and the like. To know the resources of a community, we must not only understand what various organizations offer but must also be informed about the quality and specific characteristics of their programs. The client in need of a service wants the best available for his circumstances and hopes that the worker will be able to help him get it. The worker must make an informed judgment about how good the resource is—is it a well-run nursing home?—and about the suitability of the resource for the client, or what Weissman (1977) refers to as the "best fit" between client and resource. Such knowledge is hard to come by: most practitioners are well acquainted with the resources of only a limited number of organizations, usually those they use frequently. Visiting agencies and getting feedback from clients and other workers are among the means of expanding one's knowledge of the resources of relevant organizations.

The complex bureaucracies with which social workers deal are controlled by systems of rules. Knowledge of the rules of an organization may be essential if the practitioner is to carry out his task, particularly when he is serving as a client's advocate. Often in cases of conflict, the client's cause can be advanced by knowledge of what he is entitled to under the rules of an organization. For example, it may be crucial to know, or to find out about, rules concerning appeal and fair hearing procedures if a client has been dismissed from a program and the worker is trying to get him reinstated.

Finally, an understanding of the roles of the staff of target organizations will contribute considerably to the practitioner's task work. Included here is knowledge of what relevant staff members do, organizational and professional expectations influencing their performance, and the role stresses, or job pressures, that might affect their behavior toward the client. Thus, a worker who attempts to alter the way a teacher responds to a disruptive child needs to know that the teacher cannot carry out her role unless a certain degree of order in the classroom is maintained; and he should have some sense of how much pressure she is under generally as a result of disruptive behavior in the classroom. The same consideration applies to independent task work with collaterals who are not representatives of organizations—professionals in private practice, relatives, or family members. In such cases, the collateral has a role in relation to the client, a role whose characteristics need to be understood and appreciated.

Task Review

What the client has accomplished on his task between sessions is generally reviewed at the beginning of each session. The client is asked to report on what he has accomplished; whatever record of task progress he has kept is gone over, and the practitioner introduces any evidence he may have received from collaterals or other sources. In keeping with the spirit of the model, the practitioner endeavors to obtain precise details on what the client actually did. The client's progress is recorded on a four-point scale (chapter 10). If the task was at least partially accomplished, the worker responds with approval and credits the client for his achievement. How his task achievement may have affected the problem is determined. If significant parts of the task were not accomplished, the reasons are elicited in a noncritical manner.

The review should be extended to whatever tasks the practitioner has been working on. The practitioner reports on what he has accomplished, reasons for lack of success, and so on, and responds freely to the client's inquiries. Putting both client and practitioner tasks under the same review process further emphasizes their *mutual* accountability.

Interrelationship of Activities

All the activities of the model prior to termination have been presented. At this point it may be useful to consider how these various activities are integrated as treatment proceeds. Each case begins with problem specification, which is followed by formation of the treatment contract and then task planning and implementation. A step-wise progression is followed, with return to prior activities if a step cannot be completed. That is, if it is not possible to form a treatment contract, the practitioner resumes efforts to specify the problem. If no workable tasks can be developed, one reconsiders the treatment contract with a likely return to problem specification. This structure is designed to place the activities in an orderly progression and to provide a systematic way of retracing steps to find out where things went amiss. The need for retracing most commonly arises when the practitioner attempts to proceed with task planning and implementation on the assumption that the client has agreed to a certain definition of the problem. When the client is unable to think of any actions he can take to solve the problem, rejects the worker's suggestions, or makes halfhearted and unsuccessful efforts to carry out tasks suggested by the worker, then it is likely that the client and worker are not sharing the same definition of the problem. Perhaps the practitioner did not adequately explore the client's perceptions; or the client may have gone along compliantly with the practitioner's definition without really agreeing with it. Whatever the reason for the discrepancy, one needs to go back over previous steps until a firm and clear understanding is reached.

While certain activities should occur before others are begun, once an activity has been introduced it may be used throughout the life of the case, with the purposes of its use changing as the case progresses. Thus, problem specification, as noted, is used throughout to secure additional information about the problem, monitor changes in it, or to investigate new areas of difficulty. The treatment contract may be reviewed periodically and modified, and so on. To put it another way, a case proceeds through progressive additions to activities.

Once a treatment contract has been reached, task planning and implementation become the dominant activity. The specific activities within this grouping also follow a certain progression. The first is task planning; then, when indicated, use may be made of establishing incentives and rationale, analysis of obstacles, rehearsal, and guided practice. Work with collaterals may follow if appropriate. The client then attempts to carry out the task during the interval between sessions. Task review is the next major step, often preceded or followed by exploration of developments in the problem. What then occurs depends on the results of the task review and additional problem specification. If a task has been successfully carried out, it may be simply repeated, requiring the client, in effect, to continue his new way of acting. Or a similar task at a greater level of difficulty may be developed. These options may involve relatively little work in the session. If the successfully executed task has taken the client as far as he can go in a particular direction, a new and quite different task may be developed and carried forward with use of appropriate task planning and implementation activities.

If the client has been unable to carry out the task or has only partially completed it, two options are available to the practitioner: the task may be immediately abandoned if it seems obvious upon review that it was inappropriate for the client in his particular situation, or, more commonly, the reasons why the client was unable to complete the task may be examined. This discussion may then lead to an evaluation of the incentives and rationale for the task and to an analysis of obstacles. If an adequate rationale cannot be found for the task, or if the obstacles seem unresolvable, the task may be abandoned at that point. If the task has an adequate rationale, then task planning may be used to modify the task or to develop more effective strategies for its execution. Other activities of the task planning and implementation sequence may be employed following procedures set forth earlier. These processes are repeated until a satisfactory solution to the problem(s) is arrived at or until the end of the agreed-upon period of service. When either point is reached, the practitioner and client move into the final activity: termination.

Activities and Techniques

As we have seen, work on the client's problem is organized around a set of *activities* carried out jointly by the practitioner and client or by the practitioner and others on the client's behalf. An important distinction is made between these activities and the verbal techniques the practitioner uses in carrying them out. An activity is a collaborative enterprise; techniques are the practitioner's contribution to the activity. Thus, in problem specification, an activity, both practitioner and client work on pinning down the difficulty. In this process, the practitioner may use the technique of exploration to elicit data about the problem. In operational terms, the amount of time both the practitioner and client devote to problem specification would be counted as a measure of that activity; the practitioner's use of exploration would be measured by the amount of time he devoted to that technique.

In our first version of the model (Reid and Epstein 1972), the practitioner's contribution was viewed largely in terms of such techniques as exploration, structuring, encouragement, direction, and explanation. While this structure has been retained and revised (see appendix II), it has become secondary to the present system of activities.

Activities are given greater emphasis than techniques for two reasons. First, the activities spell out the basic and distinctive strategies of the task-centered approach in its present form. While the techniques are essential to implement these strategies, they may be used as well in other forms of practice to achieve other purposes. Thus, "direction" or advice giving is a technique common to most forms of interpersonal practice, but it is used in particular ways to further certain activities in our approach (see chapter 10). Second, activities express the collaborative spirit of the model—what the practitioner and client do together to achieve common ends. This emphasis helps us move away from a view of helping in which the practitioner acts through techniques, procedures, and so on, and the client reacts by accepting or rejecting the practitioner's offerings. Although we may find it useful to examine client responses to particular practitioner techniques, the essence of our approach is better captured through examination of their joint efforts.

Chapter 8
Ending

Ending treatment is, naturally enough, the last activity in the model. As in any planned, time-limited approach, the point of termination is set in advance as part of the treatment contract. With this end point in mind, the practitioner and client formulate the last set of tasks to be worked on in the next-to-last interview. Ideally, these tasks should be repetitions or modest extensions of previously successful tasks.

The terminal interview, usually held a week later, begins with review of this final set of tasks. Attention is then turned to the main activities of termination: (1) to review and assess what was accomplished during treatment in relation to the client's problems; (2) to plan directions for the client's continuing work on these problems, if further work is needed; (3) to help the client see that the problem-solving methods he has learned in the period of service can be applied generally to problems of living.

Final Problem Review

The problem review is a systematic assessment of the status of the client's target problems, of other problems he may be facing, and of his own perception of problem change. This review not only helps the client see what has been accomplished but provides the worker and others with a basis for judging the effectiveness of treatment. Since some change for the better usually occurs in the target problem, and since the client usually has experienced at least some success in his tasks, he normally can be given genuine credit for what has been accomplished. Explicitly crediting the client serves to heighten the feelings of mastery that the client should experience at the close of treatment. In multiple-client situations, reviews may be conducted separately with each client or with all members of the client system present.

Current Description of Target Conditions

In the initial problem review, certain target conditions were identified, and the frequency of their occurrence was assessed during a retrospective baseline period, usually seven days preceding the initial interview (chapter 6). In the final review, this assessment procedure is repeated, with frequency of occurrence obtained for a comparable period prior to the last interview. Suppose the problem consisted of quarreling between mother and daughter over the daughter's responsibilities around the house. The initial baseline might have specified the frequency, duration, and intensity of the quarrels during the week prior to the initial interview. In the final interview, data on the same aspects would be obtained for the week prior to that interview.

In some cases, the problem may lack variation in frequency at either point of assessment. The initial target problem may have been specified as the client's exclusion from a work training program for which he was eligible. With the problem so defined, one would need only to determine in this portion of the final review where things stand in relation to his being admitted to the program. Such reviews, which normally take only a few minutes to complete, are conducted for each target problem. When used in conjunction with the initial reviews, they provide the client and the worker as well as an outside observer with succinct before-and-after pictures of change in each problem.

Client's Assessment of Change

The review now turns to the client's own conception of change in respect to the target conditions and the discomfort associated with them. The practitioner explores but does not challenge discrepancies between the picture of change based on the "before" and "after" assessment completed earlier and the client's view. For example, the conditions of the problem may not have changed, but the client is no longer troubled by them. Changes in other aspects of the client's life situation are also examined, with particular attention paid to areas that might have been either positively or negatively affected by the course of treatment. While the practitioner probes for specifying detail, for the client's evaluation of change, and for possible changes not spontaneously mentioned by the client, the views that matter (and are recorded) here are the client's, not the practitioner's.

Others' Assessment of Change

This part of the problem review is completed with collaterals who have firsthand knowledge of change in the client's problems and who are briefly interviewed (with the client's knowledge and consent) either in person or on the telephone. Collaterals are asked to indicate changes they perceive in the target problems as well as changes in other problems and in pertinent aspects of the client's behavior and circumstances. Collaterals may need to be advised as to how the target problems were defined, since their view of the client's difficulties may be rather different. If the collateral has been in a position to observe changes in target conditions during the terminal baseline period, his observations are elicited as a check against data obtained from the client. From the problem review, the practitioner and collateral move into a mutual assessment of what has been accomplished and possible roles the collateral may play in continued work with the client. The recording of the final problem review and ratings of problem change are illustrated in chapter 11.

Post-treatment Planning

The problem review leads naturally to planning for the post-treatment period. What the client can do to maintain the gains he has achieved, or what actions he can take on remaining problems, becomes the focus of attention. Future tasks, usually extensions of what the client has already worked on, may be planned, with discussion of potential obstacles that might occur. There also may be consideration of the client's obtaining help at a future point, either at the same agency or elsewhere.

In discussing the client's accomplishments and postservice period, the practitioner attempts to put into words the process of problem-solving the client has learned during the course of treatment. Key steps are put in nontechnical language and in a form the client can use on his own: narrowing down the problem; listing the various things that can be done about it; deciding on a course of action and planning how it should be carried out, including breaking large tasks into smaller ones; providing oneself with incentives; rehearsing and practicing what is to be done; figuring out what to do about things standing in the way; and getting others to help. Which steps are stressed will depend on what the client has done and which, in the worker's judgment, he can best comprehend and utilize. The principle is to help the client generalize from his experience, even if in a limited way, so that he can gain some conceptual understanding of the approach he has used and can apply it to future problems.

In applying this principle, practitioners often review with their clients some successful problem-solving episode that occurred during treatment to help them extract general skills from it. For example, toward the end of treatment Lila and her mother had resolved on their own a conflict over Lila's seeing Tracy. The mother had simply forbidden Lila to see her friend. When Lila pressed her mother as to what specifically was bothering her, the mother revealed that she "couldn't stand" Tracy and did not want her around the house. They then worked out a compromise: Lila would not bring Tracy home, and her mother would not "bug" Lila about seeing her friend outside the home. In the final interview, the practitioner brought up this episode and observed that they seemed to be putting into practice some ways of handling problems that they had learned during the course of service. After congratulating them on their successful resolution, the practitioner pointed out that they had specified a problem in terms they could do something about and had worked out tasks that each could do to solve it. They agreed to try to continue to use that method of resolving problems that arose between them.

An effort is currently under way to develop and test a more systematic method of teaching problem-solving skills as a part of task-centered treatment. Brown (1977a) has devised a program for this purpose. The client is first taught a general model of problem solving derived from the principles of the task-centered approach. A portion of each interview is then devoted to helping the client relate his own problem-solving work to this model. In this way, his own experiences are continually used to help him achieve a conceptual grasp of problem-solving strategies and tactics that he can apply to other problems he may face.

Recontracting and Disposition

As termination approaches, there may be reason to extend the original contract, to develop a new contract, to make a referral elsewhere, or to arrange for some other special disposition. These variations from standard termination will be briefly considered.

Limited Extensions

Brief extensions of service (normally up to four sessions) beyond the agreed-upon end point can be made to complete unfinished work. They are typically used when it appears likely that some additional time could help the client make decisive progress on a target problem. The client may have gotten off to a late start in working on the problem, or it may not have been identified until treatment was well under way. In any event, there is a reasonable expectation that further effort will make a major difference. For example, the worker and client may have hit upon a task plan that really seems to be effective with the problem, and a few more sessions might turn the tide. Just the expectation that further progress can be made with additional sessions is not reason enough to prolong treatment. Extensions made for this reason often run treatment beyond the point of diminishing returns and may be more than the client really wants. Nor does lack of progress per se constitute sufficient grounds for an extension. If little was accomplished during the regular period of service, it is not likely that a few more sessions will add much. Aside from being a waste of the practitioner's and client's time, they may increase the client's sense of failure.

Extensions may also be warranted if the problem may be resolved or significantly affected by an event expected to occur shortly—for example, discharge from an institution, a decision about a prospective job, or surrendering a child for adoption. Often the initial setting of service limits can take the timing of key events into account. Thus, the end point of service may be planned to coincide with a patient's discharge from an institution. Sometimes, however, the occurrence of such events, or their timing, cannot be foreseen. While a pending event may present an occasion for an extention, it does not in itself provide a rationale. A reason for the extension must still be established. For example, the occurrence of the event might be expected to raise issues that the client may want help in handling. If the practitioner and client have finished their work, and it is simply a question of waiting for the event to occur before wrapping things up, regular sessions can be suspended until that time.

In general, extensions are planned to accomplish a specific purpose and for a particular time span. If possible, the planning should take place before the scheduled terminal interview—usually in the preceding session.

Either the client or practitioner may propose an extension. A good deal of weight is given to the client's unsolicited request for additional sessions. Even though it is still advisable to establish a rationale for continuing treatment, client-initiated extensions are usually granted. Our principle here (and throughout) is, "When in doubt, give the client what he asks for." We have found, however, that clients seldom ask for extensions. For most, the agreed-upon period of service probably is quite sufficient. There may be some clients, however, who may want additional help but who may still "go along" with the prearranged limits simply because they have been prearranged. In fact, most of the clients who have expressed reservations about the brevity of the approach at follow-up (Reid 1977a; also chapter 10) did not ask for extensions during treatment. For reasons that are not completely clear, women are more likely than men to have these reservations (Reid and Shyne 1969; Reid 1977a; chapter 10).

It would, of course, be a simple matter to ask clients routinely if they want additional sessions. To do so, however, may undo some of the benefits of time limits and may prove disconcerting to clients who have taken the original limits seriously (as we want them to). Suggesting extensions may also give clients the possibly unwarranted impression that further help is really needed. Only if the practitioner has grounds for believing that an extension would serve a specific useful purpose (along lines suggested above) should he introduce the idea and his reasons for so doing. In the usual case, the extension should be offered as a possibility for the client to consider and not as a recommendation. In making decisions about offering extensions, practitioners need to sort out their needs from the client's. Sometimes extensions are suggested, if not urged, because the practitioner is reluctant to give up the gratification *he* is receiving from his relationship with the client.

Successive Contracts

In some cases, major target problems are identified or occur near the end of the initial contract, or have been identified earlier but set aside in favor of other problems. In any event, as termination approaches, the client is faced with a significant problem that he wants help with but has not had an opportunity to work on. In these situations, the client can be offered a second service contract to work on the problem. Practitioners must guard against the temptation to offer second contracts for problems that are of greater interest to them than to the client. If they are closely tuned to what the client wants to work on and his desire for further help, they will find that successive contracts are very much the exception.

Termination in Context of Continued Care

As noted (chapter 5), the model can be used within the context of long-term care arrangements, such as one finds in protective, correctional, or institutional work. The disposition in such cases may be to return the client to regular service or supervision provided by the same or a different worker. While termination applies to a particular course of treatment and not the case, the practitioner nevertheless conducts a terminal interview. This procedure makes sense even if he plans to retain the client. The value in reviewing the client's progress, determining generalizable aspects of his experience, and planning future directions still obtains. In addition, if the practitioner and client are to continue their contacts, they can identify specific areas for future work that can be addressed in their subsequent (and presumably) less frequent encounters.

Conversion to Open-Ended Treatment

As the brief service contract, or an extension thereof, draws to a close, the decision may be to offer a continuation of treatment on an open-ended basis. If this arrangement is made, the short-term service should be ended with a formal termination process, in the manner and for the reasons suggested above. The continuation treatment may or may not be based on task-centered methods.

While the research evidence previously cited (chapters 1 and 6) argues against frequent dispositions of this kind, there are circumstances in which they are justifiable, if not warranted. Again the client's wishes are paramount. If a client clearly expresses a desire to continue on an open-ended basis, and if to do so would not deprive another client of service, then an argument for open-ended treatment can be made. In addition, there should be reason to suppose, based on the client's use of brief treatment, that continued work would serve constructive purposes. To the extent possible, further treatment should be guided by goals agreed upon by practitioner and client. These goals may be resolution of a problem that the brief treatment program did not alleviate to the client's satisfaction or may be of a type that brief treatment is not able to accommodate—for example, extended examination of existential issues (chapter 5). To determine how well such goals are being attained, data on client progress and satisfaction should be regularly obtained and used as a basis for periodic evaluations with the client. One can still use principles of contracting and time limits to good advantage—for example, contracting with the client to continue treatment for a block of time—say, six months—with a review of accomplishments and a decision about a new contract to be made at the end of that period.

While it is hard to make a case from available evidence for routine use of open-ended treatment, the utility of this form of treatment *following* planned brief service has not been adequately tested. There is no reason to suppose that a high proportion of clients would elect this option, but we need to learn more about the fate of those who do.

Referral Elsewhere

Task-centered service may end with a decision for referral to another organization—for extended treatment, some form of nontherapeutic service, residential placement, and so on. In fact, in some cases the purpose of task-centered work may be to locate a suitable program or institution for the client and help him prepare for admission to it. In arranging for a referral, the practitioner can make use of the systematic linkage methods developed by Weissman (1976). These include providing the client with detailed information about what to expect from the resource, how to get there, and whom to see; providing the resource with information about what the client would like to gain; visiting the resource with the client or having him contact it by phone in the worker's presence; follow-up with the resource and the client to ascertain if the referral was effected as planned. Such procedures, which can also be used to refer clients to ancillary services during the course of task-centered treatment, have been found to increase the likelihood that the referral will "take" and prove satisfactory to the client.

Chapter 9
Conjoint and Group Treatment

A good deal of social work practice is conducted with systems of clients—principally couples or families seen together or in various combinations of individual and joint sessions and clients who are treated in formed groups for individual problems. While there are specialized treatment modalities designed for work with families and formed groups, the trend has been toward the development of general systems incorporating their own brands of individual, family, and group treatment (Roberts and Northen 1976).

Although this development has accentuated "schools" divisions in social treatment, it has enabled treatment systems to expand their range of application with advantages for both education and practice. It is easier and perhaps more efficient to teach and learn the principles and methods of a single system with its individual, family, and group variations than three separate approaches. If this strategy is to work, a system needs to incorporate theory and technology that meet the special requirements of these distinctive forms of practice. Since general systems tend to do this rather unevenly, practitioners must usually supplement them with borrowings from more specialized systems, particularly in the family and group treatment areas.

The task-centered approach, like a number of others, was developed primarily as a means of helping clients in one-to-one relationships. The bulk of our efforts has been in this area. Increasing emphasis has been given, however, to conjoint treatment of marital couples (Reid 1977a; Weiss 1977; Tolson 1977); to work with combinations of parents and children (Ewalt 1977; Wexler 1977);

and to treatment of individuals in formed groups (Garvin, Reid, and Epstein 1976; Garvin 1977; Rooney 1977a).

These adaptations will be the focus of the present chapter. Treatment of family units will be considered primarily from the standpoint of work with marital pairs, the best developed of our family approaches. Theory and methods of marital treatment will then be extended to other family systems. Our focus in work with families will be on conjoint treatment of problems in family relations, that is, treatment in which two or more family members are seen together for difficulties in their interaction. We prefer this form of treatment for such problems, although it may not be possible to arrange in all cases and may need to be supplemented by individual sessions. Finally, we will present a summary of our task-centered model for work with formed groups.

Problems in Marital Interaction

What are commonly described as "marital problems" in clinical social work can cover a range of difficulties, including interpersonal conflict, emotional distress associated with a marrage, dilemmas about whether or not to remain with a partner, and problems in working out a separation or a divorce. My present concern is with problems of marital *interaction,* where the target is resolving difficulty in how marital partners get along with one another. The focus for change is not the individual feelings or behavior of one person but the relationship between the two. The unit of attention can therefore be seen as a two-person system. Of all difficulties associated with marriage, problematic marital interaction is doubtless the most important and pervasive. Quite similar problems occur in other types of two-person systems. The consideration to be developed can be extended, with some modifications, to treatment of any dyad involving partners who engage in frequent, continuing interactions.

Theory and Strategy

It is assumed that most problems of marital interaction, regardless of the particular form they take, are the expression or outgrowth of the system of *rules* that characterize the interaction. This assumption has its origins in the works of Haley (1963); Jackson (1965); Watzlawick, Beavin, and Jackson (1967), and others who have used the concept of rules to organize thinking about marital and family interaction.

As I use it, the term "rule" refers to regularities in interaction, either actual or potential. Actual or *descriptive* rules characterize interaction in the past or present. When John criticizes Mary's mother, Mary gets angry and disparages John's family. As Haley (1963) has pointed out, such rules may be recognized by the partners or carried out without their being aware of the pattern, which can nevertheless be discerned by an outside observer. Or the existence of a rule may be asserted by one partner and denied by the other; or both may disagree on its characteristics.

Rules that purport to describe empirical events can be distinguished from prescriptive rules, which express conceptions of how interaction *ought to* occur, as in, "We should be able to discuss our in-laws without criticizing them." A prescriptive rule may have a close fit to actual interaction, but expresses a requirement, not a description. The difference can be appreciated in such statements as, "We shouldn't argue in front of the children, even though we do." For couples in marital conflict, descriptive rules generally describe the problem aspects of their relationship, whereas prescriptive rules usually express the kind of relationship that one or both would like to have. "We always avoid each other; we should enjoy doing things together."

Rules can be considered to be desirable (functional) or undesirable (dysfunctional) from various points of view. Clients usually evaluate rules according to how they may contribute to their satisfaction with marital and family life. The practitioner's evaluation of rules needs to take into account disagreements between clients about what rules are desirable or undesirable and must also consider the ramifications of different rules (including those not recognized by the clients) for various aspects of marital and family functioning.

Partners' references to rules that they negatively evaluate are likely to be in terms of complaints about each other's behavior. Thus, a wife may accuse her husband of criticizing her in front of company, and the husband may assert that she needs to be reminded when she is making a fool of herself. Neither is likely to put the rule in objective terms: that certain behaviors of the wife are likely to be followed by certain behaviors of the husband. As Watzlawick, Beavin, and Jackson (1967) have observed, marital partners tend to "punctuate" rules in this manner by attributing causation and blame to the other partner.

The applicability of the rule concept may at first glance be difficult to discern when one partner's behavior is defined as "the problem." "My husband is an alcoholic," a wife may say as a way of summing up the marital difficulty. Her husband may agree with her formulation of the problem. But some reflection will show that the husband's drinking behavior, no matter how much of a problem in its own right, does not define the marital difficulty. It is more accurate to say that the husband's drinking (or his behavior when drinking) causes the wife to be upset. In other words, we have the combination of a patterned action and response which form the nucleus of a rule of interaction. If the wife is not upset by the husband's drinking or associated behavior, we do not have a marital problem.

At the simplest level, an interactive rule describes two related actions of two persons: A's action and B's response. Rules become more complex when B's response in turn influences the action of A, and still more complex when A and B influence one another through a series of actions and reactions. Another kind of complexity arises when the rule is made up of the interactions of more than two persons: when Mrs. Y reprimands their son, Mr. Y criticizes Mrs. Y; Mrs. Y then attacks her husband and becomes more critical of the child, who becomes increasingly upset. Although such rules describe family rather than marital interaction per se, they may be of central importance in problems of marital conflict.

Specific rules of interaction are in turn influenced by what Haley (1963) and others have termed "metarules," or rules about rules. A *metarule* is a principle for forming or interpreting rules, for settling disputes about them, or resolving conflicts between them.

Thus, the interactive rules of most couples are guided by a principle of confirmity to social norms—role expectations—concerning married life. Rules regarding such diverse aspects as division of labor in the home, frequency of sexual activity, or the use of leisure time may be shaped by one or both partners' beliefs of what is normal for married couples to do. References to this metarule may be used by either to justify, challenge, or modify specific rules. A wife may object to her husband's practice of working at home in the evenings on grounds that husbands and wives should spend some of this time doing things together.

Metarules may be also found, as Haley (1963) suggests, in characteristic ways couples define their relationship. If one partner takes a superior (one-up) and the other a subordinate (one-down) position (a complementary relationship), then the metarule may be that the person in the dominant position will make decisions concerning rules for those aspects of the marriage for which this relationship holds. Thus, if the wife is generally the dominant partner in matters of child care, her husband may defer to her if rules of interaction need to be developed, interpreted, and so forth, in respect to that sphere. As Haley (1963) points out, however, the question of who is one-up is often a point of issue leading to conflict at the metarule level.

The types of metarules thus far described have obvious limitations as guides for interaction in most American marriages. Norms governing marital behavior are vague, often contradictory, and appear to be losing influence in the face of increasing strains in our society toward particularistic life-styles. At the same time, the long-term trend toward equality or symmetry in marital relationships appears to be continuing, with recent acceleration from the women's liberation movement. Traditional areas of dominance by wife (home and children) or husband (providing income) are becoming less distinct. Increasingly, patterns of complementarity or symmetry in marriages seem to be based on the personalities and interactive styles of the participants.

As a result of these developments, marital partners are placing increasing reliance on metarules which generally guide relations between equals. Two such rules appear to be of particular importance. One, which pertains to relations between intimates, might be called the rule of mutual devotion. According to the prescriptive statement of this rule, partners in a close relationship should be sensitive to one another's needs and desires and try to meet them out of motives of devotion, caring, love, for the other. This rule is often regarded as the ideal norm to guide interaction of intimates. It may in fact be the ideal when it works, but it is usually no longer a strong constructive force for couples who seek marital help: the willingness to sacrifice one's own needs to those of the other has generally become a victim of marital conflict. Based as it is on mutual caring, it is not a rule that can be easily restored. The partners may be striving to revive the rule but on their own terms or in ways that would in fact prevent its regeneration. Thus, a wife may complain bitterly about her husband (''If he really loved me, he wouldn't behave that way''), overlooking the role her behavior might play in his lack of affection.

The second of these rules for coequal relationships is the norm of reciprocity which calls for exchanges between partners on a quid-pro-quo basis (Jackson 1965). Reciprocity is concerned not with the partners' social roles, altruism, or dominance but rather with what each gives to the other in the spirit of fair exchange. Thus, if a couple is faced with the issue of who is to get up at night to bottle-feed their infant, the norm of reciprocity would suggest that they take turns; or if one gets up, the other will do something else in return. As studies by Gottman et al. (1976) suggest, reciprocity in marriage does not require immediate payment for value received; it demands rather that exchanges achieve an equitable balance in the long run.

Problems arise when reciprocity fails, when one or both

partners begin to feel cheated. This feeling is likely to arise when one partners believes the other is not meeting certain expectations and is not providing compensatory satisfactions in other areas. The partner who has this belief is likely to be less accommodating to the wants of the other. Vicious cycles then ensue in which each spouse is given increasingly ample justification for feeling deprived. Each becomes less likely to give to the other, and in fact may want to pay the other back with the kind of punishment each is receiving. As this process continues, the partner comes to be viewed in increasingly negative terms. Genuine contributions are minimized and faults magnified. If love is blind, marital discord has the eyes of a hawk.

This process has gone pretty far with most couples who seek a social worker's help. Usually both partners have been dissatisfied with their marriage for a considerable period of time. In some cases, the relationship is dominated by negative reciprocation—paying each other back.

Other cases seem "burnt out": the partners have given up trying; there may be a minimum of either positive or negative reciprocation. In any event, both partners are likely to feel they are deriving less than they deserve from the relationship.

In these marriages, the wished-for rules each partner would like to see control their interactions have little force. Instead, their interactions are played out according to rules or patterns that neither wants and neither has the power to change. In fact, neither may have any real understanding of the actual rules that control their lives together.

The central goal of task-centered treatment of marital conflict is to help couples resolve acknowledged problems in their interaction. To achieve this objective, the descriptive rules and metarules contributing to the difficulty are clarified; prescriptive rules suggesting desired patterns of interaction are worked out; tasks to be carried out by the partners are designed to put these new rules into operation. In the process, there is a considerable reliance on the metarule of reciprocity, which serves as a central means of justifying and organizing the couple's problem-solving efforts.

The focus of our work in marital treatment is to help couples resolve specific rule-based problems, though more fundamental (metarule) changes may occur as a by-product. To what extent this model, or in fact any approach, can bring about fundamental changes in a disturbed marriage is really unknown at this time. Modification of important rules of interaction can bring about significant change in the marital relationship as a whole under certain conditions—for example, in youthful marriages or in relationships in which strong forces for change already exist. But it is hard to predict when such major changes will occur or how lasting they will be.

Although most marital problems can be defined in terms of dysfunctional rules of interaction, some difficulties are confined to specific issues—a disagreement about buying a house, for example. Rules of interaction may determine the occurrence and shape of such difficulties but may not themselves be an integral part of them. In such cases, treatment may be confined to the issue presented, unless the partners wish to work on the ways they interact together.

Problem Specification and Analysis

Problem formulation in cases of marital conflict is a complex and often exasperating business. Not only do marital partners usually have contrary views of their problems, but their views tend to be at variance with those of the practitioner. In the typical case, the husband and wife see their problems in terms of the behavior of one another, while the practitioner is likely to see them in terms of their interaction. Moreover, a conflict-ridden marriage may breed a host of interconnected problems, making it difficult to focus on any particular issue. Finally, these difficulties have a mercurial quality, vanishing and reappearing in the well-known vicissitudes of the marital relationship. Nevertheless, as studies of short-term marital counseling have indicated (Reid and Shyne 1969), it is usually possible to identify and work with focal areas of concern.

Perhaps the first step—in fact, a convenient way of beginning the first interview, assuming the couple is seen jointly—is to determine each partner's dissatisfied wants in respect to one another's behavior and to the marriage. What does each want that he or she is not getting? In this way, the rules of interaction proving most troublesome to the couple will begin to emerge, although it is to be expected that each partner will punctuate the rule by attributing causation or blame to the other. "I withdraw from him when he gets mad at me." "It irritates me when she goes inside herself."

Sometimes the expression of dissatisfaction will state the interactive rule without the usual cross-blaming. "We don't do enough things together." "We quarrel about money." Or sometimes a partner will initially accept responsibility for the problem. Accepting total blame may, paradoxically enough, amount to an avoidance of responsibility for making specific changes. The client who says, "It's all my fault," is also likely to say, "This is the way I am; I can't change." The outlook is more hopeful if a client accepts partial responsibility—"I overreact to his criticisms."

A tendency to define the problem in terms of the other's behavior often emerges even when the difficulty has been initially attributed to the relationship. Thus, "We don't do enough things together because all he likes to do is to watch TV." Or, "We quarrel about money because she wants to spend more than I make." Relatively few persons involved in a relationship problem can be sufficiently objective and undefensive to be able to view the difficulty, as the practitioner might, in purely interactional terms. Nevertheless, when the partners are in conflict, there are strategic advantages in trying to get each to accept an interactional formulation of the problem—that is, to help them see it as a common problem (chapter 3). To do so moves each toward some recognition that each shares part of the same difficulty and sets the stage for negotiation and compromise.

Moreover, this kind of formulation more accurately defines the target of intervention—the conflict between the partners— rather than the individual behaviors of each. For example, Mrs. S may complain that Mr. S does not give her a large enough allowance. His countercomplaint is that she spends money foolishly; for this reason he doesn't give her more. The problem is best formulated in interactional terms: Mr. and Mrs. S disagree about how much money Mr. S is to give her each week. Usually, most partners in conflict will agree to this kind of problem formulation even though each may blame the other for "causing" the difficulty. The principle can be extended to problems that are less reciprocal. For example, Mr. Y may see a problem in Mrs. Y's "sloppy housekeeping," which she denies. It would probably be more advantageous to formulate the problem as "Mr. and Mrs. Y disagree about Mrs. Y's housekeeping" than as "Mr. Y doesn't like the way his wife keeps house."

An alternative approach is to obtain from each partner the problems each perceives in the other. This specification of interdependent problems is done with the understanding that each spouse will attempt to work on problems in his or her behavior that the other finds undesirable. Problems are then paired and worked on by each in the form of a reciprocal exchange. "I'll do something about the problem that you see in my behavior if you do something about the problem I see in yours." As part of the trade-off, each partner acknowledges a problem the other has attributed to him or her. Each partner may then work on his or her own "end" of the same rule of interaction. Mr. A may agree to refrain from using corporal punishment with Jerry, and Mrs. A will refrain from interfering with her husband's attempts to discipline the boy. Or each may work on their ends of separate rules.

This method of problem formulation, with some variations, has been used in a number of approaches based on reciprocity principles. For example, in a program described by Rappaport and Harrel (1972), couples are first trained in the use of reciprocity to resolve marital difficulties. Each partner then "independently prepares lists of three *specific* undesirable behaviors manifested by spouse." Partners then contract with each other to work on behaviors labeled undesirable by the other. As Rappaport and Harrel (1972) suggest, this method of problem formulation may not be suitable for couples who do not express an initial willingness to compromise on their difficulties.

In some cases, as noted, a spouse may accept responsibility

for the major part of the problem. The practitioner is still well advised to apply the norm of reciprocity to such problem formulations. If one partner owns up to the problem behavior, then an attempt should be made to get the other to do the same or at least agree to attempt some kind of change. Otherwise, the partner with the self-identified problem behavior is likely to resent having to carry the entire burden.

Given the complexities of marital interaction, it is usually a challenge to achieve the necessary understanding of the nature and causes of the difficulty. Clients may express problems in terms of segments of behavior shorn from their interactional contexts and often put in exaggerated form. ("She never wants to have sex." "He spends all his spare time playing golf.") Such behaviors may reflect a breakdown in positive reciprocity, but in order to help the partners act in more positively reciprocal ways, it is necessary to understand exactly how they are interacting. In other words, one must gain an understanding of the actual rules of their interaction and how they lead to, or express, the behaviors that each partner complains about. This kind of understanding can lay the groundwork for helping partners develop strategic actions that can reverse vicious cycles before they have progressed too far.

For example, Mrs. O. initially described the major problem in her ten-year-old marriage in very simple terms: "My husband is always flying off the handle for no reason at all, and it's making me a nervous wreck." She vividly recounted the latest incident—he had become furious and started yelling at her because she had forgotten to pay a bill. Mr. O, also present in the interview, surprisingly agreed with her definition of the problem. There was nothing wrong with his wife or marriage, as far as he was concerned. He just kept losing his temper over trivia. The social worker questioned both more closely about events preceding the temper outbursts. As a result of this exploration, he was able to piece together the following picture. The outbursts tended to occur just after Mr. O. got home from work. He often came home irritated over frustration at work but was reluctant to share any of this with his wife because of his belief (based on some prior conversations with her) that she would neither understand nor appreciate what he was going through. His frame of mind was not helped by the clutter in the living room that usually greeted him when he came in the door. For her part, Mrs. O, reacting to her prior experiences, was tense and guarded when her husband came home. She found it hard to be responsive when he did try to express his feelings about his day in a civil manner. Thus, the stage was set for interactive chains that culminated in Mr. O's "blowing his top" over "some little thing." This pattern could then be defined as a complex rule of interaction that neither partner had comprehended.

Once this descriptive rule was clarified, it became possible to identify specific steps each might take to change it. Mrs. O agreed to tidy up the living room and be more responsive to her husband when he came home. Mr. O agreed to tell his wife in a pleasant way about whatever frustrations he had experienced on the job. These tasks were within the capacities of each to perform and proved successful in altering the pattern. It would probably have been fruitless to ask Mr. O to keep from losing his temper or Mrs. O to react calmly to his outbursts, tasks that might have been derived from the initial information about the problem.

To understand marital problems, one must then understand the unwitting and unwanted rules of interaction that produce them and how these rules work against the development of positive reciprocity. The details of these repetitive sequences—who does what to whom, when—are crucial. The practitioner also needs to be aware of the beliefs that are mediating the actions of each and how these beliefs may constitute obstacles to improvement of reciprocity. For example, in the case just cited, one notes Mr. O's belief that his wife didn't appreciate his struggles at work and her likely belief that he was going to explode every time he came home from work at night and wonders how these images of the other might be contributing to their difficulties.

The practitioner normally obtains the bulk of his data on interactional problems through interviewing the participants, usually together. Supplementary individual interviews may be called for when there is reason to suppose that one partner may not be able to reveal certain information in the other's presence or when the two partners are so quarrelsome in joint interviews that it is difficult to get a clear picture of other aspects of their interaction. Whether he interviews partners together or singly, the practitioner attempts to secure agreement from them on important facts. This goal is more readily accomplished in joint than in individual interviews.

Task Planning

Once a problem and the rules of interaction producing it have been identified, tasks designed to modify the problem and the interaction are developed with each partner. Two modes of task formulation can be used. One involves an expansion of task-formulation procedures with the individual client. The practitioner may elicit task possibilities from each partner, suggest tasks to either or both, and help the pair arrive at feasible tasks that are acceptable to each. In the second approach, the practitioner uses some form of structured interaction between the partners as a vehicle for task formulation. He may ask the partners in effect to discuss task possibilities between themselves and to come up with tasks each might carry out. The practitioner then takes on the role of facilitator, intervening in the couple's dialogue to keep them focused on the subject, to help them clarify what they are saying to one another, to encourage each to express alternative actions his partner might undertake, and to make agreements firmer.

It is particularly important, as Patterson and Hops (1972) suggest, to help partners "pinpoint" behaviors in the other they would like to see changed. Thus, if a wife says she would like her husband to be more "considerate of her feelings," the practitioner would ask her to specify the ways she would like to have her husband show consideration in respect to particular feelings. This approach has the advantage of giving more initiative and responsibility to the partners and may promote their learning of ways to negotiate with one another. It may be difficult to use, however, with partners so torn with conflict that they are unable to communicate with each another in a rational manner. Moreover, this method might not be the best when problems are the product of complex interaction chains that the couple may not comprehend even after they have been clarified. In such cases, the practitioner may have a better perspective than the partners on what tasks might be the most strategic.

As has been previously suggested, probably the ideal tasks are those that will enable the partners to modify dysfunctional rules of interaction. In order to accomplish this purpose, the tasks may need to be directed at actions that take place early in the cycle, before the partners have reached a point where they can no longer control their reactions toward one another.

The development of such strategic tasks is dependent upon understanding the patterns of interaction that produce the problem. It may take several sessions to clarify these patterns. Our experience suggests that task formulation should not be delayed to that point. Rather, it is important, I think, that at least one shared or set of reciprocal tasks be developed in the first session, even if the tasks are less than ideal and even if the session needs to be rather lengthy (two hours or so). It is also important that the initial tasks be relatively easy for the partners to carry out. The rationale for this strategy is to capitalize on their motivation before it wanes and to help them achieve a quick demonstration that they have the capacity to change. As Rappaport and Harrel (1972) have noted: "If the first behavioral exchange results in mutual satisfaction for both partners, a positive pattern will be created and the couple will most likely want to continue bargaining to further enhance their marriage" (p. 205). Failure to carry out the tasks can expose barriers to the improvement of the relationship and can provide diagnostic information to be used as a basis for constructing tasks that might have a better chance of success.

Tasks addressed to problems of marital interaction can be divided into reciprocal, shared, and individual types. Each type has a different structure and different planning requirements. Reciprocal tasks call for different actions by each partner on the basis of a quid-pro-quo exchange. Since the actions are paired by the notion of reciprocity, each partner must value the intended actions of the other and must perceive those actions to be a reasonable exchange for his (or her) efforts. The details of the actions need to be planned, but with allowance being made for variations that may be indicated by circumstances. Planning needs to take account of how both partners may react if certain contingencies arise. For example, if a husband's task is to call home when he is delayed at work and his wife's reciprocal task is to respond in a calm, accepting manner when her husband calls, one might consider such contingencies as the husband's not being able to get to a phone and the wife's being out when he calls.

The manner in which the tasks are to be carried out becomes important when, as in the example, above, the tasks require interaction. Thus, the husband and wife could accomplish their tasks in a subtly attacking or disparaging manner that could discourage further work on them or create additional problems. A planning procedure suggested by Azrin, Naster, and Jones (1973) might be used to avoid such difficulties. They suggest simply that the partners be asked to carry out agreed-upon behaviors in a manner that each thinks would be pleasing to the other.

Another contingency that needs to be considered is that one partner will not carry out his part of the bargain. In setting up the task, it is desirable to have each partner make a commitment to do his part even if the other does not. If one is able to complete the task, the other may be stimulated to follow through at a later point or at least make some positive response. The double commitment also helps avoid interactions in which both back away from doing their tasks because each perceives the other to be shirking responsibility or because neither wants to take the first step.

Shared tasks call for the partners to work closely together in a cooperative manner. A single task statement beginning with the names of the partners is used rather than separate but paired statements, as in the case of reciprocal tasks. Thus, partners may agree to work out a budget together or to plan some activity. I shall briefly discuss three types of commonly used shared tasks: joint problem-solving tasks, conversation tasks, and enjoyable-activity tasks.

In *joint problem-solving tasks,* partners undertake to resolve some specific issue or modify a rule of interaction through face-to-face communication. The partners attempt to clarify the issue or rule, discuss alternative means of resolution or change, and try to formulate a plan of action. If a descriptive rule of interaction is under consideration, the couple, with the practitioner's assistance, may try to develop a prescriptive rule they can both agree on. Thus, the partners may wish to change their pattern (descriptive rule) of the husband's leaving the house in a temper in response to criticism from his wife. The prescriptive rule they work out may call for the wife to overlook certain behaviors of the husband that normally provoke her criticism, while he, in exchange, may agree to try to maintain normal interaction when his wife does say something critical.

Tasks to be carried out in their day-to-day interaction can then be devised to implement plans that emanate from this problem-solving process, although often couples will carry out necessary action on their own initiative once they have agreed what is to be done. Joint problem-solving tasks can either be worked on in the session (as will be shown later) or at home.

Conversation tasks may be designed to help a couple resolve problems in face-to-face communication. Thus, a couple's task may be to discuss one or more issues without making reference to each other's past misdeeds, to refer only to the actual behavior as opposed to inferred motives or attitudes of the other, to stick to one topic for a certain length of time, or to avoid interrupting one another.

A third common type of shared task calls for the couple to engage in some mutually enjoyable activity, such as going out to the movies together, sharing a cocktail and a pleasant chat before dinner, or having sexual relations. Such *enjoyable-activity tasks* are designed to reduce distance and isolation and to help the partners find ways of deriving pleasure from their relationship. Such tasks are often suggested by the worker. Instigation of enjoyable activities may enable partners to "get out of a rut," to break up existing patterns of mutual withdrawal and isolative behavior that neither particular wants but that neither is able to take the initiative to alter. For example, a spouse may be reluctant to propose an activity because of fears of rejection by the other but may welcome the worker's suggesting it. That the activity is cast as part of treatment adds to its legitimacy. Obviously, timing is important; enjoyable-activity tasks will be rejected or may be counterproductive if the marital relationship is seething with conflict. It is also important that both partners regard the proposed activity as enjoyable. If only one does, and the activity would still serve a useful purpose, then it is better to set reciprocal tasks; for example, the husband will take his wife to see a particular movie (which he doesn't want to see) if she will do something in exchange for him.

Unlike reciprocal or shared tasks, individual tasks are carried out independently by each partner. Although individual tasks are guided by the norm of reciprocity, they are not paired in explicit quid-pro-quo fashion as are reciprocal tasks. For example, a couple may agree on a set of reciprocal and shared tasks but one partner may agree to take on an extra task. Or each partner may carry out a task unrelated to the task of the other and without an understanding that completion of the two tasks represents an exchange.

Individual tasks are used in several ways in marital treatment. First, there may be need for one partner to work on a problem in which the other is not involved but that is still affecting the marital relationship. For example, difficulties at work may be affecting the way a wife relates to her husband. Second, one spouse may be willing and able to do more than the other during a given phase of treatment; individual tasks can be used as the means. The temporary assumption of greater responsibility by one partner does not necessarily run counter to the norm of reciprocity. Whatever one partner does can eventually be repaid by the other, or the partner willing to do more may in fact already be in the other's debt. In any event the practitioner is usually advised to take advantage of initiatives for constructive change whenever they occur, reciprocity or other metarules notwithstanding. Finally, use of individual tasks may be indicated when the degree of overt antagonism or mistrustfulness in a relationship is too great for the development or execution of reciprocal or shared tasks. In such situations the individual tasks may need to be limited to whatever each partner is willing to do in whatever area of the relationship he or she is willing to do it. For example, in one case where the husband and wife were having a running battle in the treatment sessions and at home over a half dozen or so poorly defined issues, the best that could be done at the beginning was for the husband to make an effort to engage his adolescent son in a conversation about his school problems and for the wife to make a listing of their numerous debts.

A similar approach has been developed by Weiss and his associates (Weiss, Birchler, and Vincent, 1974; Weiss, 1975). Taking note of the difficulty conflicted couples frequently have in carrying out quid-pro-quo exchanges, they devised the "parallel contract." Each partner agrees to effect a change in behavior which is rewarded if accomplished, regardless of what the other partner has done. A husband may agree to take care of the children on Saturday afternoon with a reward of an extra evening of bowling if he does. His wife may agree to have meals ready on time during the week with the purchase of a new dress as her reward. As Jacobson and Martin (1976) suggest, contracts of this kind may be a strategic way of beginning treatment with marital partners who are not yet able to effect the more efficient and possibly more effective quid-pro-quo exchanges.

Task Implementation

The task-implementation activities previously discussed (chapter 7) are applied in work with marital pairs. I shall consider here only those aspects that differ when husband and wife are treated simultaneously.

Incentives and rationales for reciprocal, shared, and individual tasks need to be established with each partner before the task plan is settled. The incentive for each in reciprocal tasks is usually the anticipated change in the other's behavior. As suggested earlier, parity in the exchange is a crucial consideration. Neither partner should feel that he (she) is carrying an unfair burden. This criterion does not mean that the tasks themselves need to be "equal" in any particular exchange. What counts is each partner's *perception* of fairness, which can be influenced by many factors. The metarule of social norms can affect their perception: one partner may be willing to take on a more onerous task because his (her) behavior represents greater deviation than the other's from their conception of the norms of married life. Thus, a husband may agree to come home from work without his customary two-hour layover in a tavern in exchange for a pleasant greeting from his wife. One partner may be willing to do more than the other with the expectation of being paid back at a later point or in some other way. The practitioner needs to determine how each partner perceives these temporarily unbalanced exchanges and to ensure that neither feels put upon or is covertly anticipating some "payoff" that might not be realized.

Often the connection between tasks and the rules of intervention they are designed to change needs to be made explicit. This is particularly indicated if a task strikes either partner as trivial or disconnected from the main issues of the marriage. Thus, in one case (Tolson 1977) a shared problem-solving task was devised to work on the high frequency of interruptions that occurred in the couple's communication. Since interruptions seemed, to the wife at least, to be a relatively minor concern, the practitioner explained that the problem expressed a struggle for control in their interaction. Moreover, given their high rate of interrupting one another, they could not use face-to-face communication to the best advantage in work on more important problems in their relationship. The clarification enabled the couple to put the task into proper perspective and to work on it productively.

In task-centered treatment of marital interaction, considerable stress is placed on in-session work on joint problem-solving and *conversation tasks* through simulation and guided practice with the partners. These two activities can be considered together since the line between simulated and actual task behavior is difficult to draw when the couple is interacting in the practitioner's presence.

The practitioner assumes the role of a task "coach." He observes the partners' performance, praises actions that further the task, structures their communication, pinpoints difficulties, and provides feedback to help correct them. He may suggest alterations in joint problem-solving tasks or raise questions about alternatives that the partners suggest. Through role-play he may model desirable responses or may demonstrate how new ways of responding can affect subsequent interaction.

Tape recordings of the couple's communication are used extensively. Playbacks of recordings can give partners a vivid picture of what has just occurred between them and enables the practitioner to point out specific aspects of their interaction that may need further work. While videotaping provides the most complete record of interaction, the cost of the equipment and difficulties using it in a treatment session are obvious drawbacks. Inexpensive audio cassette recorders do almost as well. Confidentiality problems can be avoided, if need be, by erasing the tapes before the end of the session.

After setting up the task, the pracitioner usually permits the couple to work on it without interruption for a few minutes at least. Normally couples begin to interact in a natural manner. If the practitioner's presence seems to be inhibiting, he can assign his observational function to his tape recorder and leave the room until the partners have a chance to "warm up." The practitioner will usually find reason to interrupt the interaction before it has achieved its immediate objective. At these stopping points, he may wish to play back sections of the preceding interactions. His interventions may range from a comment to a fairly lengthy coaching session with role-play and subsequent discussion. Or he may suggest that the task be revised or replaced. He makes a particular effort to comment on positive aspects of task performance and to keep the focus on their interaction ("See, when each of you started to express some appreciation for the other's efforts, things began to go more smoothly"). Criticism of one partner's actions should be balanced, although not necessarily at once, with criticism of the other's. In keeping with the basic strategy of the model, in-session work on conversation and joint problem-solving tasks serves as practice for tasks that are carried out between sessions. Since a good deal may have been accomplished in the sessions itself, the task may need to be modified or extended for a work at home.

Because three persons are present, role-play can assume a variety of forms. The practitioner can model desirable responses with each partner in turn. Thus, he can play the husband with the wife, the wife with the husband. We have used this procedure following taped playback of preceding problematic communication between the partners. The role-plays and subsequent discussion then show each how the dialogue might have been conducted differently. Simulations along these lines or those in which husband and wife simply play themselves can also be used to help each rehearse reciprocal or shared tasks to be conducted between sessions.

Procedures developed by Thomas (1976) for helping couples resolve specific communication problems and make decisions are particularly germane to work on conversation and joint problem-solving tasks. Thomas provides a catalogue of common marital communication problems, methods for their assessment, and a "corrective feedback and instruction" program for their modification. His step-by-step procedures for marital decision making would be particularly useful in joint problem-solving tasks that called for couples to reach such decisions as whether or not to move or adopt a child.

In problems of marital interaction, analysis of obstacles is primarily addressed to beliefs partners have about one another and about the rules of their interaction. Partners who view one another in negative terms or who disagree about the rules of their interaction are not likely to complete conflict-reducing tasks.

In general, the more conflict-ridden the marriage, the more likely the partners are to develop distorted conceptions of each other. Anxiety, frustration, and hostility breed unrealistically negative and oversimplified images. A wife who may lose her temper with the children two or three times a week and only upon considerable provocation is seen by her husband as "always blowing her top at the kids." The wife regards her husband, whom most would see as merely cautious in money matters, as a "miser." Often one finds that spouses tend to think of one another in terms of pejorative labels and that they lack balanced, differentiated conceptions of each other. Negative, distorted beliefs are likely to become even more dominant during periods of acute conflict; under emotional stress the pejorative label may closely reflect the image the partner has of the other. The husband who in anger shouts at his wife that she is an "imbecile" may well see her at that moment as grossly limited in intelligence. In the absence of stress, partners may appraise—or be able to appraise—the attributes of their partners more objectively.

The practitioner can help marital partners acquire more accurate and discriminating pictures of each other in several ways. At a minimal level, he can call attention to negative stereotypes and raise question about their validity. Through further probing, he can try to elicit instances of behavior that would give each partner a better-differentiated picture of the other. He may also try to help each view the other's attributes or behaviors within their motivational and situational contexts. Thus, the husband who thinks of his wife as a pepper pot with the children may be asked how often she loses her temper with them and under what circumstances. He may begin to see that this behavior occurs less often than he thinks and to realize that it may be understandable in view of her day-long child-care responsibilities and the children's provocations.

In carrying out this kind of image reconstruction in joint interviews, the practitioner usually forms a temporary alliance with the partner who is being stereotyped. In the example just cited, the wife should be able to supply evidence that would help break down her husband's negative image. The practitioner would then try to take up one of her stereotypes of him, and then ally, again temporarily, with the other partner. Teaching clients how to respond empathically to one another on the basis of realistic images of each other (Guzzetta 1976), having each depict in writing characteristics of the other, or having them collect data on occurrences of certain behaviors are other ways of undoing negative stereotypes.

Beliefs about rules of interaction become obstacles when there is disagreement between the partners about what these rules (or metarules) should be. The disputes then concern the prescriptive rules that the partners want to have govern their interaction. Mrs. A believes that she and her husband should have dinner out once a week; her husband believes they should eat out only on special occasions; Mr. B thinks the children should be in bed by 9 P.M.; Mrs. B believes in a flexible schedule, and so on.

While such disagreements may emerge as obstacles to tasks already planned and attempted, they frequently enter the picture during task planning. Often they can best be seen as facets of the problem. In any event, some resolution may be necessary before tasks can be satisfactorily planned.

The practitioner's role in these disagreements resembles that of a negotiator. In this role, he does not attempt to impose his own rules on the couple but may support one partner's position or may suggest ways of reformulating the rules. In some cases, the key to the solution may be found in a metarule that defines norms of marital relationships. The rule needs to be one that both partners accept; both also need to agree that it applies to the dispute at hand.

In one case, for example, a dispute occurred over a husband's not calling his wife to say he would be home late when an afternoon "crisis" occurred at his plant (where he was a foreman). It was possible to relate the problem to a higher-order principle—that marital partners should let each other know if they can not show up at appointed times. While the wife valued this metarule more than the husband, he could recognize its legitimacy, and this recognition made him more willing to make concessions.

A solution can sometimes be found in applications of the more general metarule of reciprocity. One partner accepts a rule proposed by the other but receives something of equal value in exchange. A wife will accept her husband's prescription that she support him in his disciplining of the children, but in exchange the husband agrees to accept her prescription that they discuss disciplinary actions before they are administered.

Another general metarule of interaction—the principle of compromising differences—can also be brought into play. Although similar in function to reciprocity, compromising emphasizes mutual concessions toward some central position rather than parity in exchange. For a compromise to be effected, each partner must recognize the legitimacy of the other's wants, and the disagreement must be stated in terms that permit each to give ground. Azrin, Naster, and Jones (1973) have developed a useful technique—"the frequency fulfillment procedure"—for accomplishing the latter. In this procedure the wants of each partner are translated "into a continuum of possible activities such as a statement of frequency, duration or situation" (p. 323). In this way, the partners can be helped to move away from "all-or-none" positions. Thus, a husband may want his wife to accompany him every Sunday afternoon on visits to his parents, which she refuses to do. Each partner can be asked to state desirable frequencies and durations of visits together to his parents. Once the disagreement is put in such terms, it then becomes possible to negotiate a mutually acceptable compromise.

Parent–Child Interaction

The theory and methods developed for treatment of marital pairs can be extended with some modifications to work with parents and children on interaction problems.* This variation is designed primarily for a parent and an older child, one at least old enough to participate as a client in processes of problem and task formulation. With children too young to become involved in these processes, treatment proceeds with the parent as client, following the

---

*For purposes of discussion, a parent-child dyad is assumed. Situations involving more than one parent or child are taken up in conjoint family treatment below.

general model as presented in earlier chapters, even though the parent's interaction with the child may still be the primary focus.

Like marital pairs, parent-child dyads are rule-governed systems. The metarules that pertain to marital interaction (social norms, mutual devotion, reciprocity, and so forth) have their counterparts in parent-child relations. Still, there are important differences. In our society, metarules for marriages are based to a large extent on the assumption that the partners are coequals, whereas dominant social norms for parent and child relationships are based on assumptions of inequality. Parents are accorded authority (within limits) over their children who are (within limits) to obey them. Their greater physical strength and sophistication (with younger children) and their control of family resources give parents power to enforce the rule. In most problems of parent-child interaction, children are not behaving as parents want them to. Hence, the metarule of parental authority almost inevitably is an issue. Either parents view the origin of the problem as rebellion against their authority or they attempt to impose their authority as a means of resolution.

In formulating tasks, practitioners need to be sensitive to the parents' conception and implementation of this metarule. For example, parents may object to the idea of carrying out reciprocal tasks with their children on grounds that the children should do what they are supposed to whether or not parents do anything in return. Or they may give lip service to such tasks but either not do them or do them in a way that defeats their purpose.

In much of our work with parent-child dyads, task plans are designed to create a more rational, benign, and effective authority structure. A type of plan frequently used is modeled after the behavioral contracts used by Stuart in his work with families of delinquents (1971). Contracts were established between parents and delinquent children in which children earned privileges for carrying out agreed-on responsibilities. Sanctions (usually withholding of privileges) were applied if children did not carry out responsibilities. Bonuses (in addition to the stipulated privileges) were given for "extended periods of near-flawless compliance with contractual responsibilities" (p. 7). The use of contracts was found to "predispose family conflicts towards successful resolution" (Stuart and Lott 1972), although no relation was found between characteristics of contracts and outcome. Although Stuart does not make the point explicit, the contracts seemed to provide metarules for the exercise of parental authority. Privileges, bonuses, and sanctions were bestowed or withheld by the parents, not the children.

Task plans built along these lines can be used to particular advantage in parent-child conflicts in which both parent and child are willing to negotiate rules to establish a mutually acceptable structure for parental authority. For the parent, the approach provides a means of reestablishing control over the child's behavior, and thus may prove attractive even though prerogatives to exercise arbitrary discipline may have to be surrendered. The child can see (or be helped to see) the advantage of a more stable and equitable system in which he has at least some voice.

Parent-child conflict cannot always be reduced to issues concerning parental authority and discipline, however. Children may desire changes in other aspects of parental behavior—they may want parents to give them more time, not to favor siblings, and so forth. Parental tasks to these ends can be undertaken as part of reciprocal exchanges in which the child's compliance with certain parental demands is part of the bargain.

In some cases, particularly those involving adolescents, conflict may have reached the point of no return. The child may be unwilling to submit to parental authority unless major concessions are granted. The only viable approach may be to negotiate with the parents and child as coequals. If parents are reluctant to do so, it may be necessary to point out that they have already lost their capacity to control the child and that this may be their only means of regaining it. For example, in his work with runaways and their parents (where the point of no return had been reached in a literal sense), Bass (1977) obtained from the child a list of wants that would have to be met as a condition for his returning and remaining home. From the parents was obtained (in a separate interview) a comparable list of the behaviors they wanted their child to change. The parent(s) and child were then seen together to negotiate their demands and develop reciprocal tasks to implement those mutually agreed on.

Shared tasks to be worked on both within and after the session follow the general structure for marital pairs. The practitioner's coaching and modeling may be directed more toward the parent in tasks designed to improve on communication, since the parent may be better able to use this kind of intervention. The parents' authority role must, of course, be carefully taken into account in joint problem-solving tasks and in arranging for shared-activity tasks outside the interview. Use may be made of available programs designed to help parents and children work on interaction problems in the treatment session (Martin and Twentyman 1976; Corson 1976; Christophersen, Rainey, and Barnard 1973; Alexander and Parsons 1973).

Treatment of Family Interaction

I have thus far considered conjoint treatment of marital and parent-child dyads. The strategies and methods that have been suggested will now be extended to simultaneous treatment of larger combinations of family members.

Understanding Family Interaction

A family may be thought of as a higher-order system that incorporates marital, parent-child, and sibling subsystems. Like the systems it incorporates, it may be characterized in terms of rules governing the interaction of its members, which in turn are governed by metarules. Rules describing family interaction as a whole are naturally more numerous and complex since they incorporate both dyadic rules and rules of interaction among family triads, quatrads, and so on. While metarules at the family level are built from the dimensions thus far considered—social norms, reciprocity, and so forth—they likewise are more complex.

Additional principles and concepts from systems theory have been used to understand these complexities (Watzlawick, Beavin, and Jackson 1967). Thus rules of interaction can be pictured as being maintained in a steady state (homeostasis) through actions of family members (negative feedback mechanisms) that reduce deviations from these rules. The usual intractability of well-established patterns of family interaction can then be explained through the operation of these mechanisms. The principle of equifinality can be used to account for the common observation that interactive sequences among family members appear to gravitate toward familiar patterns despite diverse points of origin ("No matter where we start, we always wind up having the same fight"). Systems theory can, of course, be applied in this manner to any of the subsystems (marital, parent-child, siblings) that make up family systems.

While systems theory provides a promising way of understanding family interaction, its practical utility has been limited by difficulties in operationalizing key concepts and by lack of systematic knowledge about the functioning of families *as systems*. For example, we have not yet developed satisfactory means of isolating rules of interaction and determining their stability over time. Without adequate baseline data to define rule stability or homeostasis, it is impossible to delineate the operation of feedback mechanisms or other processes that involve system stability. If a rule cannot be specified, we cannot very well say that particular actions serve to maintain or change it. Until we can calibrate such concepts, we can hardly expect to carry out the systematic studies needed to provide data for theory building and testing.

Other theoretical prespectives (Olson 1970) are, like family systems theory, useful largely as a way of organizing thought and observation about family interaction. No body of theory yet provides much specific guidance for the practitioner in his work with families. It is thus not surprising that in its study of family therapy the Group for the Advancement of Psychiatry (1970) found "a striking gap between theory and practice; the conceptual approach formulated by family therapists bears only a tenuous relationship to their actual conduct of treatment'' (p. 535).

Despite the limited utility of present theories, a systems view of family interaction provides a useful orientation in working with any type of problem involving family relations, whether the unit of attention is a single family member or some combination of members. This perspective will not take the practitioner very far, but it will orient him in the right direction.

Seeing the Family Together

Application of the task-centered model in conjoint work with family units larger than dyads has been limited largely to treatment of parent-child interaction problems involving both parents and one or more children or a single parent and two or more children. In these cases, issues in marital interaction have been taken up in family sessions as they relate to the parent-child problem or dealt with in sessions with just the marital partners. Thus, a triangular conflict between father, mother, and child over discipline would be taken up in a session involving all three family members. Conflict between the parents (over sex, finances, and so on) in which the child was not directly involved would be taken up with them alone.

This strategy, which is consistent with our concentration on delimited problem areas, has the advantage of sharpening focus of work and of enabling marital partners to discuss their difficulties without feeling inhibited by their children's presence. It is also in keeping with our generally cautious approach to conjoint family treatment. It is a highly complex mode of intervention whose processes and outcomes have not yet received much systematic study. Until we can learn more about its range of possible effects on family functioning, it may be well to restrict its use, at least in our framework, to clear-cut problems of parent-child interaction. Our efforts to develop and test task-centered methods in this area have been limited by a number of factors, including lack of intact families in the settings in which we have carried out most of our work.

At a technical level, task-centered family treatment makes use of strategic methods of problem specification, task planning, and implementation previously outlined for work with marital and parent-child dyads. Rules of interaction that define or underlie relational problems are identified and clarified, and tasks are designed to change them. Individual, reciprocal, and shared tasks are utilized with different combinations of family members.

Work with Formed Groups

The principles of conjoint treatment that have been presented can be applied to any situation in which target problems involve interaction of members of *natural groups*—that is, groups that have a life apart from the treatment session. Thus, we have used conjoint variations of the model to treat problems of aggressive behavior occurring within a natural group of children in a school setting. Somewhat different principles apply when clients are treated for individual problems within the context of a formed group; that is, a group created to help individuals with their own concerns. The ultimate change target against which success is measured is not interaction of group members outside the session but rather resolution of the separate problems of each. Within the task-centered framework, the term "group treatment" is used to describe this form of intervention. The strategies and methods of task-centered group treatment have been presented elsewhere in detail (Garvin 1974; Garvin, Reid, and Epstein 1976; Garvin 1977; Rooney 1977a). The following summary is intended to provide only a general orientation to this approach and to fit it to the current framework of the model.*

In task-centered group treatment, the group process is used to further the basic activities of the model. Group members, guided

* The summary draws heavily upon Garvin, Reid, and Epstein (1976). I am particularly indebted to Charles Garvin for the generous loan of his basic formulations.

by the leader, help one another to specify problems, plan tasks, rehearse and practice behavior, analyze obstacles to task achievement, review task progress, and so on. The leader's role is to make effective use of this process through orchestrating his own interventions with the contributions of group members.

In order that the contribution of members can be used to best advantage, groups are made relatively homogeneous in respect to target problems. Thus, a group may be formed around problems of academic achievement or posthospitalization adjustment. As a result, group members have firsthand knowledge of the kind of problems others are experiencing and are thus in a good position to provide support and guidance. Moreover, members can more readily apply lessons learned from the task work of others to their own situations.

While it does not permit the kind of sustained, focused attention on individual problems and tasks possible in one-to-one treatment, the group mode has certain distinct advantages. Group members in the aggregate may possess more detailed knowledge than the leader about intricacies of the target problems. Given this experiential knowledge base, the group can often suggest task possibilities that may not have occurred to either the leader or the member being helped at the moment. Gaining recognition from a group provides an incentive for task accomplishment not available in individual treatment. As noted, vicarious learning is possible in group treatment; in particular, a member who carries out a task successfully can serve as a model to others. These advantages are not always realized, however. Groups may become unfocused and discordant. Members may become competitive and overly critical. Certain participants may become objects of group hostility—the well-known scapegoating phenomenon.

In order to exploit the potentials of this medium and to avoid its pitfalls, the group leader needs to exert a constructive influence on the dynamics of the group. The purpose of the group needs to be clarified and kept in view. The general purpose of any task-centered group is to help individual members with their target problems, but this purpose needs to be geared down to specific situations. At one point, the goal may be to analyze an obstacle to task progress that several members have in common. At another, it may be to help a particular member plan the details of implementing a task. Explicit statements and reminders of purpose serve to organize activities of the members.

The communications of the participants need to be channeled in relation to the purpose. Task-centered groups, unlike some others, are not oriented toward freeranging communication among its members. While all members are encouraged to contribute, and an effort is made to draw out silent members, communication within the group should further an explicit, agreed-upon purpose within the framework of the model.

Beliefs that members have about one another and about appropriate behavior in the group influence the sociometric and normative structures of the group. The practitioner attempts to encourage beliefs that are functional for the group's purpose: for example, that each participant is a worthwhile person who deserves help in working out his problems; that each has to find a solution that is right for him; that each has a right to his fair share of attention and assistance from the leader and the group. Shared beliefs about how the group should conduct itself become the basis for group control of the behavior of its members. The practitioner attempts to foster group-control efforts that will maintain focus on problems and tasks; that will facilitate sharing of relevant information (but discourage prying into aspects of the members' lives not germane to work on their problems); and that will stress positive reactions to task accomplishment over negative responses to task failure.

Leadership within the group is an additional facet that needs to be attended to and used constructively. Although the practitioner normally assumes the primary leadership role in task-centered groups, he may use members as coleaders for particular purposes—one member may be particularly adept at reducing tension in the group; another at keeping the group focused on the business at hand.

The initial step in group treatment is preliminary individual interviews with prospective group members. The interview has several purposes: to determine the general nature of the applicant's problems in order to see if at least one of major concern to him falls within the projected focus of the group; to orient him to the general structure and purpose of the group-treatment model and to answer whatever questions he may have about it; to ascertain if he wants to join the group, to receive individual help, or to deal with his problems on his own. In general, clients who wish to be admitted are accepted for group treatment if they have problems that seem likely to fit the model in general (chapter 3), are in accord with the group's focus, and if they meet whatever fixed criteria (relating to age, sex, and the like) have been set up. In some instances, groups may be formed on the basis of certain client statuses that tend to yield similar problems. Thus, a group may be formed for patients about to be discharged from a mental institution with the expectation (conveyed to prospective members) that the group will focus on problems associated with their status.

The practitioner may explore the client's willingness to reveal his problems to others, his comfort in group situations, and other factors that may bear upon his capacity to make use of the group experience. While the resulting information may be used to help the client reach a decision, the choice is left to him. We have not yet developed criteria by which we can select out clients who might be either particularly suited or unsuited for our form of group treatment.

The basic decisions the practitioner needs to make are whether or not to form the group and the size and duration of the group. Generally, a decision to form a group is based on some evidence that a number of persons with similar problems can be recruited. Practitioner interest and skill in working with groups is a major consideration. In some circumstances, group treatment may provide a saving of practitioner time. The size of task-centered groups tends to be rather small: the preferred range is four to six members. A limiting factor is the amount of time and effort it takes to review and plan tasks for each member at each session. If the group is too large, the sessions become excessively long and tiring. In keeping with the rationale of the model, group treatment is brief and time-limited. As in the one-to-one model, a range from eight to twelve sessions once or twice a week is generally used.

In the initial group meeting, clients are asked to state the problems they wish to work on and to assist one another in problem exploration and specification. The group leader provides instruction and guidance to help members carry out this process and in addition participates himself. The practitioner may assume an active role to ensure that each client specifies his problem with adequate clarity. A preliminary treatment contract will have been formed with each client in the screening sessions prior to the first group meeting. These understandings serve as the basis for a contract with the group. In the first group session this contract, which covers the purpose and duration of the group, is reviewed and affirmed.

Once problems are specified, tasks are developed and worked on, as in applications of the model with individual clients. The essential difference is that task planning, implementation, and review activities are carried out collaboratively by the practitioner and group members. Following Garvin's original formulation, various approaches have been developed and tested in experimental work conducted by Ronald H. Rooney.*

In one format, these activities are carried out by the group as a whole. Proceeding in turn, each member formulates, plans, and reviews tasks with the help of the practitioner and other group members. The remaining activities of the task-planning and implementation sequence are used as needed.

A somewhat different format may be used if problems of group members are sufficiently similar to allow the development of common tasks that each member can carry out in his own way. Thus, in one group of adolescents the common problem was ''not having friends.'' It was possible for the members to develop and plan certain common tasks designed to help them develop ''friend-

* The remainder of this section reflects the results of Rooney's efforts. It also owes much to the pioneering work of Ellen Washington, who has used the task-centered model in more than 20 adolescent groups.

making" skills (e.g., initiating conversations), which were then practiced in the group through role-plays with one another.

In a third approach, use is made of the "consulting-pairs" method (Rooney 1977a). In the initial or second session the group is divided into member pairs who help each other specify problems and work on tasks. Before the group is subdivided, the leader instructs the members in the use of the model. He provides roving supervision once they have begun their work. Before the end of the session, the group is reassembled, and the pairs report on what they have accomplished. Stating the tasks they have developed to the group as a whole serves the function of summarization (chapter 7) in the individual treatment model. The group then may help certain members complete or refine work on tasks. Subsequent sessions follow a similar format. The leader continues to provide instructions in the use of the model at the beginning of the session, concentrating on those activities the pairs are likely to use in their work. Task reviews are conducted within the pairs, with results reported to the group. In adolescent groups, peer counselors who have received special training in the model may be used to work with the dyads. The consulting-pairs format has the advantage of increasing the amount of individualized attention each member receives—which is particularly useful when the group is large or problems are somewhat dissimilar. In addition, by making the operation of the model explicit and by putting members into "practitioner" roles, this format may enhance the client's grasp of problem-solving skills and his ability to generalize them to problems other than the ones he has worked on.

These formats can, of course, be used in different combinations. All variations of the group model can be supplemented with individual work with particular clients. Practitioner tasks take the form of intervention on behalf of a single client or the group as a whole. Group members may also take on the equivalent of practitioner tasks to help their peers—for example, by providing "wake-up" calls or serving as companions on visits to clinics.

While data on problem alleviation and task progress have been collected for various approaches, they have not yet been tested in controlled experiments. Results in a number of trials have been encouraging (Garvin, Reid, Epstein 1976; Rooney 1977a), but more developmental work needs to be done before rigorous testing is attempted.

Chapter 10
A Study of Effectiveness

The task-centered approach was designed to be developed and tested through empirical research. Accordingly, a program of study was undertaken while the model was still in its formative stages and has continued to the present. Early studies of the model consisted largely of exploratory tests of its application to a variety of types of problems and clients in a variety of settings (Reid and Epstein 1972; Reid and Epstein 1977). These tests provided valuable information on the range of application of the approach, helped us identify promising innovations, and exposed areas needing further work. They did not, however, give us definitive data on the effectiveness of our methods. Although outcome data were accumulated, none of the studies was adequately controlled; that is, we did not use control groups or equivalent procedures that would permit us to conclude that the treatment methods made a difference in how the cases turned out. We had decided to defer more rigorous tests of outcome until we were reasonably satisfied with both our research *and* treatment methods.

Our first controlled test of task-centered methods consisted of an attempt to assess the effectiveness of a set of in-session activities (task planning, establishing incentives and rationale, analysis of obstacles, simulation, guided practice) as a means of helping clients achieve particular tasks (Reid 1975a). In brief, 32 clients (largely children from a school setting) were randomly assigned to experimental and control conditions. Sixteen student practitioners each carried one experimental and one control case. Experimental and control clients received the same form of task-centered treatment until the fourth interview (approximately) in each case. At this point the two cases were treated differently: in the experimental case, a task was formulated with the client, and these activities were applied to it. In the control case, a task was formulated in a similar fashion, but nothing further was done in the interview. No systematic differences could be found in the characteristics of the experimental and control tasks. Progress on each task was reviewed by the practitioner in his next session with the client. On the basis of tape recordings of these reviews, judges independently made ratings of task progress, not knowing which cases were experimental or control. These ratings revealed that almost 70 percent of the experimental tasks in contrast to only 20 percent of the control tasks had been substantially or completely achieved, a statistically significant difference.

The results suggested that the activities tested were instrumental in helping clients achieve specific tasks. The next logical step seemed to be to determine whether or not task-centered methods were an effective means of alleviating *target problems*. It was one thing to show that concentrated practitioner effort might help a client carry out an isolated task; it was quite another to ascertain if such a task-centered effort made a measurable difference in respect to problem change. Moreover, we had tested only certain methods. We were interested in conducting a test of the full range of practitioner activities directed at problem alleviation.

Study Purpose, Design, and Method

This next step was taken in a more ambitious experiment, addressed to several goals. First, as indicated, we were interested in determining the extent to which task-centered methods contributed to change in target problems. Second, we wanted to see if effectiveness varied according to particular characteristics of the client, problem, or practitioner. Third, we wished to obtain a description of how practitioners actually used the model and to find out if the use of particular kinds of activities and techniques were associated with task achievement and problem change. Fourth, we hoped to ascertain the durability of change following treatment and to obtain a picture of the client's assessment of the model.

These purposes called for a study in which treatment could be experimentally manipulated and a high degree of control could be exercised over practitioner behavior. These criteria could be best met through our task-centered program at the School of Social Service Administration (chapter 1). The program would provide students to serve as practitioners at fieldwork agencies receptive and accustomed to our research and development efforts. It would also be possible to provide (as part of our educational program) intensive training and supervision of the student practitioners in use of the methods we wished to test.

An overview of the design will first be presented, followed by a more detailed presentation of key elements of the plan of the study. The study consisted of two similar experiments, each of which took one academic year to complete. Although the second experiment varied from the first in some details (to be discussed subsequently), the two were sufficiently alike to be treated as one undertaking. The design is set forth in schematic form in Table 10.1.

In brief, each student practitioner participating in the project was assigned two cases. In both cases, the practitioner and client formulated target problems (Phase I). Then, through a random procedure, one of the cases was designated experimental (A) and the other control (B). In the experimental case, the practitioner and client immediately began to work on the target problems with the practitioner making intensive use of task-centered methods for a period of three weeks (Phase II). During the same phase, the control cases received three weeks of "supportive attention," a form of placebo treatment in which the practitioner made no active efforts to alleviate the target problems. Measures of the amount of problem change occurring in this phase were used to assess the effectiveness of the task-centered methods tested. The methods tested consisted of the activities and techniques described in chapter 7 (and operationally defined in appendix II). In other

Table 10.1 Schematic Presentation of Design

Group A	Group B
Project Cases *Randomly assigned to*	
Phase I (2 weeks)	
Problem identification and formulation	Problem identification and formulation
Collection of baseline data on problems (first problem review)	Collection of baseline data on problems (first problem review)
Phase II (3 weeks)	
Task-centered methods	Supportive attention
Phase III (3 weeks)	
Reassessment of problems (second problem review)	Reassessment of problems (second problem review)
Continued treatment	Task-centered methods
Case closing	
Phase IV (3 weeks)	
	Reassessment of problems (third problem review)
	Continued treatment
	Case closing
Phase V (12 weeks)	
Two-month (average) post-treatment follow-up	Two-month (average) post-treatment follow-up

words, we tested the interventions that normally occur in the middle stage of the model—between the initial specification of the problem and termination.

So far the design has followed the model of the classic experiment, inasmuch as an experimental treatment has been provided one group of subjects and withheld from another. To gain additional information about the effectiveness of the methods tested, a crossover* feature was added: following three weeks of supportive

---

* We had considered, but eventually rejected, using a complete crossover design, in which the A cases would be given supportive attention while the B cases were receiving the experimental treatment, followed by an additional comparison of problem change between the two cases. Although such a design would have theoretically given us more information about the effectiveness of the experimental treatment, it seemed unworkable for two reasons: one could expect "carry-over" effects from prior treatment in the A cases, a major contraindication for use of the full crossover design; practitioners and their supervisors thought it would be difficult to shut treatment off once momentum had been built up.

attention (Phase II), the control (B) clients received three weeks of the experimental treatment. For these clients, the amount of problem change that occurred during the control phase (Phase II) was compared with the amount of problem change occurring during the period of treatment (Phase III) that followed. If treatment was in fact effective, one would expect a greater amount of problem alleviation to occur in these cases during Phase III than Phase II. In this way, the B cases were used as their own control to provide an additional assessment of the experimental interventions. The A cases, meanwhile, were allowed to "run their course" during Phase III; no further comparisons with the B cases were made. Follow-up interviews were held with accessible clients and collaterals from one to three months following case closing. The major purpose of the follow-up was to obtain an assessment of the *durability* of change achieved during treatment in both A and B cases. All interviews in the research phases of the cases and the follow-up interviews were tape recorded.

Practitioners and Settings

The practitioners ($n = 44$) who conducted the experimental and control treatments were first-year graduate students in the task-centered sequence at the School of Social Service Administration. Their project work was a part of their field training in clinical practice and research. Each practitioner carried an experimental and control case, with the exception of one who carried a control case only.

Although they were just beginning their graduate training in social work, they were by no means inexperienced in helping roles. About three-quarters had prior paid work experience in social work or closely related occupations (usually more than a year), and almost all who did not had similar (though less lengthy) experience as volunteers or student interns. Their experience and training levels presented both disadvantages and advantages for the project. They were more or less novices in social treatment, and most lacked familiarity with the type of client groups and settings used in the project; these were handicaps in their application of the model. On the positive side, the students were receptive and open to the task-centered approach and had not developed strong points of view or habits of work that would interfere with their learning it. Moreover, as a group, the students were not dissimilar from the kind of relatively inexperienced, untrained practitioners that largely make up the staffs of many of our social agencies. How the students fared with the model might be a good indicator of how well it could be taken over by such agency practitioners.

Prior to beginning their project cases, the student practitioners received approximately 11 weeks of combined class and field training in task-centered methods and applied on a pretest the treatment and research procedures they were to use in the project. Project cases were then supervised in group and individual sessions; all supervisors were graduate social workers trained and experienced in use of the model.

Clients were drawn primarily from two types of setting: a public school system and a psychiatric outpatient clinic. As indicated, we chose these sites because our experience with them in previous research and development efforts had been quite positive, and both were receptive to the kind of experimental design we had developed. Moreover, both sites served the kind of low-income clientele of particular concern to social work, and, in combination, the sites offered the variety of client and problem types we wanted to have in order to assess the differential effectiveness of our approach.

Case Assignment and Phase I

Assignment of cases to the project began each year on a predetermined target date (early in January). Cases referred to social-service units in the schools and clinic were assigned to student practitioners without prior screening or selection, to avoid hand picking cases for which the model might seem especially well suited. Our usual approach in the beginning phase was modified somewhat for the sake of the experiment. Practitioners were, in fact, instructed to avoid interventions that might affect the clients' problems during this phase, although at any point help could be given in emergencies.

When the client referred was a child, the usual referral in the school settings, the practitioner initiated contact with the parents, who often became clients themselves. In some cases, the problem for which the referral was made directly involved the parents, as in problems of tardiness or truancy. In others, an attempt was made to engage the parents in work on the client's problem if they could contribute to its solution. For example, parents might play an important role in helping a child who was doing poorly in his studies but might not be able to do much about a problem of disruptive classroom behavior. Sometimes the relationship between the child and a parent or difficulties concerning other children become the basis for target problems. When the person referred was an adult or couple, the usual referral in the psychiatric clinic, the practitioner generally formulated target problems with the individual or family members referred.

Criteria for target problems followed general principles of the model: problems were to be specific, agreed to jointly by client and worker, and capable of being alleviated through their combined efforts. Problem specification followed guidelines presented in chapter 6. Once the problem areas had been generally described and agreed on, the practitioner systematically reviewed each target problem with the client (or clients in cases involving work with more than one family member). In this review (the first problem review), the specific behaviors and circumstances to be changed were spelled out, and variations in the frequency of problem behavior or conditions were specified for a baseline period, usually seven days, preceding the interview. In addition, data on problem characteristics and frequency were elicited from collaterals, usually schoolteachers with direct knowledge of the client's problem. These problem reviews were recorded on special tapes for subsequent analysis (see "Measurement of Change," below). In this way target problems for both cases were formulated. One of each pair of cases was designated as experimental and the other as control through a random assignment procedure. Practitioners were not informed which case was which until problem reviews had been completed on one of the two cases, that is, until one of their cases had completed Phase I. Most pairs of cases finished Phase I at about the same time.*

The majority of the cases (68 percent) initially referred to the project and seen by practitioners completed Phase I and were randomly assigned to experimental and control conditions. Terminations during Phase I occurred mostly in the psychiatric facility for what seemed to be the variety of usual reasons that produce dropouts in outpatient settings after one or two sessions. Some applicants decided their problems were solved, could not be helped, or would be better dealt with by other means. Each dropout was replaced by the next case referred; a process that had to be repeated more than once for a few of the practitioners. In addition, two B cases dropped out during Phase II, too late to be replaced. Consequently their matched A cases were deprived of the controls essential to the research design and hence could not be counted as project cases. Although lost cases inevitably add some measure of uncertainty to the results of an experiment, it is difficult to see how the turnover reported above might have favored either the experimental or control conditions, particularly since most of it occurred before the cases were randomly assigned to these conditions.

Task-Centered Treatment versus Supportive Attention

After target problems had been formulated and reviewed, task-centered treatment was begun if the case was experimental (A), or the client received supportive attention if the case was control (B). This phase of the experiment continued for three weeks.

---

*It would have been desirable to withhold information about assignment until problem reviews had been completed on both cases to avoid possible biasing effects on problem formulation in the remaining case. To have done so, however, would have created difficulties if problem formulation in one case lagged behind the other, or if one case dropped out and had to be replaced. The case completed first would not have been able to move into the next phase. As a result, an unwanted and unstandardized "control" period would have been introduced into cases so delayed.

The experimental treatment was designed to follow the sequence of activities presented in chapter 7. There were approximately two client sessions per week for each case plus related work with collaterals. How the experimental treatment was actually carried out will be taken up in the presentation of study findings. The rationale for the three-week treatment phase merits some comment, however.

Our decision about the span of treatment resulted from the balancing of two considerations: on the one hand, there was need for a period long enough to enable the treatment program to produce measurable change in target problems; on the other hand, we wished to keep the time span sufficiently short so as not to create an excessive delay in providing a possibly effective treatment for clients assigned to the control conditions. Moreover, the longer the control phase was extended, the greater might be the attrition from the control group, particularly in the outpatient clinic. The three-week period seemed to be a reasonable compromise between these factors. The solution had one drawback, however. One could not expect the experimental treatment, even if effective, to show a *great* margin of change over the control condition in a three-week period consisting of, at most, six treatment sessions.

Supportive attention was designed as a placebo treatment that would acomplish three purposes. First, it was to provide some control for the "nonspecific" effects of treatment—benefits that might result from ventilating one's concerns to a sympathetic listener or receiving attention from an understanding person in an authority position. Such benefits might be expected from almost any form of interpersonal treatment or from even a friendly relationship. In order to test the specific contribution of task-centered methods to problem change, we wanted to control for ingredients common to any benign relationship. The second purpose of the control treatment was to minimize problems of bias that may result when clients are asked to report on changes that have occurred during a period of treatment. Clients may exaggerate the amount of change that has occurred in order to satisfy the expectations of the practitioner or to justify their own investment in treatment.

Giving control clients a form of treatment would equalize the effects of this kind of bias in comparisons of problem change between experimental and nonexperimental conditions. Finally, the control treatment was to be used as a means of maintaining the client's interest in treatment and of providing practitioner availability should emergency needs arise.

Practitioners were given various options in conducting supportive attention sessions. They could let the client discuss immediate concerns, explore historical material, obtain further information about the client's problems or social situation, or, with children, engage in play activities. They were not, however, to develop tasks, use any of the task-centered activities, employ such change-oriented techniques as advice giving or providing explanations of the client's behavior, or to take any actions in the client's social system aimed at alleviating his problems.

For use of supportive attention as a means of controlling for nonspecific effects of treatment and client bias in reporting change, it would have been desirable to have as many supportive attention sessions in the control cases as task-centered sessions in the experimental cases. Because of difficulties anticipated by practitioners in refraining from using active treatment interventions in supportive attention sessions and ethical considerations (for example, having clients make repeated visits to the outpatient clinic for placebo treatment), we decided to limit the number of supportive attention sessions to no more than one a week.

Second and Third Problem Reviews

A second, separately taped problem review was conducted by the practitioner, usually within five to seven days following completion of the three weeks of supportive attention or task-centered treatment in Phase II. In the reviews, normally conducted at the beginning of the first interview of Phase III, the practitioner elicited data from clients on the following: (1) the status of the original target problems during the period following the termination of Phase II; (2) the status of additional target problems identified and dealt with since the first review and on other areas of difficulty that had emerged during the second phase; and (3) the client's own assessment of change in the target problems since the first problem review. In addition, the practitioners obtained (on the same tape) the reports of collaterals on problem status and change.

Following the second problem review, the control (B) cases began a three-week course of task-centered treatment, which was to be a replication of the treatment given during the experimental phase of the A cases. At the conclusion of this phase a third problem review (identical in form to the second) was conducted by the practitioners.

Practitioners, rather than research interviewers, were given responsibility for collecting change data for two reasons: first, it was assumed that clients (many of whom were not highly verbal) would give more complete and accurate data to practitioners with whom they were accustomed to sharing information about their problems; second, in the B cases, it would have been logistically difficult, and somewhat burdensome for the client, to sandwich a research interview between termination of the control phase and beginning of the treatment phase. Possible effects of practitioner bias in conducting the problem review were, of course, a source of concern, since the practitioner naturally hoped his experimental case would do better. As a counterblancing factor, practitioners had to (and did) follow a standard format in conducting the reviews, which in the second year was supplemented by lists of specific questions about the problem status of their clients. The lists were prepared by researchers who analyzed the first problem reviews without knowing which case was experimental and which, control. Moreover, students knew that not only tapes of their problem reviews but their entire cases would be subjected to intensive analysis. These factors, we assume, kept an effective check on the influence of the practitioners' bias.

Measurement of Problem Change

Measures of outcome were centered on assessing change in the client's specific problems and his overall problem situation during the treatment and control phases of the experiment. Measures were obtained by having two judges listen to tapes of problem reviews obtained by the practitioners and rating the extent of problem change. First, the initial and second problem reviews were compared for each case to determine change in the experimental phase of the A cases and the control phase of the B cases. Then the judges compared second and third problem reviews of the B cases to determine change during the treatment phases of those cases. The problem reviews, recorded on special tapes, contained no references to treatment. Judges did not know which cases had received treatment and, in addition, were given erroneous information about the design of the study.

Change in specific target problems was rated on five- and ten-point scales devised to fit data of different quality.* When a target problem was specified in terms of counts of behavior, change was assessed using a scale anchored to percentages of decrease or increase in the behavior. Suppose a client's problem was failure to complete and hand in homework assignments and that the initial problem review had recorded such failure to do so each of six baseline days. If after the second problem review it was reported that the client had failed to hand in completed assignments on only two of the previous six school days, a 67 percent alleviation of the problem would be recorded by the judge. A percentage of alleviation within this range (61–80 percent) was considered to represent "considerable alleviation," or an eight on a ten-point scale. Over a third of the ratings were made on scales based on such frequency counts. Less precise data were fitted to scales in which the judge was given more discretion. In some instances, frequencies of problem occurrence were approximate and qualified in various ways (40 percent of the ratings). In other instances (24 percent of the ratings), frequencies were inapplicable (for example, when the problem was defined as a lack of a resource) or not obtained. The first judge rating a case would select the scale to be used. If the

* On a ten-point scale, 10 represented maximum positive change in the problem (problem no longer present; 5, no change; 1, considerable worsening. Corresponding values for five-point scales were 5, 3, and 1. The scales and related instruments are presented in full in Reid 1977c.

second judge disagreed with the selection (an infrequent occurrence) differences were resolved through a conference. The scales were applied to data elicited from clients and collaterals. This variable scaling approach, we hoped, provided a set of measurements that would best "mine" a given set of data to its limits. To these scales, based on objective data obtained from clients (client objective rating), were added (during the second year of the project) a rating of the client's own opinion of change (client subjective rating).

A second focus of assessment was change in the client's overall problem situation. In making the overall ratings, judges took into account both changes in specific target problems and in other problematic aspects of the client's situation that had been identified but not dealt with. During the first year of the project, data obtained from collaterals and the client's subjective assessment of change were included as part of the base the judges used in their ratings. These aspects were rated separately during the second year. Also during the second year separate overall problem-change ratings were made for each client in multiple-client cases.

The additional ratings of change in specific problems and the overall problem situation during the second year were in the interest of securing more discriminating measurements. Since the same rating procedures in each year were applied to experimental and control conditions, it was assumed that the additions would not affect comparisons between experimental and control outcomes.

Interjudge reliabilities of problem-change ratings were computed by type of scale, type of data used by the judges, the phases judged, and project year; 23 correlations (Pearson r's) were computed. For the first year of the project, the median correlation was .62; for the second year, .80. The increase was probably the result of improvements in instruments and training. During both years, correlations were highest for scales based on frequency counts (median $r = .96$), and for assessments of change during Phase II (median $r = .76$). All but two of the seven low coefficients (below .50) involved judging of change during Phase III (experimental treatment of the B cases). In sum, while interjudge reliability was generally satisfactory, we can place more confidence in ratings involving second-year cases, scales based on frequency counts and Phase II changes. Each pair of judge ratings was averaged to create mean judge ratings for each measure in each case. To facilitate analysis ratings on five-point scales were converted to ten point equivalents.

Two measures of problem change were then computed: changes in the main target problem and changes in the client's overall problem situation. It was assumed that most significant aspects of problem change could be captured by these measures. In recording problems, the practitioners were instructed to record the problem of greatest importance to the client first. This problem was used as "the main problem." (In the majority of cases this was the only problem formulated.) Changes in remaining target problems were taken into account in the measure of overall problem change. Mean judge ratings were averaged across different measures of change to create composite change scores for both the main problem and the overall problem situation. The composite scores were made up of ratings of change based on both the client's and collateral's accounts.*

* The intercorrelations of sets of mean judge ratings provide justification for creating the composite scores.

Correlations
(Pearson's r)
Mean Ratings of Problem Change for A and B Cases, Phase II

	Main Problem	Overall
Client objective-client subjective	.30 [a]	.79 [a]
Client objective-collateral	.44	.88 [a]
Client subjective-collateral	.41 [a]	.62 [a]

Mean Ratings of Problem Change, B Cases, Phase III

	Main Problem	Overall
Client objective-client subjective	.37 [a]	.67 [a]
Client objective-collateral	.36	.74 [a]
Client subjective-collateral	−.08a [a]	.48 [a]

[a] Second year cases only

All the intercorrelations were statistically significant (p < .05) with the exception of the client subjective-collateral pairing for the main problem, Phase III. This correlation is based on only nine pairs of ratings, in five of which there was perfect agreement between the client and collateral ratings. The negative correlation results from a major discrepancy in

Case Characteristics

The project sample consisted of 87 cases: 47 from the public school system; 38 from the psychiatric clinic; and 2 from a youth service facility, where one of the student practitioners was placed. Since the experimental and control groups were quite similar in respect to all measured characteristics, data will be reported for the group as a whole.

The project families were predominantly black (92 percent); the great majority could be defined as low-income. The median gross annual income of the families was $6,400, well below the (1973) Chicago city worker's "low standard" family budget of $8,635, which defined a minimum income needed for the basic consumption needs of a family of four. Twenty-four percent were receiving public assistance. The great bulk of employed adult wage earners in the sample held unskilled or semiskilled jobs and had no more than a high school education.

In addition to the pervasive problems of low income, the families as a group were disadvantaged in other respects. Most lived in inner-city areas plagued by high crime rates. More than a quarter lived in deteriorated housing. Forty percent reported significant physical or mental health problems in at least one family member; about the same percentage of families was headed by a single person, usually a mother with children at home.

A total of 156 target problems was formulated for the sample as a whole; or somewhat fewer than two per case on the average. While these problems were distributed across all categories of our problem typology (chapter 3), certain categories accounted for most: about a third were classified as problems of role performance, most of which were further specified as problems in the

---

one case. As can be seen, correlations are uniformly higher for the overall problem situation than the main problem, for reasons that are not completely clear. The overall level of association was thought to be high enough to warrant averaging of client-objective, client-subjective, and collateral-change ratings for the main problem and overall problem situation, a procedure that not only reduced the data to single measures for each case but also produced uniform measures across both years of the project.

role of student, usually in some aspect of classroom behavior or academic performance. Another third of the problems were interpersonal (interpersonal conflict or dissatisfaction in social relations) involving largely family members, teachers, or peers.

In a third of the cases, work on target problems involved in-person interviews with one or more family members in addition to the client seen most (the primary client). Of the primary clients, 57 percent were children (13 or under); 3 percent adolescents (14–17); and 40 percent adults (18 and over). A little over half (52 percent) were female. The client group assumes a more adult cast when other family members who could be considered clients are involved; these were mainly parents or spouses of the primary clients.

Problem Change

Problem Change: A versus B Cases, Phase II

Given the design of the experiment, the best test of the effectiveness of the task-centered methods can be made by comparing problem change in the A and B cases, following the experimental or control treatments during Phase II of the study. As table 10.2 shows, the A cases surpassed their B counterparts on both measures at acceptable levels of significance. The results suggest that the experimental treatment did, in fact, make a contribution to change in respect to both the specific problem of greatest concern to the client and to the client's general problem situation. As might be expected, a greater amount of change was achieved in the more limited specific problem than in the client's general problem state, which included difficulties not dealt with in treatment.

Table 10.3 presents the data of table 10.2 in terms of the distribution of cases across different categories of problem change. The last change category needs some explanation, since it groups together different types of change. Actually, most cases in this bracket showed minimal positive change (5 to 5.9) in both main

Table 10.2 Mean Change, Main Problem and Overall, A and B Cases, Phase II

	Mean Change by Type of Case		
	A (Task-Centered Methods)	B (Supportive Attention)	Significance (t-test, paired means) p <
Main problem	7.7	6.8	.02
Overall problem situation	7.2	6.5	.03

problem and overall problem situation. Four cases showed some worsening on the main problem, and an equal number (though not necessarily the same cases) were judged to be worse in respect to the overall problem. All but one of these cases fell in the control (B) group.

When the two categories of alleviation (considerable and moderate) are examined, we see that the spread between A and B cases is greater in the former. Thus, if considerable alleviation is

Table 10.3 Change in Main Problem and Overall Problem Situation, A and B Cases, Phase II, by Change Categories

Categories of Change		A Cases		B Cases	
		N	%	N	%
Main problem					
Considerable alleviation	(8–10)	18	(42)	11	(26)
Moderate alleviation	(6–7.9)	21	(49)	20	(46)
Minimal or no change; worse	(less than 6)	4	(9)	12	(28)
		43	100	43	100
Overall problem situation					
Considerable alleviation	(8–10)	18	(42)	8	(19)
Moderate alleviation	(6–7.9)	17	(40)	22	(51)
Minimal or no change; worse	(less than 6)	8	(19)	13	(30)
		43	100	43	100

used as the criterion to define successful resolution of the problem, we find that more than 40 percent of the A cases meet it on both measures, while it is met by only a quarter or a fifth of the B cases, depending on the measure.

Table 10.3 also provides some clues as to the nature of the experimental effect. If we first consider the spread of the B cases across categories of change in the main problem, we find a symmetrical distribution: about half the cases scored moderate gains, with a little over a quarter falling on either side of this range. This distribution might be taken as an estimate of problem change without systematic intervention for the type of case studied. The distribution for the A cases (main problem) is quite different: while about half the cases also fall in the middle category, almost as many are found in the "considerably alleviated" classification, with relatively few showing only minimal gain or less. Quite possibly the task-centered interventions, by accentuating to some degree factors promoting positive change, served to pull some cases that otherwise would have fallen into the last category into the middle one; and, in turn, some cases that otherwise would have showed only moderate problem alleviation came into the "considerably alleviated" category. Consequently, the distribution of the A and B cases would show no differences in the middle category but would differ at the top and bottom. This explanation seems more plausible than the alternative: that the experimental treatment had a positive strong effect on cases that normally would show little change (jumping them from the last to the first category), and had no effect on cases that would achieve moderate alleviation without treatment. A similar pattern can be discerned for changes in the overall problem situation; perhaps for similar reasons. There is a higher proportion of B than A cases in the moderately alleviated category, but again the B group does less well than the A group at the extremes.

As might be expected, the two measures of problem change (main problem and overall) were positively correlated ($r = .59$). Although changes in the main problem seem quite influential in ratings of change in the overall problem situation, this influence was less strong if the main problem was highly delimited (e.g., difficulties in completing classroom work in a particular subject), if other problems were worked on, or if major changes occurred in problem areas not directly dealt with in treatment.

Supportive Attention versus Task-Centered Phases, B Cases Only

It will be recalled that following a three-week supportive attention phase, the B cases received a three-week period of task-centered intervention. Ratings of problem change during the treatment phase were compared with similar ratings of change during the supportive attention phase. If the experimental interventions were effective, one would expect a greater degree of change occurring during the treatment phase. In the top half of table 10.4, we see that for the experiment as a whole this hypothesis was supported, to a statistically significant degree, for measures of overall problem change; for main problems the differences between the task-centered and supportive attention phases of the B cases were in the expected direction but did not reach statistical significance.

Table 10.4 Mean Change, Main Problem and Overall, B Cases, Control and Experimental Phases

	Mean Changes by Phase All Cases (N =35)		
	Supportive Attention (Phase II)	Task-Centered Methods (Phase III)	Significance (t-test, paired means) $p<$
Main problem	6.7	7.2	N.S.
Overall problem situation	6.4	7.3	.01
	Second-year Cases (N =19)		
Main problem	6.3	7.2	.05
Overall problem situation	6.5	7.2	.05

The findings must be interpreted with a great deal of caution, since a significant number of the B cases (nine) terminated before they received the experimental treatment. In some of these cases, clients had done well during the supportive attention phase and appeared to want no further help; in others the clients had done poorly and perhaps had terminated for that reason. On overall problem change during Phase II, the dropouts had achieved a mean rating slightly higher than those remaining. It is difficult to say how the findings might have been altered had the dropouts completed the experiment.

All but two of the dropouts occurred during the first year, however. In the second year, workers were instructed to make special efforts to hold on to B cases until the end of the experimental phase; perhaps as a result, fewer cases terminated prematurely. One of the two cases that dropped out during the second year achieved above-average change ratings during the supportive attention phase; the ratings for the other were below average. Since the second-year cases were relatively free of selection bias resulting from dropouts, they perhaps provided a better test of the hypothesis. Data on these cases alone, which are given in the bottom half of table 10.4, support the hypothesis across both measures of problem change.

In table 10.5, we see the pattern of change in the overall problem situation that resulted when cases crossed over from the control to the treatment phase. If the diagonal of the table is exam-

Table 10.5 Pattern of Change in Overall Problem Situation during Supportive Attention and Task-Centered Treatment: 35 B Cases

Problem Alleviation during Supportive Attention		Problem Alleviation during Task-Centered Treatment			
		cons.	mod.	min.	total
Considerable	(8–10)	4	1		5
Moderate	(6–7.9)	5	12	2	19
Minimal	(below 6)	4	4	3	11
		13	17	5	35

ined, we see that the majority of cases (19) continued to progress at generally the same rate after treatment was begun, a finding that reminds us of the potency of nontreatment factors in change. We can also see, however, that in thirteen cases (below the diagonal) the rate of improvement was accelerated after the crossover, while it declined in only three cases (above the diagonal). Thus, following the crossover from the control to the treatment conditions, the B cases tended either to maintain or increase their rate of improvement. The acceleration of improvement during the treatment phase seemed consistent with the pattern of change that was suggested for the A cases. Of the 13 cases showing improvement following the crossover, 9 showed a modest degree of acceleration (one category) and only 4 a marked degree (two categories). Again, it seems as if treatment served to accentuate existing trends toward positive change. The pattern for the main problem was similar although less marked.

The data presented thus far are based on means of the several judge ratings. Additional analyses were carried out to determine if similar differences between experimental and control conditions would obtain if ratings were not averaged or if different combinations of ratings were used (see p. 237). With one exception, differences reported as significant in tables 10.2 and 10.4 were also found to be significant ($p < .05$) when analyses were limited to the ratings based on objective data obtained from clients or when these ratings were averaged with available collateral ratings. The one exception was the significant change reported (table 10.4) in the main problem for the second-year B (control) cases during the experimental phase. When the client subjective ratings of change were extracted, this change, while favoring the experimental condition by over a half a point, was no longer significant. The client's subjective ratings alone, available on the second-year cases only, showed significant ($p < .05$) differences in favor of the experimental conditions for the main problem but not for the overall problem situation ($p < .10$).

As noted, collateral data, when available, were averaged with other ratings since these data were not obtained on all cases. A separate analysis of collateral ratings alone was carried out for the A–B case comparison in respect to the main problem—the only data set in which there were sufficient number of paired collateral ratings to warrant analysis. Although data from collaterals were obtained on 38 cases, ratings were not always obtained for A and B pairs. In a given pair of cases, a collateral rating might be germane or available for one case but not the other. Paired ratings were secured for 24 cases, or 12 pairs. Mean change for the main problem, based on collateral data only for these pairs, was 7.8 for A cases and 7.0 for B cases. This difference is approximately the same as the one reported in table 10.2, yet given the small number of cases, it was not statistically significant.

On the whole, the findings suggest that the task-centered methods tested in the project contributed to the alleviation of the client's target problems above and beyond what clients achieved on their own or in response to a placebo treatment. This conclusion receives its strongest support from the comparison between the experimental cases and their matched controls. In that comparison the effects of spontaneous remission and other extraneous factors appear to be reasonably well controlled. While such factors were not controlled when the B cases were compared with themselves, the changes observed in these cases following the crossover do provide further evidence that the experimental treatment was effective.

Initial Characteristics and Problem Change

The findings presented thus far suggest that the experimental intervention had an overall positive effect on problem change. Additional analyses were carried out to determine if particular characteristics of the client, problem, or practitioner had any apparent influence on the effectiveness of the model. In other words, was there evidence that the model worked better with certain types of clients, problems, or practitioners than others? In answering this question, we must distinguish between a simple association with outcome and the influence of a characteristic on the effectiveness of treatment. Thus, highly motivated clients might have better outcomes than poorly motivated ones simply as a function of their better motivation; that is, the association would obtain even if the treatment was totally ineffective. Motivation would be said to have an influence on treatment if treatment effects systematically varied between different levels of motivation; for example, if treatment was found to work better with highly, than poorly, motivated clients. To make such a determination, one needs to control for change due to factors other than the treatment being tested. In the present analysis, we attempted to achieve partial control through use of change ratings obtained during the supportive attention phase of each case, making use of the matched pairs and own control features of the design to the extent possible.

This analysis failed to produce strong evidence that characteristics of client, problem, or practitioner influenced the effectiveness of treatment. Two findings are worthy of note, however. Adults (18 or older) seemed to do somewhat better under treatment conditions than children (13 and under); that is, the spread in change ratings between adults in experimental and control phases was greater than the comparable spread in ratings for children. The differences were the greatest in respect to the main problem and approached significance ($p < .10$, two-tailed test) when client change in the main problem during the experimental phase of the B cases was measured against change in the control phase of these cases. In these own control cases, about two-thirds of the adults did better under treatment than control conditions as compared to only half the children.

While the adult-child differences may be the result of chance, they were of some interest to us because their direction was opposite from what we had expected. We had thought that the model would have been more effective with the more circumscribed problems of children than the more complex problems of adults, particularly adults drawn from a population of psychiatric outpatients. With hindsight, it seemed likely that whatever advantage the children might have had in respect to problem complexity was outweighed by motivational factors: almost all the adults entered the treatment program as applicants seeking help; for almost all the children treatment was initiated by others.

The second interesting difference emerged when results from the first year of the project were compared with those of the second. We had expected the second-year cases to do better, since the model and training procedures during the second year had presumably profited from our first year's experience. While the "years" comparison involves various factors, it can be considered to be a practitioner variable since improvements in our operations would matter only if they affected practitioner performance. Differences were consistently in the expected direction, reaching statistical significance ($p < .05$ one-tailed) in respect to changes in the main problem during Phase II of the experiment. In the second year, the margin of difference in change ratings between experimentals and controls for the main problem was noticeably greater than in the first year. In 40 percent of the second-year cases, the mean change ratings for the experimental cases exceeded their matched controls by more than 2.5 points; in only one pair of first-year cases did we find this great a margin of superiority for the experimental condition. That differences between the two years occurred largely in the main problem might well have been the result of our stressing work on that problem much more during our second-year training program than the first.

Task Characteristics and Progress

A task is a source of both service and outcome variables. The characteristics of tasks describe a central component of the service structure. Task achievement provides an intermediate measure of outcome that should logically be linked to problem change. The data to be presented will concern the service and outcome aspects of *operational* tasks. While general tasks were frequently used to organize treatment, they were not subjected to systematic analysis.

Practitioners recorded a total of 440 operational tasks, or about five per case on the average. The great bulk of the tasks called for specific actions the client was to work on between sessions. There were relatively few recorded practitioner tasks, since the conceptualization of worker activity as tasks had not been developed when the project was begun. However, a good deal of worker activity that would have been so labeled took place, as will be subsequently shown. The majority of the tasks (60 percent) involved recurring actions (for example, doing one hour of homework each evening); the remainder specified unique actions (e.g., keeping an appointment at a clinic). Most of the tasks (75 percent) could be carried out by the client alone (as in the examples above); the remaining quarter required the cooperation of another person (e.g., having a friendly conversation with a coworker). Somewhat more than a third of the tasks were repeated, some as many as six times. Ideas for tasks were more likely to come from the worker (75 percent) than the client (20 percent). Collaterals were the source of the remainder. These data do not give us a picture, however, of the role of practitioner-client collaboration in task formulation.

Practitioners completed task-achievement ratings on 370 (84 percent) of the recorded tasks. The major reason for not securing progress ratings was the lack of opportunity for the client to carry out the task, though in some cases practitioners failed to conduct task reviews or record ratings. Although a good level of agreement was obtained between practitioner task-progress ratings and those recorded by independent judges who listened to tape recordings of task reviews (see chapter 11), it is possible that outcomes of less successful tasks were underreported. Also, the results reported below include only the ratings of the last trial of repeated tasks, which were often (though not always) more successful than earlier trials.

The majority of tasks (55 percent) were reported as having been completely achieved; an additional 16 percent were substantially achieved. About a fifth (22 percent) showed no progress, and 7 percent showed partial achievement. Several factors were found to be associated with task progress.* Consistent with earlier find-

* Because there were usually several tasks per case, one could not assume that task progress ratings were independent events. Therefore tests of statistical significance were not applied to these relations.

ings on problem change, tasks in the second year of the project had more successful outcomes than during the first year. Differences in task achievement between the two years were more marked, however, than differences in problem change. In the first year, 65 percent of the tasks were achieved (completely or substantially) in contrast to an achievement rate of 84 percent in the second year—another reflection, perhaps, of improvements in both training and treatment procedures following the first year.

As expected (see chapter 7), the degree of the client's apparent commitment or expressed willingness to work on the task was positively related to task progress. The practitioners were asked to rate commitment on a five-point scale immediately after the session in which the task was planned. The possible effects of commitment are most clearly revealed in respect to tasks rated as completely achieved. When commitment was rated as low or neutral (points 1 through 3 on a five-point scale), we find that about 30 percent of the tasks were rated as fully carried out, as opposed to 63 percent when commitment was judged to be moderately high (4) and 76 percent when commitment was rated as high (5). Low or neutral ratings of client commitment did not necessarily foreshadow failure to accomplish the task: about half the tasks given such ratings were carried out at least substantially. These findings must be interpreted cautiously, however, since we did not exercise tight control on when practitioner ratings of commitment were made. Some practitioners may have rated client commitment following task review; it was thus possible that information from the review could have influenced some of the ratings.

The success of repeated tasks bore an interesting relation to the number of times the task was repeated. When the final achievement ratings of repeated tasks were examined, it was found that tasks repeated twice (after the first try) had the best outcomes: 93 percent substantially or completely achieved. For tasks repeated only once or tasks repeated more than twice, outcomes were less favorable—64 percent and 71 percent respectively. Thus, while persistence seemed to pay off, the rate of payoff seemed to decline after the second repetition.

Finally, the lack of strong association in one instance merits comment because of the theoretical importance of the variable tested: tasks initially suggested by clients had outcomes only slightly more favorable (78 percent achieved) than tasks initially proposed by workers (69 percent). Most of this difference, however, occurred in relation to complete achievement—62 percent for client-suggested tasks and 53 percent for worker-suggested tasks.

Given the structure of the model, there should be a positive relation between task progress and problem change. This relation was investigated through correlating mean task-progress ratings with mean ratings of overall problem change during the experimental phase of each case. The resulting coefficient for all cases was .39 (p<.01); for first-year cases, .27 (p<.05); second-year cases, .50 (p < .05). Although a somewhat higher overall correlations had been hoped for, one would not expect the relation between task progress and problem change to be perfect, even if work on tasks was entirely responsible for problem alleviation. A problem may be alleviated through a single successful task following several unsuccessful efforts or through a series of partially accomplished tasks. The increase in the level of correlation during the last year of the project provides additional evidence that the model operated "truer to form" on the second try..

Interview Characteristics

In order to make use of the results of an experiment, one needs to be able to describe the characteristics of the experimental treatments. It does little good to demonstrate that a particular method is effective if we are not clear about what is actually tested. One aspect of project services—use of tasks—has already been considered in relation to project outcomes. We shall now turn to a more detailed analysis of service patterns, beginning with the interviews between practitioners and clients.

In respect to numbers and distribution of client interviews, both the experimental and control treatments were carried out in

reasonably close approximation to the original plan. Problem specification (Phase I) consumed a mean of three interviews in both A
and B cases. The experimental phases contained a mean of 6.0 interviews in the A cases and 5.8 interviews in the B cases. Three
interviews on the average were devoted to the supportive attention
phase in the B cases. Both experimental and control cases received
about the same number of interviews (a mean of 11) when interviews following the experimental phases in each case are included.
The overwhelming majority of interviews (92 percent) were with
single clients. Of the remainder, most were with single parents and
children or with husbands and wives.

Content Analysis of Service Interviews

The major focus of our study of interview characteristics was a
content analysis of communication between practitioners and
clients. We selected for analysis all audible tape recordings of
task-centered treatment sessions conducted during the experimental
phase of the A cases. Given limited resources, we decided to concentrate on this phase because it represented the more decisive of
the two tests of the model and because we thought we could obtain
a better picture of the working of the model and its relation to outcome by a thorough analysis of this set of cases than by sampling
cases, interviews, or interview segments from both experimental
phases. In making this decision, we assumed that the task-centered
interventions studied would not differ greatly from those in the experimental phase of the B cases.

Of 43 possible A cases, 5 could not be coded because of the
poor sound quality of the tape recordings. The 38 remaining cases
yielded a total of 209 codable interviews in the experimental
phase. Using tape recordings of these interviews, judges coded
both the *activities* engaged in by practitioner and client and the
techniques used by the practitioners. The instrument (appendix II)
followed closely the system of activities and techniques described
in chapter 7.

An activity was interpreted as an event that started with relevant statements on the part of either practitioner or client and continued until a new activity was begun. The example below, in which the client's task was to tell his mother he planned to get his own apartment, will illustrate the coding procedure.

Task Review   1. C: I started to tell her, but I couldn't follow through.

                2. P: What did you say?

                3. C: Well, I said how crowded things were, but we got

Analysis of   off on another subject and I let it drop. I've been

Obstacles   trying to figure out why I did, I mean, let it drop. I

                    suppose I just didn't want her to start in about how

                    lonely she would be.

                4. P: That would have made you feel guilty?

                5. C: Yes.

As the example shows, judges made no distinction between practitioner and client inputs in coding activities. The total amount of time spent in each activity was calculated from a recording device on the playback machine.

Judges assigned each coded activity to the problem and task to which it pertained, when possible to do so. For this purpose judges were given lists of problems and tasks taken from the practitioners' written recordings. As might be expected, the tape recordings revealed some problems and tasks that the practitioners had not recorded—usually problems and tasks that were considered but not worked on. Judges added these unrecorded problems and tasks to the list and assigned activities to them as well.

The coding scheme for techniques was applied simultaneously but only, of course, to the practitioner's contribution. The basic coding unit was the practitioner's response. In the example above, practitioner responses 3 and 4 were coded as "exploration." This unit was modified to permit coding of more than one technique in complex responses (see appendix II). The amount of time practitioners devoted to each technique was then computed.

The reliability of coding of both activities and techniques was assessed by having a sample of interviews independently coded by a second judge: one interview was selected at random from each case. The median percentage of agreement between judges was 78 for activities and 76 for techniques. While not inordinately high, these levels of reliability are usually considered quite satisfactory for content-analysis instruments of the type used.*

Activities

Our first interest in the analysis of the process data was to construct a picture of what the experimental treatment looked like. In this way we could learn what interventions were actually tested in the experiment and get a sense of how the model worked in practice. Emphasis was given to activities because of their greater importance in defining the processes of the model (chapter 7). Various ways of describing practitioner and client activities in the experimental phases of the A cases are presented in table 10.6. The overall percentage distribution (column 1) suggests that all activities outlined in the model were used but with a different order of emphasis than we had anticipated. The biggest surprise was that problem specification emerged as the single most heavily used activity in a sequence of interviews taking place after the target problems had been presumably specified. We had expected it to be used throughout the treatment phase as a means of refining understanding of the problem, incorporating new information about it, and of monitoring problem change but had not expected it to overshadow all other activities. Listening to samples of tapes suggested that the bulk of problem specification in the treatment phase was devoted to exploration of ongoing or new manifestations of the problem. For example, in one case a wife was trying to cope with an alcoholic, abusive husband. In each session his current behavior and their interactions were explored in considerable detail as a basis for devising tasks. In reviewing such examples, we con-

---

* In determining percent of agreement for activities, variations of less than three seconds between judges in respect to when each thought a particular activity began or ended were discounted. Thus one judge might record that a given activity began a second or so after the other judge. Such discrepancies seemed to be more the result of the mechanics of recording and playback than substantive disagreement.

Table 10.6 Profile of In-session Activities, A Cases, Experimental Phase

Activity [a]	Percent Time, All Interviews	Mean Time per Interview (minutes)	Percent Cases in Which Used	Percent Tasks in Which Used
Problem specification	38.1	9.68	100.0	30.3 [b]
Task planning (total)	(29.1)	(7.39)	(100.0)	(91.9)
Generating alternatives	(9.5)	2.41	92.1	71.1
Task agreement	0.8	0.21	97.6	54.2
Planning details of implementation	15.9	4.03	100.0	76.9
Summarization	2.9	0.74	100.0	48.0
Establishing incentives and rationale	5.4	1.38	100.0	48.0
Analyzing obstacles	5.8	1.46	84.2	32.3
Simulation	1.9	0.48	57.9	11.1
Guided practice	5.9	1.48	21.0	3.8
Client task review	11.8	3.00	100.0	66.1
Practitioner task	1.2	0.31	4.8	6.1
Total	100.0	25.36		

[a] For definitions see chapter 7 and appendix II. Excludes time spent on certain structuring activities (e.g. arranging for appointments) and on non-treatment matters
[b] Allocated to task to which most closely related when possible to do so

cluded that we had probably underestimated a valid need for ongoing problem specification. On the other hand, it still seemed to be used excessively in many instances: sometimes to the point that insufficient time remained for adequate task planning.

Of all activities directly concerned with work on tasks, task planning was clearly dominant, with most of the time spent, as would be expected, in generating alternatives and planning details of implementation. Remaining activities concerned with helping the client prepare for task performance (establishing incentives, analysis of obstacles, simulation, and guided practice) were given less emphasis than we expected or than is suggested by the model. When we add to the foregoing the observation that a relatively large amount of time was given to task review, we can conclude that the bulk of practitioner and client time in the treatment phase of the experiment was devoted to continuing problem specification, task planning, and task review.

The remaining columns of the table provide additional perspectives on use of activities. In the second column, the average amount of time per case devoted to various activities is shown. As can be seen, the average amount of time was less than one-half hour per interview. The interviews themselves were somewhat longer, since small talk, setting appointments, and so on, were not counted. (It should also be noted that interviews with adults tended to be lengthier than those with children.)

Percentages and average amounts of time spent in different activities do not tell the whole story, however. Certain activities, such as task agreement and summarization, may not consume much time, yet can be extremely important. The last two columns of table 10.6 show percentages of cases and tasks for which each activity was used, regardless of the time spent on it. As can be seen, most of the activities of the model were used in most cases, and some in all of them. There was considerably less breadth of application at the task level, however. This was expected, since it was never intended that all activities be used for each task. For example, many tasks are variants of earlier tasks and may require little in the way of additional task planning or establishing incentives. For some tasks, there would be no obstacles to analyze, and so forth. Still, we had expected higher percentages of use per task for certain activities—in particular, task agreement and task review. Although evidences of task agreement were found on half the tasks, this activity, theoretically at least, should have been uniformly present. In some instances, nonverbal agreements (head nods) were obtained but not revealed on the tape. In others, practitioners seemed to assume the client was in agreement with the task plan unless he raised questions about it.

By the same logic, reviews of task progress should have occurred more frequently. As with task agreement, limitations of the coding process may have led to an underestimation of use: data on task progress were frequently picked up in discussions of developments in the client's problem. Three activities—guided practice, simulation, and communication relating to practitioner tasks— were particularly infrequent (less than 12 percent of the tasks).

Guided practice, used largely for academic learning problems, was given a considerable amount of time (20 minutes per task on the average) for those tasks in which it was used; its potential range of possible application appeared to be quite limited in the project cases, though it could have been used more in communication problems. Simulation, which has a much broader range of application, seemed underused, particularly with adult clients. Communication relating to practitioner tasks, which also might have been greater, reflects, of course, only the in-session portion of this type of activity, which, as noted, was not well defined when the study was undertaken and hence was probably under-coded.

Additional analyses were carried out to determine if proportional use of activities varied according to case characteristics. The only significant source of variation was found in comparison between adults and children. Significantly greater use was made of problem specification with adults (a mean of 46 percent of time per case) than with children (29 percent per case).* Various activities, however, were used to a significantly greater extent with children than adults: summarization, 4.6 percent versus 2.2 percent; simulation, 3.9 versus .8 percent; guided practice, 12.2 percent versus .4 percent. The differences are understandable: the problem situations presented by the adult clients were probably more complex and required more ongoing analysis. Summarization (going over the task plan) would be more likely to be emphasized with children; children were also more likely to have tasks requiring guided practice (e.g., tasks to develop study skills) than adults in the project. As noted, it may be more difficult to involve adults in simulation. It is of interest, however, that for most activities there were no significant differences between children and adults.†

Extensive analyses were carried out to determine what rela-

* Mean percentages of time per case for each activity were compared, treating the percentages as scores. Only differences significant at $p < .05$ (t-test) are reported.

† It should be kept in mind that these findings are based on differences in *percentage distributions*. Since interviews with adults tended to be longer, a somewhat different picture is obtained when *time spent* on activities is used as the dependent variable. (See Fortune 1977.)

tion might exist between use of particular activities and outcomes measured both in terms of task progress and problem change.* None was found. Although it would have been gratifying to find an association between activities and outcomes, that we failed to do so is perhaps not surprising. Activities were measured in terms of their presence or absence and the amount of time devoted to each. Qualitative aspects, such as the skill with which they were applied, were not assessed. To relate our measures to outcome would be somewhat analogous to predicting the success of surgery from amounts of time surgeons spent in making incisions, suturing, and so forth. Moreover, these measures did not take into account work within the social system, which, as will be shown, was considerable. Finally, we lack the theory, knowledge, and data to enable us to develop and test the complex equations that would be needed to predict outcomes from amount and type of intervention. Thus, an activity might be generally quite effective, but this effectiveness would be difficult to detect if it were used heavily in less responsive cases that might have poor outcomes in any event. At present, we can say only that the "package" of interventions used apparently contained effective ingredients. We cannot specify which ingredients within the package were particularly effective.

Techniques

Within the framework of the activities of the model, the practitioners made use of various techniques (chapter 7; appendix II). Although, for reasons already explained, techniques were given secondary emphasis, they do provide an important dimension of the service input. The bulk of the practitioners' in-session communication with clients could be accounted for by the four categories of techniques presented in table 10.7. The only other technique that merits comment was encouragement, used primarily to

---

*In these analyses both percentage distribution of activities and time spent on activities were used as independent variables. Both univariate and multivariate analyses (step-wise multiple regression) were conducted. Changes in main problem, the overall problem situation, and task-achievement ratings were used as the dependent variables.

Table 10.7 Most Common Techniques:
Frequency and Characteristics of Use

Technique	Percent of Time Used	How Primarily Used
Exploration	26	To elicit data from client on problems and task progress
Structuring of communication in the interview	20	To focus client communication on problems and tasks
Direction (or advice giving)	14	To suggest possible tasks or means of implementation
Explanations of client's actions, actions of others, or his social situation	28	To clarify problems; to help client plan tasks and analyze obstacles
Total, major techniques	88	

express confidence or approval in relation to the client's task performance. Since it often appeared in the form of short phrases ("Good, I'm proud of you"), its frequency of use was greater than its share of time (4 percent) would suggest. As was the case with activities, and probably for the same reasons, no relation was found between time devoted to different techniques and outcome. A more elaborate analysis of the relation between the experimental interventions and outcomes (Fortune 1977) is in progress and, it is hoped, may reveal some connections between these variables.

As has been indicated, techniques were applied in special ways within the task-centered framework. It also seems that the proportional use of techniques differed from more usual (psychosocial) practice. These differences become apparent when one compares the data presented above with results of analysis of practitioner interventions in various studies of psychosocial casework. In some of these studies (Reid and Shyne 1969; Pinkus 1968; Lish 1973), techniques were classified with an earlier version of the scheme used in the present project. In others (Hollis 1972; Mullen 1968), the coding scheme used was similar enough to the present one to permit comparisons in certain categories.

The most striking quantitative differences occur in respect to three categories: exploration, structuring, and direction. In general there was much less use of exploration but greater use of structur-

260 A Study of Effectiveness

ing and direction in the present experiment than in the various studies of psychosocial practice. First, restricting comparisons to those studies of psychosocial treatment in which versions of the present coding scheme were used with adult clients (Reid and Shyne 1969; Pinkus 1968), we find that exploration ranges from 46 to 51 percent of total input in these studies contrasted to 20 percent for adult clients in the present study; in the comparative studies the range for structuring is 5 to 7 percent, and for direction is 1 to 4 percent; the comparable percentages in the present project are 19 and 18. Even when the comparison is limited to planned short-term psychosocial treatment (included in the data reported by Reid and Shyne 1969), the differences, while somewhat less, are of comparable magnitude. Studies of psychosocial practice analyzed by use of techniques in the Hollis system also reveal differences similar to those reported earlier (Hollis 1972; Mullen 1968). Task-centered work with children can be compared to one study (Lish 1973) in which social workers used psychodynamically-oriented verbal and play-therapy techniques with children. Differences between these workers and ours were of a magnitude similar to those observed in the comparison of task-centered and psychosocial practice with adults.

While the amount of time devoted to explanation in the project interviews does not appear to differ substantially from time devoted to similar techniques in the comparative studies, it seems to have been used much differently in the task-centered cases. On the whole, the comparisons suggest that the purposes and structure of the model have produced a profile of techniques that differs substantially from that of one major form of social work practice.

Work with Collaterals

Turning from client interviews to the practitioner's efforts within the client's social system, we find that in the great majority of cases (80 percent) such efforts occurred: in 71 percent, one or more in-person contacts with a collateral took place. Since, as noted, present conceptualizations of this aspect of the model were not well developed when the experiment was undertaken, and since work within the social system is inherently difficult to measure, the quality of our data leaves something to be desired. We were able, however, to get a sense of the scope and emphasis of intervention in the social system through a content analysis of the practitioners' narrative recordings. Discrete practitioner actions (N = 260) in work with collaterals (excluding problem reviews) were identified and coded according to their apparent purpose. The most common type, accounting for 44 percent of the total, was actions designed to *elicit* information—usually about resources the client might need, about the collaterals' perceptions or expectations of the client, or their suggestions for possible client tasks. In an additional 17 percent, the apparent purpose of the practitioners' actions was to *convey* information to collaterals, usually in the form of progress reports. About a fifth of the practitioners' actions concerned work with collaterals on their responses to client task performance or the development of reciprocal or shared tasks to be carried out with the client. The remainder of the practitioner's interventions in the social system—another fifth of the total—consisted of practitioner tasks and other actions addressed to a wide variety of purposes, including straightening out misunderstandings between the clients and organizations, helping collaterals deal with client behavior, and arranging for referrals. In children's cases, most of the practitioner's interventions in the social system involved teachers and parents not defined as clients; in adult cases, other clinic personnel and social agencies. Despite the extent and variety of such activity and its possible importance, it is still fair to say that the great bulk of the practitioner's time and effort was spent in face-to-face work with clients.

Findings at Follow-Up

Follow-up interviews with clients and collaterals were obtained with two major objectives in mind: first, to determine the durability of whatever gains might have been achieved during the treatment program; second, to elicit the client's evaluation of the service program. The interviews were conducted by trained research interviewers approximately two months (on the average) following case termination, which usually took place shortly after completion of the experimental phase in each case. The shortness of the follow-up period was dictated in large part by the need to assess school-related problems before the end of the school year. Of the 87 project cases, follow-up interviews with clients were obtained on 77, or 89 percent.* In addition, data from collaterals were secured when they had knowledge of the problem and were available; collaterals were interviewed in about half the cases.

Problem Change Following Service

The initial portion of the follow-up interviews consisted of a problem review similar to the one previously conducted by the practitioners. (Interviewers were given copies of the practitioners' description of the clients' problems prior to treatment.) From the reviews at follow-up, we obtained from both clients and collaterals a picture of the status of each problem and the clients' overall problem situation.

Change following treatment was measured by having a judge compare data obtained at the end of the treatment period with the follow-up data.† Change was rated on a three-point scale: improved, no change, worse. To check reliability, a second judge in-

---

* Although the major reason for failure to follow up clients was difficulty in locating them, the clients not interviewed had a lower mean overall problem-change rating (6.5) at completion of the experimental phases of treatment than did the clients who were interviewed (7.4). Given this fact, it is likely that if the missing clients had been interviewed, evaluations of service would have been somewhat less positive than are subsequently reported; but at the same time the "relapse rate" would probably have been slightly lower, since the missing clients did not have as much to lose as those interviewed.

† The follow-up sample included some B cases (five) that terminated prior to a problem review. In these cases, status of the client's problem at follow-up was compared with the status of these problems as described in the last recorded contact with the client. It should be noted that the percentages to be reported subsequently would not be materially affected by the exclusion of these cases.

dependently rated half the cases. The judges agreed 75 percent of the time for the main problem and 80 percent for the overall problem situation. All disagreements involved adjacent steps of the scale.

On the whole, findings (based on the ratings of the first judge) indicated that gains were either maintained or improved upon during the post-treatment period: for the overall problem situation, 21 percent of the cases showed improvement, 70 percent no change, and 9 percent deterioration. The distribution for the main problem had a similar shape but with lower percentages showing either improvement or deterioration. Only ten cases in all were rated as showing deterioration either in the main problem or in the overall problem situation.

In addition to providing factual information on the status of problems at the point of follow-up, clients and collaterals were asked directly for their evaluations of problem change following treatment. The overwhelming majority of clients (80 percent) thought their overall problem situation had changed for the better during the follow-up period; the remainder said their problems as a whole had not changed, with the exception of one client who felt they had gotten worse. In the opinion of collaterals, the overall problem situation of 60 percent of the clients had shown a change for the better; in the remaining 40 percent they thought that no change had occurred. A similar distribution was obtained for both client and collateral opinions with respect to the main problem.

As can be seen, a more optimistic picture of post-treatment change is obtained from client and collateral reports than from the analysis of the judges, though one notes that collaterals were less optimistic than clients. Perhaps the judges were more conservative because they were basing their ratings on presumably factual data, whereas the clients and collaterals were simply asked to give their opinions about change. In this connection, the judges were not influenced by desires to say what interviewers might be expected to hear. All sources of data are consistent on one important point, however: that clients were at least able to hold on to gains achieved during the treatment period.

Client Evaluations of Service

As a part of the follow-up interview, clients were asked a number of questions to elicit their appraisals of the service program. The items covered the client's reactions to various aspects of the service structure and methods and their assessment of service as a whole. (The instrument appears in Reid and Epstein 1977, pp. 291–92.) In general, client evaluations were positive, with 70 percent or more of the clients responding in a direction clearly favorable to the service on all items but one.

The one exception was, "I thought service was a little too short—I could have used a few more interviews"; about half (46 percent) of the clients agreed with this statement. At first glance this finding might suggest a major negative reaction to the durational limits of the model. It seemed likely, however, that some of these responses were the result of a social-desirability effect: some clients might have thought it would be "polite" or socially correct to say that they did not get quite enough service, as a departing guest might say to his host: "The visit was too short." Evidence for this assumption was found in apparently inconsistent responses to certain other items. Many of the respondents who thought service was a little too short also *agreed* with the statement: "We met just about the right number of times" and *disagreed* with: "There were a lot of things on my mind we didn't have time to talk about." To get a more valid measure of negative appraisal of time limits, we considered such a reaction to occur when a client responded that service was either "a little" or "much too short" *and* gave a socially *undesirable* response to a related item, such as disagreeing with, "We met about the right number of times" and agreeing with, "There was a lot on my mind we didn't have time to talk about."

The responses of a quarter of the clients were found to meet this criterion for dissatisfaction with the time constraints of the model. Interestingly enough, almost all of the respondents who had said service was a little too brief but mentioned nothing else "negative" about durational limits were children who had been referred by teachers for learning or behavior problems. It seemed more likely that these children, many of whom were reluctant clients, were responding in a socially desirable way than complaining about not having enough service.

But that as many as a fourth of the clients seemed to have genuine reservations about time limits was a matter of concern. Additional analysis revealed that adults, particularly women, were overrepresented in this subgroup, though not to a statistically significant degree. Clients in this group also reported significantly less change on the main problem (p. < .05, chi square) and somewhat less change in their overall problem situations. Surprisingly, clients who thought service was too short were in treatment almost exactly the same length of time as those who did not have this complaint. These findings are in accord with those obtained in a study of short-term treatment of largely middle-class clients for family problems (Reid 1977; Reid and Shyne 1969). In those studies as well, respectable minorities of clients, disproportionately female, expressed reservations about service limits.

Responses to one item in particular were indicative of the clients' general satisfaction with service: 86 percent thought that they had been "helped considerably" by service or "could not have gotten along without it"; an additional 13 percent indicated that they had been helped slightly; only 1 percent (one client) indicated that service had not been helped at all. This level of satisfaction is roughly the same as obtained in a previous test of the model with low-income black clients for largely individual problems (Reid and Epstein 1972) and exceeds the level reported in an application of the model with primarily white, middle-class clients treated for marital difficulties (Reid 1977a). Responses to three other items suggested that one of the purposes of the model—to provide the clients with a constructive problem-solving experience (chapter 5) had been achieved in the respondents' opinion: 88 percent reported satisfaction with their own accomplishments; 91 percent thought their experience would help them with new problems; and 78 percent said they would see a social worker again.

While collaterals were not asked directly to evaluate the service program, their opinions about problem change suggest that they were reasonably satisfied with progress clients made on their target problems. Almost half the collaterals (45 percent) did indicate, however, that they thought that clients had problems that could have been worked on but were not. From this finding, one might infer that these collaterals, most of whom were teachers in the school setting, were expressing some reservations about the focus and scope of service. In some instances, collaterals probably had wanted practitioners to concentrate on problems of concern to *them* rather than on client-defined problems. In other instances the collaterals might have wanted clients to have a lengthier period of treatment. In any event, the data suggest the need for more effective interpretation of the task-centered model to collaterals than was apparently achieved in the experiment.

Discussion

Having already commented on most findings of interest, I shall devote this section to review of methodology and results relating to the most important question that can be asked about the data: How did task-centered methods contribute to problem change? This question subsumes several more specific issues: Did treatment make any contribution to change? How much of an impact did it have? What were the means by which its effects, if any, were achieved?

A complex field experiment cannot be expected to produce a completely unequivocal answer to the question of how much a method of treatment has affected psychosocial problems. In the present case there are a number of reasons for being less than certain about results relating to outcome.

At least three factors might have limited the margin of superiority attained by the experimental treatment. First, practitioners had little training or experience in use of the model and lacked familiarity with the settings in which the experiment took place. Second, measurement of treatment effects was based on six sessions over a three-week period—a somewhat shorter and more rigidly bounded duration than one might desire. Finally, the model had to compete with itself in respect to the crucial problem-specification phase. If we assume that a problem carefully defined is one partially solved, then the control cases probably benefited from application of the first stage of task-centered treatment. This limitation was difficult to avoid if target problems were to be comparable in both experimental and control conditions prior to treatment.

Other factors may have worked to the advantage of the experimental treatment, however. First, the non-specific effects of treatment, such as the benefits of friendly listening, were imperfectly controlled, in as much as there were fewer sessions in supportive attention than in task-centered intervention. Thus there was greater opportunity for those effects to operate in the experimental conditions. Second, outcome data were based to a large extent on client self-reports as obtained by their practitioners. Two sources of bias are possible here. Clients may have tended to exaggerate gains perceived to be the result of a systematic program of treatment in which they had made an investment. This bias may have benefited the experimental more than the control condition, since the client's investment in terms of time and effort was greater in the former. Practitioners, who undoubtedly wanted their clients to do better under the experimental condition, may have conducted problem reviews with clients and collaterals in ways that favored that condition. We made efforts to control such bias by having practitioners ask stipulated questions in the review and requiring inadequate reviews to be redone, but it may have occurred in ways too subtle to be caught by our control procedures. Finally, it must be recognized that various forms of bias may be present in an experiment in which the principal investigators and staff hope to obtain a positive outcome, as was the case in the present undertaking. Under such circumstances, various kinds of decisions, such as whether or not to pursue a client who has dropped out of the program or to accept evidence secured with some degree of variance from preestablished rules, may unwittingly be made in favor of the experimental treatment. While conscious efforts were made to avoid bias in such decision making, subjective influences on judgment are difficult to control. The importance of this form of bias or "experimental demand" has been well documented by Rosenthal (1967).

Such limitations are difficult to avoid in experimental tests of methods of social work intervention. Problems in controlling nonspecific treatment efforts seem inevitable. If simple a "no treatment" control group is used, as is frequently done, there is, of course, no control at all for these effects. It is hard to construct a "lesser" treatment that can provide these effects in equal measure to the experimental treatment, since the distinction between nonspecific and experimental effects is never clear cut. When target problems occur outside the observational orbit of researchers or accessible others, as is often the case, one must rely on the client's own accounts; nor can we assume that collaterals, if available, are unbiased in their views. The use of researchers, rather than practitioners, to collect data from clients does not eliminate problems of interviewer bias. The interviewers may also expect that the treatment program should work; and it is impossible to assume that they will not learn which clients they interview have received treatment. If research methods are to be used to assess and improve treatment, model developers need to perform at least initial tests of their own creations and hence may fall prey to the effects of experimental demand.

Replication of experimental tests of treatment methods by investigators who played no part in developing them provides an answer to some of these problems (but not all). Such tests are not easily replicated, however, and for this reason, among others, replication has not yet become a routine practice in clinical research. Practically speaking, I think, we must give weight to the results of yet unreplicated, imperfect experiments, if only because they may yield knowledge that is somewhat more reliable than untested convictions.

If we assume that the treatment program made a difference in the lives of the clients, what can be said about the extent and nature of its impact? Whether or not a task-centered approach was used, the client's problems appeared to be eased. The experimental treatment seemed, however, to augment the upward direction of problem change: for example, one could say that a client who would have experienced a moderate amount of problem alleviation without receiving treatment was likely to experience a considerable amount of problem alleviation if he did receive it. Moreover, treatment seemed to have a positive impact on the client's problems in general. There was no evidence that alleviation of specific target problems was undone by outcroppings of "substitute" problems.

Changes in the client's problems seemed relatively durable over a two-month span following treatment. This time period is short, but it is long enough to provide some reassurance that changes achieved could survive without continuing practitioner activity, and that these changes were not being immediately offset by problems arising in other areas. The course of problem change following treatment still seemed to be in an upward direction, possibly reflecting the natural processes of change for the problems studied. Whether these processes would have continued in the same direction or whether the problems would have eventually gotten worse is open to conjecture. In any case one would expect that, sooner or later, similar problems or other equally troublesome difficulties would arise, not because of the insufficiency of treatment, but rather because problems are an inevitable part of human existence.

How the task-centered methods may have produced problem change can be inferred from the data gathered on service inputs. It is clear that treatment to a large extent consisted of helping clients select and plan specific tasks that they agreed to carry out and then attempted. This approach did seem to be an effective means of problem solving. In this respect, the findings are in accord with our previous experiment (Reid 1975a) and with other previous research. In their review of studies relating to client compliance with practitioner instigations, Levy and Carter (1976) observe that client actions planned with practitioners are more likely to be carried out if these actions are described in "specific detail," and if the client gives "overt indication of intent" to implement the action (p. 190). These predictors of client performance were essential characteristics of the tasks used by project practitioners.

In the present experiment, tasks that were selected and planned were usually carried out, particularly, it seems, if the client strongly expressed a willingness to try them. When tasks were successful, problem alleviation was more likely to occur. The data provide no clues about the relative effectiveness of particular task-centered activities and techniques but do suggest that the intervention as a whole placed considerable emphasis on certain activities—problem specification, task planning, and task review—and more stress than has been usual in social treatment on certain techniques—direction and structuring. Practitioner efforts within the client's social system were less clearly delineated, but a good part of them apparently served to facilitate problem specification and the planning, review, and implementation of client tasks.

In a program of model research and development, there are inevitable discrepancies between the model on paper and the model as used in a given test. Modifications in the model may be made after the experiment is under way, or the test may reveal aspects of a model's operations that were not taken into account in its prior formulations. One then needs to decide if these novel features contributed to the model's effectiveness or detracted from it.

In the present instance, the notion of practitioner tasks and related theory were incorporated into the model after the test was under way. Moreover, the data from the experiment indicated that one activity—problem specification—was stressed more in the middle phase of treatment than one would have expected from the written statement of the model, whereas other activities, such as simulation, received less emphasis than would have been expected. Since no relation was found between the amount of use of any activity and outcome, one cannot tell from the data whether or not these deviations from the model were useful. Some judgments can be made, however.

It appears that practitioners regarded continued emphasis on problem specification as necessary to carry out other activities, particularly with adults. Given lack of information of the role it played, and given the fact that the model as a whole tended to be relatively successful with adults, more emphasis on this activity, as a part of the middle phase of treatment, seems warranted. Certainly an effort needs to be made to delineate how this activity should be used in relation to others and to isolate its components.

Use of simulation did not appear to be necessary to the effectiveness of the model, since it was hardly used at all with the more successful adult cases. Since other evidence exists that simulation is an effective means of promoting action (McFall and Twentyman 1973), we need perhaps to place greater stress on this activity in training practitioners to use the model, particularly in work with adult clients.

In presenting the model for use by others we must reconcile the formulations that guided the test with the picture of practice that was obtained from it. Perhaps we can say that the task-centered activities and techniques presented in chapters 7 and 8 were tested in substance and found to be effective with certain samples of clients and problems. But we must add some qualifications: certain activities, particularly practitioner tasks and simulation, were not well implemented; and more extensive use was made of problem specification than is suggested by the written formulations. As the statement implies, applications of the model to problems of family interaction (chapter 9) were not systematically tested, even though some use was made of these applications in certain project cases.

Chapter 11
Systematic Case Information

Clinical social work is usually a part of a larger program of services provided by the agency. These services are supervised, organized, and managed by personnel who are not directly responsible for carrying them out; they are largely financed by the public, either through taxes or through voluntary contributions.

Efforts to help clients often involve combinations of different practitioners and agencies. High rates of staff turnover may add to the number of practitioners involved with a client, particularly one under long-term care.

In essence, who the client is and what happens to him concerns not only a single practitioner but an entire network of individuals and organizations. Communication of accurate information about the client is essential in order to supervise, plan, and manage services and to make sure these services are provided with proper coordination and continuity. Administrative needs for such information have been heightened by increasing emphasis on agency accountability to funding sources and to the public; by the growing use of methods of "scientific management" in the administration of social agencies; and by the tightening of social welfare budgets. In an era of scarce resources, the modern agency administrator wants to know with some precision what services are being provided, to which clients, with what effect, and at what cost.

This information becomes particularly important when the agency attempts to utilize methods whose effectiveness has been tested in systematic research, such as in the study just reported. That a model has demonstrated a certain level of effectiveness in a controlled experiment is no guarantee that it will achieve a comparable level in routine agency practice with a different kind of clientele, under a different program of staff training and supervision. Moreover, ways must be devised to obtain service and outcome data on ongoing applications of a model to provide a basis for on-site assessment and development. One cannot expect that the resulting data will attain the level of rigor or control possible in a small-scale experiment, but they can provide some gauge of how things are working, particularly if measures are roughly comparable to those used in the experimental tests.

At the same time, practitioners themselves need recorded information about their own cases that can help them determine what was done and how well it worked. When the practitioner, as often happens, has a large number of cases to keep in mind, this information becomes essential. Moreover, practitioners are interested not only in their own cases but also in those of other practitioners that might help them in their work. A practitioner faced with a specific type of case situation, particularly one he is unfamiliar with, is helped if he can determine how the situation was handled by other workers. Usually he acquires such information in a somewhat unsystematic way from colleagues and supervisors. For this purpose, well-organized case records can often provide better information more efficiently.

To satisfy these traditional and emerging information needs, agencies and practitioners are turning increasingly to methods for recording and utilizing what might be called *systematic case information*. I use this expression generically to refer to specific, well-organized, and readily communicated data on client characteristics, problems, service processes, and outcomes. The chapter will focus on our efforts to develop and use this kind of information base within the task-centered system of practice.

Recording Approaches

Systematic case information is collected, usually by the practitioner, through some type of structured recording format, which organizes the record according to predetermined divisions or headings and specifies the kind of information to be placed in each. Some formats, such as the problem-oriented record (Weed 1969; Martens and Holmstrup 1974; Kane 1974; Burril 1976), provide ways of structuring narrative (word) records. Other formats, such as the one developed by Seaburg (1965), call for numerical coding of case data. Structured formats are usually accompanied by instructions, sometimes in the form of elaborate manuals, which specify the kinds of information to be recorded or how it is to be coded.

Structured recording formats have a number of advantages over traditional forms of discursive narrative recording, in which the practitioner puts down pretty much what he chooses, usually reporting on events in the case in a chronological fashion. This recording style tends to produce unwieldy records, uneven in content and coverage. Structured formats, on the other hand, produce better-organized, more usable records in which there are fewer omissions of important data. Moreover, they provide the practitioner with a structure for his work on the case.

Finally, the information they produce can be more readily put into forms that can be stored, retrieved, and manipulated by computers. Computerized information systems can quickly provide administrators and practitioners with displays of data serving a wide variety of purposes, from program assessment to case management (Fein 1975; Reid 1975b; Volland 1976). The actual and potential value of such systems has placed an even greater premium on collecting data that can be readily put into computer-acceptable forms.

Structured formats, and the information they produce, have their limitations, however. Organization does not guarantee accuracy. The structure of the record may make it difficult to capture important sequences and configurations of events. Formats that require largely coded information may not provide enough qualifying or other detail for many uses, and the codes themselves may be so crude or used with such variation that the resulting data may be of questionable quality. Finally, formats may impose dysfunctional restrictions on practice. A good deal more developmental work on structured formats is needed before their potential can be realized and their pitfalls avoided.

Structured Recording of Task-Centered Practice

Over the past several years, we have attempted to develop means of collecting and recording systematic case information for multiple uses within the task-centered system. Our efforts have been guided by certain assumptions: (1) In view of cost and feasibility considerations, primary reliance would need to be placed on case-record data provided by practitioners, but concomitantly methods would need to be developed to assess the reliability of such data and to correct for possible distortion resulting from practitioner errors or bias. (2) Data obtained should be of direct value to the practitioner, enhancing both the quality of his practice and the accuracy, meaningfulness, and completeness of the data themselves. (3) The data should capture *specific* characteristics of target problems, the service processes, and outcome. (4) The data should be in a form that would enable comparison to be made with results of our experimental tests.

We have experimented with a variety of recording formats in several hundred cases (including those in the experiment, chapter 10) from school, mental health, corrections, family service, and public welfare settings. The format presented and illustrated here is a revised version of one that has been used in our most recent work. Unlike most formats, it is designed to be used with a particular service model and can be taken as an example of how model-specific formats might be structured.

Recording Format: Case Illustration

I. Identifying and Basic Social Data
   1. Name of Client(s)___Harriet Alls___   Worker _Joan Nash____
      referred or applying
   2. Address _1201 Willow Street, Apt. 2A_ Phone _691-7081_____

3. Race __White__   4. Marital Status __Divorced__
5. Income __$350 per month__ 6. Source of Income __Alimony & Child__
7. Referral Source __Dr. Gershwin, Pediatrician__   Support
8. Date of Referral __1/16/75__
9. Data on Clients and Members of Social System [List clients and important members of social system and provide requested information, as relevant.]

Name	Relation to Client	Sex	Age	Education	Occupation	Check If Living with Client
Harriet Alls	--	F	22	H.S.	unemployed	
Debbie	daughter	F	4	--		X
Tim	son	M	2½	--		X
Tina	daughter	F	2½	--		X
Rona Smith	sister	F	26	H.S.	beautician	
Gerald Alls	ex-husband	M	24	one yr. coll.	salesman	

II. Problems as Initially Stated
A. By Clients

Mrs. A feels "overwhelmed" and "exhausted" because of burden of caring for three young children. Has no life of her own. Ex-husband does not provide enough money for a decent place to live.

B. By Referral Source or Collateral

According to Dr. G, Mrs. A is a distraught and depressed young woman who has problems about being a mother. Her situation could lead to child neglect, if it hasn't already.

III. Target Problems [explicitly agreed on by practitioner and client] Problem #1
Summary Statement
Mrs. A is not providing adequate care for her three preschool-age children.

Specification

By the time Mrs. A gets up in the morning (after 10 a.m., (5/7*),
the children have been up, undressed, and unfed for several hours.
During the rest of the day she has difficulty controlling their
behavior, she slaps and screams at them when they get into things
or when they make noise. She tries to get Debbie to do things to
keep the twins occupied and gets angry at her when she doesn't
cooperate. There are no regular mealtimes. The children are fed
when Mrs. A eats, mostly snacks throughout the day, or they get
food themselves. During the last few weeks she has been "taking
walks," leaving them alone in the apartment for an hour or more
(2/7).

Problem Duration
One year, worse in past month.

Problem #2 †
Summary Statement
Mrs. A is dissatisfied with her housing situation.

Specification

Mrs. A and the three children live in a small, second floor
walk-up apartment; children crowded into one tiny bedroom, Mrs. A
in another; major appliances always breaking down; poor cooperation from landlord, who would like them to leave; downstairs neigh-
bor complains of noise, particularly in the morning.

Problem Duration
One year.

IV. Problem, Client, Situation Characteristics (not previously presented)

Mrs. A has been depressed and overwhelmed with child care,
housing, and financial problems since her divorce from
husband a year ago, which she initiated after he "walked
out". He has moved to another city, visits children ir-
regularly. She expressed considerable resentment at him

---

* Indicates frequency of occurrence (five times) during baseline period (seven-day period)
† Additional problems may be added to this section as well as to section VIII below.

for leaving her in her present "mess." She has been barely able to manage on his monthly payments. He is now one month behind. She moved into present apartment on a temporary basis; now feels permanently trapped. She has not thought of working, has no job skills and no one to take care of children. The only person in her social system she turns to is her older married sister, who lives about two miles away and whom she sees or talks to about once a week. Because the sister works full time, she hasn't been of much help during the week, although she does take Mrs. A's children now and then on weekends. Mrs. A has currently few friends and, since the divorce, practically no social life.

Mrs. A is a thin, tense woman who appears to be bright and perceptive. She talks freely about her difficulties, crying occasionally but recovering quickly. She expresses concern about the children which seems genuine despite her (understandable) resentment over her present situation.

Additional Data

Home visit (1/30/75) confirmed Mrs. A's picture of inadequacy of apartment, but I found it to be tastefully decorated. Twins are active, noisy; Debbie, quiet, tends to cling to mother.

V. Problem Assessment and Planning

A vicious circle of interaction has developed between Mrs. A and her children (problem 1). Her avoiding child-care responsibilities (e.g., by sleeping late, leaving the house) leads to uncontrolled behavior on their part, which in turn aggravates her avoidance reaction. When she does intervene, it is often at a point when their behavior is "out of control," and she reacts with impulsive and excessively harsh discipline (screaming, slapping), which further exacerbates their behavior problems. Her belief that Debbie, age four, should be of help to her with the twins adds to her frustration and anger at the child's behavior. Her inability to cope with the problem is further impaired by an unsatisfactory housing situation (problem 2). Her ex-husband's delinquencies in providing alimony and support payments, together with problems in coping with children, have prevented her from finding a more suitable place. She seems anxious at this point to try to "get on top" of her situation and is willing to "try anything." In addition to helping her de-

velop tasks relating to the care of her children in the
home, the possibility of day-care facility for oldest child
and/or homemaker should be considered, as well as a consultation with Legal Aid concerning her ex-husband's payments.

VI. Contract [In addition to agreement to work on target problems previously listed]
 A. Goals
 1. Adequate care for children.
 2. A larger apartment.

 B. Service Duration
 Ten interviews over six-week period
 3/21 Recontracted for additional two weeks (two sessions) to
 complete work on housing problem.

 C. Other Service Characteristics
 Office interviews with Mrs. A following one session at home.
 She will bring children to sessions.

VII. Task Schedule [Tasks given for problem 1 only]
*Task #*1

Mrs. A is to make up schedule for herself and children,
setting down times for getting up, meals, housework,
naps, etc.

Problem to which related __1__   Session formulated __2__
Origin of Task: Client _____   Practitioner __X__   Other (specify) _____
Client's Initial Commitment __4__*

Task Reviewed: Session # __3__ ____ ____ ____ ____ ____ ____
Task Achievement Rating: __2__* ____ ____ ____ ____ ____ ____

Comments
She has done some work on schedule, but it was not complete.
We finished it in session.

*Numbers refer to ratings on scales previously presented (chapter 10). In brief, the Com-
mitment Scale refers to degree of willingness to work on task (5 high, 1 low). The Task-
Achievement Scale measures the client's or worker's success in carrying out task (4, completely achieved; 3, substantially achieved; 2, partially achieved; 1, not achieved or mini-
mally achieved).

Task #2

Mrs. A. is to get up at 9 a.m. to prepare her own and children's breakfast. If she does not, she is to get up when first awakened by children.

Problem to which related __1__   Session formulated __3__
Origin of Task: Client __X__   Practitioner _____   Other (specify) _____
Client's Initial Commitment __4__

Task Reviewed: Session # __4__ __5__ ____ ____ ____ ____ ____
Task Achievement Rating: __2__ __2__ ____ ____ ____ ____ ____

Comments

Session 4. She got up before nine once on her own initiative and once when awakened by the twins (out of five days). She has been trying to get up but "can't seem to quite make it." She began to do much better after Debbie began nursery school. This task, then, became incorporated as a part of task 4 (below).

Task #3

Practitioner will attempt to locate nursery schools and day-care centers that might take Debbie.

Problem to which related __1__   Session formulated __2__
Origin of Task: Client _____   Practitioner __X__   Other (specify) _____
Client's Initial Commitment __NA__

Task Reviewed: Session # __3__ ____ ____ ____ ____ ____ ____
Task Achievement Rating: __4__ ____ ____ ____ ____ ____ ____

Comments

Mrs. A had mixed feelings about this plan because of her problems in "getting going" in the morning, having to dress and take twins along to drop and pick up Debbie; worried about cost. After a number of tries, I located day-care center (operated by Community Consultation Service) which agreed to take Debbie in morning group on emergency basis after I explained her situation. I also arranged for volunteer driver (Mrs. Green from agency pool) who can take Debbie to and from the school three days a week. Mrs. A responded favorably to these arrangements. She would try to take Debbie there herself the first time so she could see the school.

*Task #*4

Mrs. A will get up and get Debbie ready for nursery school
pick-up by 9 a.m.

Problem to which related __1__   Session formulated __3__
Origin of Task: Client __X__   Practitioner ____   Other (specify) ____
Client's Initial Commitment __5__

Task Reviewed: Session #   __5__ __6__ __7__ __8__ __9__ __10__ ____
Task Achievement Rating: __4__ __4__ __2__ __3__ __3__ __4__ ____

Comments

Task Review, Session 7. Mrs. A "overslept" two mornings the
preceding week. Volunteer driver rang bell and awakened her;
waited until she got Debbie ready. Brief telephone conference
with driver after first morning on how to handle this problem.

*Task #*5

Mrs. A will spend an hour in the afternoon with children in
which she will try to teach them how to play together.

Problem to which related __1__   Session formulated __5·__
Origin of Task: Client __X__   Practitioner __X__   Other (specify) ____
Client's Initial Commitment __4__

Task Reviewed: Session #   __8__ __9__ __10__ ____ ____ ____ ____
Task Achievement Rating: __3__ __3__ __3__ ____ ____ ____ ____

Comments

Idea for task grew out of Mrs. A's insistence that Debbie
could do more to help her with the twins. In its final form,
task was designed to help Mrs. A structure her time with
children in constructive ways to help her and children do
things together. In office session (6) with Mrs. A and children, I modeled ways of getting children involved in games,
drawing on a game Debbie had learned in nursery school. Mrs.
A then took over and I took on coaching role. Major problem
was impatience with Debbie, whom she sees as slow. Later discussed her expectations of Debbie. She could see that she
wanted Debbie at times to be a "little governess."

VIII. Final Problem Review
   1. Target Problems (Major changes in target problem since beginning of treatment)

Problem #1

Mrs. A was not providing adequate care for three preschool-age children.

The major changes in this problem occurred after arrangements were made to have Debbie taken to a nursery school for a half-day. Mrs. A began to get up in the morning to get Debbie ready for school and as a result began to take better care of the twins during the morning. She has been able to spend some structured time in the afternoon with the three children and has made some progress toward establishing a regular evening mealtime for them. She says she has not left them unattended since coming to the agency.

Problem #2.

Mrs. A was dissatisfied with her housing situation.

Both Mrs. A and worker attempted to locate better housing but could find nothing that she liked or could afford. That the landlord had her stove fixed and has been friendlier has made her a little less dissatisfied with her current arrangements.

Change in Other Areas: New Problems

Her financial situation remains about the same. Practitioner was advised by Legal Aid that it would do little good, and possible harm, to put legal pressure on Mr. A regarding the payments. Mrs. A decided she did not want to take action on this anyway until she got herself and the children "straightened out." No other problems have emerged.

IX. Rating of Problem Change

| | Assessed by | | |
Problem	Client	Collateral	Practitioner
1	8	—	8
2	6	—	5
3	—	—	—
Overall problem situation	8	—	7

Scale

10	9	8	7	6	5	4	3	2	1

Completely resolved	Considerably alleviated	No change	Considerably aggravated	Greatly aggravated

X. Post-Treatment Planning and Disposition

```
Mrs. A wants to pursue three goals following treatment: (a) to
get a larger apartment, (b) to get her ex-husband to pay her the
money he owes her (by "putting it to him" directly next time he
visits children), (c) to begin to develop some sort of social
life, possibly with the help of her sister. Some next steps
toward these goals were discussed, as well as her long-range
interest in job training and employment. Arranged to call Mrs. A
for telephone follow-up in about one month.
```

Utility of the Format

The case itself provides, of course, another illustration of task-centered practice and may be viewed from that perspective. Our concern here, however, is with case recording. As can be seen, the recording guide is an attempt to organize case data in a compact, accessible form through use of a combination of structured narrative recording and practitioner ratings. Unlike a chronological narrative, the data, regardless of when they are obtained, are incorporated under predetermined headings. As a result, the user can quickly locate pertinent information. Thus, observational data on the children and Mrs. A's housing situation can be found by going directly to the section in the record where they logically belong rather than having to be searched for through a long series of recorded contacts. The organization also facilitates recording since it provides structure and limits for the practitioner's responses.

The format is organized around the central elements of a case record in the task-centered system—data on clients and problems, tasks, and outcome. The separation and numbering of problems (as is done in the problem-oriented record) and of tasks facilitates identification and location of these elements. What may be distinctive about the format is the display of the basic service structure through the enumeration of tasks. Thus, even without the "comments," one can quickly ascertain from the review of the task statements the main outline of the service strategy with Mrs. A.

The importance of the recording format as a means of training practitioners and of shaping practice can hardly be overestimated. The practitioner is not only reminded about the basic structural features of the model (target problem, contract, task formulation and review, and so on) but is required to practice within this framework in order to complete the guide in a reasonably correct and honest fashion. Moreover, the practitioner's grasp of these features is readily revealed, particularly by his problem specifications and task statements. Misunderstandings can be pinpointed and corrected.

Ratings relating to tasks and problem change can be easily coded and entered into a case-information system. Additional coding (for example, or problem and task types) would be necessary if the case information is to be used to maximum advantage. Given the form and structure of the data, coding of this kind can be easily accomplished by technical personnel with a modest amount of training.

The format, or the amount of recording required for particular items, can be modified to meet particular purposes. If practitioners have high caseloads and little time to record, the comments under "tasks" may be restricted (or even omitted), and only the more important tasks may be listed. For students, the format can be supplemented with process recordings of interviews or structured recording of activities. (An example of the latter may be found in chapter 12.)

Reliability of Practitioner Ratings

Whether the recording is detailed or condensed, practitioners are expected to make ratings of problem change and task progress. While practitioner ratings of service outcomes are a feature of many information systems, usually no way is provided to assess the accuracy of the practitioner's judgments. An obvious credibility question arises, since the practitioner is to some extent being asked to rate the results of his own efforts. His personal involvement or "stake" in the outcome could be expected to result in a certain amount of bias, either in the direction of exaggerating improvement (out of wishful thinking or a desire to "look good") or of minimizing gains (to avoid appearing immodest or because of self-critical tendencies).

A major reason practitioner outcome ratings have gone unchecked in information systems has been the difficulty in obtaining adequate corroborative evidence. While independently obtained client ratings can be obtained, client appraisals may also be affected by personal involvement and may be based on different perspectives from those of the practitioner.

The field experiment (chapter 10) provided us with an opportunity to assess practitioner ratings of problem change against the presumably more objective ratings of the judges. A comparison was made of practitioner and mean judge ratings of overall problem change during Phase II, in which cases either received task-centered treatment or supportive attention. Both practitioners and judges used the same scale, but to simulate rating conditions that might obtain in ordinary practice situations, the practitioners were given only brief instructions on the use of the scale. They were not trained in its use and were provided little time in which to make the ratings. (The scales were introduced and the ratings obtained in group sessions.) In one important respect the rating situation was unusual: the practitioners knew that independent judges would be making comparable ratings based on analysis of tape-recorded problem reviews with the clients. It is reasonable to suppose that this awareness placed some constraints on practitioner bias.

Interest was centered on the comparison of ratings for the experimental cases which, like cases in an ongoing agency program, received treatment that the practitioners thought to be effective. The results were most revealing. The correlation between practitioner and client ratings was surprisingly high: ($r = .84$), indicating a considerable amount of congruence between the two sets of ratings. But the magnitude of the correlation notwithstanding, the practitioners' ratings were consistently higher than the judges': of a total of 43 pairs of ratings, the practitioners' and judges' ratings were identical in 12; of the remaining 31 pairs, the practitioners' ratings were higher in 28, lower in only 3. The differences were generally small; few were greater than a point. The overall "inflation rate" (the algebraic average of the differences between practitioner and judge ratings) was about a half-point per case. Thus, while the two sets of ratings covaried closely (accounting for the high correlation), the practitioners' ratings generally edged those of the judges. The margin of difference seemed to reflect optimistic practitioner bias.

This interpretation is supported by the practitioner and judge ratings for problem change during the control phase of the B cases. Of 42 pairs of ratings compared, 5 were identical; the practitioner ratings were higher in 16 and lower in 21. The correlation between the two sets of ratings was lower ($r = .47$) than for the A cases, and margins of differences between them were greater. However, since differences tended to counterbalance one another, the practitioners' ratings were only about a tenth of a point below the judges when averaged algebraically over all cases. This slight pessimistic bias in the practitioners' ratings overall probably reflected a conviction that the control cases would not show significant positive change without systematic intervention, though some practitioners who thought their supportive attention had done some good may have been biased in the opposite direction. The findings for the B case ratings make the point that practitioners were not generally more optimistic than judges but more optimistic only when their involvement in the success of treatment was presumably high.

A second outcome assessment routinely obtained in applications of the model is the practitioner's rating of task progress. This rating is of particular utility both in clinical work and in service-oriented information systems since it provides a means of evaluating specific treatment strategies.

Again the reliability of the practitioners' ratings is of central concern. Our first investigation of the reliability of task-progress ratings was carried out as a part of the field experiment on task implementation Reid (1975a) and briefly described in the preceding chapter. The correlation between practitioners' ratings of task progress and the mean ratings of two independent judges was high ($r = .79$). The practitioners' ratings were only a trifle higher, on the average, than the judges'. In that experiment, however, a considerable amount of attention on the part of practitioners and judges was focused on a single task per case, and the total sample of tasks was small ($n = 32$).

Our second investigation, conducted as a part of the field experiment reported in the last chapter, examined the reliability of practitioner task-progress ratings under more ordinary conditions. While the ratings were obtained as part of an experiment, the focus of attention was on problem change, not task progress; in fact, practitioners were not told that their task-progress ratings would be checked. Moreover, a much larger number of tasks ($n = 220$) was used. Reliability data were obtained in the course of the content analysis of the treatment interviews of the experimental phases of the A cases. In addition to coding activities and techniques, judges made ratings of task progress based on listening to the practitioners' task reviews with the client. The practitioner-judge correlation, while not as high as the one obtained earlier, was still quite respectable ($r = .68$). Practitioners and judges were in perfect agreement on 67 percent of the task ratings. The inflation factor was minimal—practitioner ratings exceeded those made by judges by less than one-tenth of a point per task. It is possible, however, that practitioners might have underrecorded less successful tasks (see chapter 10).

These reliability studies provide a rationale for using ratings made by practitioners as estimates of task progress. The lack of optimistiç bias in the ratings is particularly encouraging. In this respect the task-progress ratings look better than ratings of problem change, in which the "inflation factor" was sizable enough so that it would need to be taken into account in their use.

A note of caution must be injected, however. The reliability data for both problem change and task-progress ratings were obtained under conditions in which practitioners knew that independent verification was at least possible. The same set of conditions is difficult to reproduce in routine agency operations.

But even in normal agency practice it is possible to set up procedures through which practitioner judgments can be verified. (The amount of checking *actually* done is probably less important than the practitioners' awareness that it *can be* done.)

Two approaches may be feasible. A sample of clients could be interviewed by a research technician (or a trained volunteer). The interview, which might take place at any point during the course of service or shortly after termination, could be used as the vehicle for collecting independent data on task progress and problem change. Alternatively, practitioners could tape record samples of their in-session work with clients, including task and problem reviews. The tapes could also be used both for supervisory purposes and as a source of independent data on practitioner judgments about outcome. Only a small fraction of the tapes would need to be used for either purpose. Since tapes are reusable, there is no cost in making tapes that are not used.

Practitioners may not welcome such auditing procedures, but it would be hard for them to find a rationale to oppose them. No client has to be either taped or interviewed against his wishes, and there is no reason to suppose either procedure does him any harm. On the contrary, auditing would serve the client's interest by helping maintain and improve service standards.

Although they may resist the idea, professionals would generally concede that their work should be open to some form of independent evaluation conducted by someone who can observe their efforts or their immediate results. What is proposed here is not even a direct evaluation of the social worker's performance, but rather procedures for assessing the adequacy of his judgments about the outcome of his efforts.

Cumulative Data

Thus far we have considered systematic case information from the standpoint of recording formats and of methods to test and improve the reliability of the data they yield. We shall now consider the utility of such information after it has been extracted from individual case records. Our major undertaking in this area has been an attempt to develop a system for organizing cumulative data on problems and tasks. The intent was to design a system that could provide practitioners, supervisors, and model developers with information on types of tasks and task outcome for particular types of problems.

Suppose a practitioner is attempting to help a child with a problem of aggressive behavior. The practitioner may not have had a great deal of experience with this kind of problem or with the task-centered approach. He might ask: "What kinds of tasks should be considered for such a problem?" "Is there any way of predicting which tasks would work best?" A supervisor or model developer might also be interested in learning if particular kinds of tasks used by practitioners proved especially fruitful or fruitless with this sort of problem. More successful tasks might be recommended to supervisees or stressed in the model. The less successful could be examined to determine reasons for failure. It might be then decided that certain varieties of tasks were not particularly useful or that some modification in their use was indicated.

Partial answers to these questions might be obtained from a distillation of the accumulated experience of practitioners' use of tasks to treat this kind of problem. The practitioner, supervisor as model developer would like to be able to have immediate access to information about the range of tasks used and the degree of success experience with different types.

A project was undertaken to create a design for an information system component that would meet the needs stated above. Data from 240 task-centered cases accumulated over a period of several years were reviewed. The cases had been carried by 71 practitioners, including students and trained workers, as a part of both special projects and routine practice. The cases yielded a total of 386 target problems and 1,114 tasks.

The first step was to classify the target problems: approximately 40 specific categories were constructed. Then tasks used for each type of problem were identified and where feasible were also classified. Practitioner ratings of task progress were used to compute achievement ratings for each type of task.

Through this structuring of the data we were able to retrieve information on tasks used for various types of problem. Our intent was not to produce a large amount of information of immediate applicability in practice but rather to determine the feasibility and potential usefulness of this mode of organizing data.

Information on problems and tasks was compiled in an 100-page document (Fortune 1976). The examples below illustrate how this kind of "information text" can be used.

The first example is useful for one interested in an output of task data relating to a specific problem encountered in a case. Suppose the problem at issue is a youngster's poor study habits. The user locates the problem in the text and finds the following output:

Problem: Role performance, student: poor study habits
Task Types and Data
1. Task type: To complete schoolwork according to a planned schedule
   Illustration: To do one class assignment each day for one week
   Average achievement rating: 3.2*
   Additional information: Task achievement tends to be client-specific
2. Task type: To spend time studying according to a schedule
   Illustration: Each evening to review for 15 minutes the main points her math teacher made in class
   Average achievement rating by task variation:
   a. Reward upon task completion   2.7
   b. No reward upon task completion   2.5
   c. Studying to be assisted by parent or sibling   2.0 (see critique)
   Additional information: Task achievement tends to be client-specific

Under additional information the user reads that achievement for both types of task tends to be "client-specific," which, as the text explains, means that how well a client achieves one task of a type is a good predictor of how well he will achieve other tasks of that type. In relation to the third variant of the second type of task

* On Task Achievement Scale previously described.

(studying with the assistance of other family members), the user is informed that a critique of prior experience with the task is available. If he were interested in that variation, he could refer to the critique which would inform him that in using this task variant, workers normally had not involved other family members in setting up the study schedule and this factor might have accounted for the relatively low achievement rate.

Information of this kind could be valuable if used judiciously. In general, the user might be helped by simply seeing what types of task had been employed with a problem of poor study habits. More specifically, he would learn that a straightforward effort to help a child schedule study assignments seemed to work relatively well in relation to other alternatives. Or if he were helping the child structure his study time, then he could see that tasks calling for solitary study, particularly with a reward, have been more successful than tasks involving the child's studying with a family member. If the later were to be tried, it might make sense to engage the family member in task planning.

In using such information wisely, the practitioner would need to remember that it is based simply on cumulative experience and that it is limited in respect to contingencies that might affect task selection and performance. Thus a task type may have a mediocre "track record" because of deficiencies in how it was used (as the example above illustrates) or because of certain typical obstacles that may not be present in the case at hand.

The information system has already been used to good advantage to locate types or features of tasks that were not working as well as might be expected. In one analysis of tasks with children, we found, surprisingly, that provision for tangible rewards upon task completion did not appreciably raise achievement rates. (Usually the difference between rewarded and nonrewarded tasks was less than the slight margin noted in the previous example). An examination of samples of the tasks and related recording revealed that many practitioners were routinely suggesting gold stars and food treats as rewards, without determining the child's interest in receiving them. There was reason to suppose in many cases that the reward had little value for the child or did not add much to such built-in reinforcers as the practitioner's and others' approval and the child's own sense of accomplishment. On the basis of this conclusion, we took steps to emphasize in practitioner training and supervision how tangible reinforcers should be selected and used (chapter 7).

The system has also been used to identify types of tasks that seem to work particularly well, or at least better than alternative types in more common use. A good example is tasks calling for affiliative actions—making friendly overtures, responding positively, and so on. Affiliative tasks seemed to be quite successful in helping shy or isolated clients make friends and surprisingly were somewhat more likely to be accomplished than alternative task types for problems of aggressive behavior in children. The most common type of task used with the latter problem is to have the client avoid persons, situations, or actions contributing to his aggression. But it was found that tasks in which the client tried to "make friends" or at least "make peace" with an antagonist had somewhat higher accomplishment rates and seemed to offer more definitive and constructive solutions to the problem of aggressive behavior.

The usefulness of a system of this kind could be obviously enhanced by adding ratings of problem change (a step that has already been incorporated), by refining methods of task classification, and by utilizing additional data on clients and service inputs. The potential payoff would grow as the number of clients, problems, and tasks in given categories accumulated.

Information on clients, problems, and tasks could be stored in computerized systems and then manipulated and recalled for various purposes. For example, let us return to the practitioner working with a child who has a problem in aggressive behavior. Now let us put the practitioner in front of a terminal (similar to the ones used by airlines personnel to make reservations). The terminal is connected to an information system which contains data from a large number of cases involving similar clients and problems. By typing in certain codes, the practitioner can ask the system to produce information on the particular type of case at hand—a male child between the ages of five and ten with a problem of aggressive behavior with peers. He then gets an immediate printout or visual display of alternative task programs that have been found to work well with this particular type of case situation, plus additional information about what interventions have or have not been effective. If he had not specified that the child was male or female, the "computer" could have asked him to do so before proceeding to process the initial inquiry. All of this may sound futuristic, but a number of computerized systems that perform comparable functions are already in operation in the helping professions (Reid 1975b).

Chapter 12
Dissemination
Laura Epstein, Eleanor R. Tolson,

and William J. Reid

No matter how elegant it is on paper, a system of practice will be of little value unless practitioners can be adequately trained to carry it out effectively. A practice system should come equipped with means of dissemination—that is, with methods for translating its abstract information into practitioner performance. In this chapter we shall first review the more important aspects of dissemination and the shape they take in the present system. Our work in one area—skill assessment—will then be examined in detail.

Aspects of Dissemination

First, to accommodate the wide variation in levels of training in social work, a practice system should be laddered so it can be used, at one end, with a reasonable measure of effectiveness and safety by practitioners with little training and, on the other end, with greater sophistication and presumably greater efficacy by better-trained practitioners. The laddering of the task-centered system has been better developed at the lower rungs than at the upper end. If we assume that the basic purpose of the approach is to facilitate the client's own problem-solving efforts, then practitioners with only a few hours training and supervised practice can help the client develop and work on commonsense tasks compatible with these efforts without serious danger of making matters worse. At what would have to be the bottom rung of the ladder, high school students in one project were trained to use methods of task-centered group treatment with younger students having difficulties with the school system (Rooney 1977a). At this point our ladder takes us through about one academic year of graduate training in the task-centered system. As we go beyond this level, it becomes less certain how advanced knowledge of human functioning and change can be utilized to increase the effectiveness of the model. Although we can provide some general directions, we cannot spell out the details at this point.

Second, it should be clear what kind of academic program is needed to train students in the essentials of the system. Since the amounts of time and resources available to train social work students in direct-service methods are limited, the educational program should be as condensed and economical as possible. Judging from our experience over the past seven years in student training at the School of Social Service Administration, we think that a program of one academic year should be sufficient to impart the basics of the approach to students without prior social work education. A viable program in task-centered methods would include the following: a year of classroom methods and field instruction; courses in human behavior and the social environment (with particular stress on learning theory) and in small-group processes; and finally, a practicum in clinical research built around the student's own fieldwork cases.

Third, if a system of practice is to be disseminated, ways must be found to provide adequate in-service training in its use to workers in the field. In our experience, the typical means of accomplishing this purpose—one- or two-day workshops or week-long institutes—is rather limited. While workshops provide an adequate mechanism for orienting workers to the basic ideas of an approach, they really do not equip them to carry it out. Our own observations received support from a study of efforts to implement task-centered methods in public agencies (Bogaty and Farrow 1977).

In order to learn a treatment model, practitioners need, we

think, an opportunity to use it and to get feedback on their performance. One format that has worked reasonably well, we have found, is to space out a relatively small number of training sessions over a period of several months (Golan 1977). After an orientation to the approach, practitioners try it out on one or two of their own cases. Subsequent sessions (at least several weeks apart) are organized around the resulting case material, giving practitioners an opportunity to learn the model through application and discussion of their own experiences with it.

The last aspect to be considered is supervision, a process central to both staff and student training. The content of supervision—that is, the concepts and methods to be taught—can be derived in a straightforward fashion from the practice system itself. A system may or may not require a special supervisory technique. What supervisors do need, however, is a means of assessing skills of practitioners who use the system. Skill assessment provides a central link between the content of the system and the practitioner behaviors to be affected by the supervisory process. Thus, a practice model may call for the worker to do a thorough exploration of the client's problem and may describe what this means. But the model would ordinarily neither delineate different worker behaviors representing varying degrees of thoroughness in problem exploration nor provide procedures for evaluating these behaviors. Skill assessment, then, is a method of determining the extent to which practitioner behavior meets specified criteria of performance set forth by a practice system. It works to provide the practitioner with corrective feedback on his performance and to evaluate his level of competence.

The practitioner's skill or competence must be assessed, since decisions on how well he is doing need to be made for various purposes (instruction, grading, promotion). Usually supervisors or others apply broad, unexplicated criteria without any independent checks on the reliability of their judgment. Obviously, a first step in developing better methods of skill assessment is to explicate standards of performance: the practitioner behaviors that indicate a particular level of skill in carrying out some prescribed method.

Procedures for applying the criteria to samples of practice and for judging different levels of skill would need to be worked out. The reliability of the rating system would need to he tested by having independent judges apply it to the same practice samples and comparing their level of agreement.

The obstacles to adequate skill assessment are enormous, and some cannot be satisfactorily solved at this time. Generally, our assessments of social work practice are based on implementation of methods of undetermined effectiveness. One usually cannot say that the practitioner's operations were skilled in the sense of producing a successful outcome, but only that they followed some untested conception on how something should be done.The paradox of ''skilled'' but possibly ineffective performance is one troubling consequence. Since conceptions of desirable practice abound, evaluation of skill must always be seen within the limits of a particular model or method of treatment. Statements about a practitioner's skill must then be accordingly qualified: he may be skilled in one approach but not another. We doubt at this point if we can identify a set of generic practice skills that would be common to all systems of practice. Even such likely candidates as exploring the client's presenting request would probably be interpreted differently from the viewpoints of different practice systems.

Even within a system, it is difficult to develop precise standards for the complex practitioner behavior that usually needs to be judged. Ideally, one must not only specify the action to be carried out but also the conditions under which its execution is appropriate. An interpretation of the client's behavior may be well executed but may occur at the wrong time. For many if not most contingencies of practice, the treatment system itself may not provide adequate guidelines for such fine, but essential, discriminations.

The last difficulty to be mentioned is theoretically the most easily solved, but its solution is costly. Assessments of practice skill are usually based on the practitioner's report of his activities. Given the opportunities for inaccuracy and distortion in the practitioner's written and oral accounts, it is uncertain whether we are judging skill in practice or in communication about practice. To a large extent, this limitation can be overcome through use of direct or indirect observation (tape recording) of a practitioner's work. The time and effort required to obtain and analyze even samples of observed practice are major reasons why this solution is not often used in routine supervision.

While we have not developed a special form of supervision to be used with the task-centered approach, we have begun work on a method of skill assessment, the Profile of Practice Skills. Although it has not yet overcome many of the limitations we have just discussed, it does represent, we think, some progress toward a difficult objective.

The Profile of Practice Skills

The Profile of Practice Skills has been used for several years in student training in the task-centered program at the School of Social Service Administration. The profile is presented as it has been used in this program. Its adaptation for use in agency practice will then be considered.

At present, the profile serves the following functions:

1. It describes behaviors that should guide students in carrying out task-centered treatment.
2. It delineates the skills the student is expected to learn by explaining the items and criteria upon which his performance will be evaluated or assessed.
3. It states what the instructors (classroom and field) are required to teach in order to provide the students with the necessary learning experiences. It is understood that a field site or seminar may fail to produce an adequate supply of identified learning experiences. The student is not responsible for learning or being evaluated on information and experiences to which he has had no exposure or inadequate exposure.

The profile is written to distinguish between a basic level of skill expected by the end of the first academic quarter, or roughly three months; and an advanced level expected by the end of nine months of education. Because of considerable individual differences among students, changing agency conditions, and the equivocal nature of any descriptions of skill, including our own, it has not been possible to develop a differentiation of an intermediate level of performance.

The original profile was developed by the senior author of this chapter in 1973. It was received by students with unusual enthusiasm because it explained what was expected of them. Since its introduction, the profile has been revised yearly. In 1976, Eleanor Tolson organized the profile to identify levels of performance. The Profile of Skills is reproduced in table 12.1.

Each skill is rated on the following scale: (3) advanced, (2) acceptable, (1) unacceptable, (U) appropriately not used. A rating of 3 is given if performance of the skill meets the criteria set forth in the boxed-in portions of the scale; a 2, if it meets only the criteria contained in the unboxed portions. The lack of an "advanced level" in the definition of a skill means only that we have thus far been unable to work out an adequate way of defining that level. The rating of unacceptable (1) is used for skills that in the rater's judgment are poorly performed or not in evidence when they should be. Use of the U rating will be made clear in the illustration below.

Evidence for rating the student is obtained from a structured recording guide, essentially a more detailed and somewhat differently organized version of the one illustrated in chapter 11. The student's written recording is supplemented with selective listening to tape recordings of sessions with clients. The recording guide permits the instructor to rate practice skills for each interview as a basis for summary ratings and to provide students with immediate feedback on their performance.

This use of the profile is illustrated by the following segment of a recording guide. The practitioner had helped the client, Amy, age nine, develop a task in which she was "to use a multiplication fact sheet when she worked on her math problems." In the record-

Table 12.1 Profile of Practice Skills in Task-Centered Treatment

Note: Boxed words in the skill items on the left-hand side of the page are explained in the boxes on the right-hand side of the page. The unboxed items and explanations depict level of performance expected at the end of the first quarter or three months; boxed items describe the level expected at the end of the academic year. Numbers in parentheses are used to identify particular skills.

I. *Interviewing*

A. Enables client role induction

Client to be provided with means and opportunity to understand both his and the practitioner's rules purposes, and expectations from treatment and what it will be like

1. Explains practitioner and client roles and purpose of treatment appropriately

(1) Explains and demonstrates what the practitioner can and will do and the reason for practitioner-client association. Repeats explanations when client gives evidence that his understanding of roles and purposes is unclear

2. Explains procedures appropriately

(2) Explains how treatment will proceed. Repeats explanations of role, purpose, and procedures as needed. Attaches verbal explanations to the treatment activity: for example, when formulating tasks, "Recall that we said we would find ways to reduce this problem. This is what we are doing when we think of tasks"

B. Explores thoroughly and selectively

(3) Asks questions, makes observations, and gathers information to learn what and how client is doing, thinking, feeling; judges directions for movement. Limits information-gathering activity to areas related to the target problem and the development of an assessment of the target problem

C. Obtains necessary facts

(4) Obtains facts about the client's "objective reality" (e.g., address, age, family constellation, job, income or other means of support, marital status, custody of children, school placement and achievement, health)

D. Is disciplined and empathetic

Adopts the preferred professional posture: self-control of preferences and wishes in dealing with clients to avoid exploiting them for personal

1. Disciplines own feelings

(5) reasons; appropriate feeling responses expressed to clients revealing respect and understanding; selectively communicating advocacy of client

2. Demonstrates accurate empathy

(6) interests. Demonstrations of empathy are characterized by accurate knowledge and specific expressions about how this person feels in his plight

II. *Initial phase of treatment*

A. Identifies appropriate
   target problems

(7) Identifies to client and in recordings the problem(s) to be focused upon. Identifies the target problem the client wants changed

B. Develops a specification
   of each target problem
   in quantifiable terms

(8) Determines the conditions that describe each target problem and the frequency with which each occurs within a stated baseline period. Shares this information with client. The conditions of each target problem and their frequency of occurrence within a stated period of time are sufficiently specific to enable progress or outcome on each problem to be assessed

C. Sets appropriate goals

(9) Makes a judgment with client on desired, expectable outcome. Works with client to arrive at a desired outcome statement which is feasible and related to the target problems

D. Sets duration and uses
   to enhance treatment

(10) Specifies the number of treatment interviews which are determined by worker-client agreement by the end of the initial phase

The client is frequently reminded of the number of interviews remaining. The time limits are kept firmly and continuously in mind to intensify effort

E. Determines appropriate
   priorities with respect
   to target problems

(11) Lists problems in the order in which they are to be focused upon when they are too numerous to be worked on simultaneously

Priorities are set, taking into account the following: stated wishes of the client; judged urgency of the problem; capability of combining (whenever possible) work on several aspects of the problem or several related problems in order to heighten effect and maintain involvement of significant others at an effective level

F. Arrives at a treatment
   contract

(12) Summarizes the work in the initial phase by making a verbal or written agreement with the client as to how long treatment will be, what will be worked on, and to what end (duration, target problem, general tasks, goal). Contracts to be altered if a basic change in the agreement occurs

III. *Assessment*

A. Makes early inclusive
    assessment

(13) Develops an assessment of the target problem(s) by making connections between the characteristics of the person, his situation, and the problem. Similar to "diagnosis" but without inferences of "medical" or "disease" model

		Takes into account both the influence of the environment (external factors) and personal characteristics (internal factors)
B. Revises assessment when necessary	(14)	Revises the assessment of the target problem(s) from time to time
		This is done when new information indicates that a modification will better fit the facts

IV. *Middle phase of treatment*

A. Concentrates on target problems — (15) Concentrates on actions by client, practitioner, and others to create the desired outcome. Alleviation of target problems, to the degree set forth in the contract, or the contract as altered. When time has prohibited working on all target problems, and if it appears that more time is likely to yield problem alleviation, and client wishes to, the contracted period of time is extended

B. Reviews problem status in quantifiable terms — (16) Explores to identify changes in the state of the target problem in each interview. States changes in problem status according to the specification of each target problem; that is, obtains the frequency of occurrence of each specifying condition within a stated period of time as in the initial phase of treatment

C. Generates tasks and task alternatives — (17) Identifies, with the client, an activity or behavior likely to lead to problem reduction

Attempts to engage the client in locating several such behaviors

D. Elicits task agreement — (18) Secures the client's agreement to perform the task

E. Plans details of task implementation thoroughly — (19) Plans, with the client, when, where, for how long, and with whom the task is to be performed. Does so in detail

F. Establishes sufficient rationale and incentives — (20) Discusses with the client the potential gains to be had from performing the task

Identifies and/or provides the client with rationales and rewards that motivate the client to perform the task

G. Carries out simulations and guided practice — (21) Engages the client in rehearsing or practicing the task or models the task behavior for the client

H. Analyzes and resolves obstacles — (22) Anticipates, with the client, potential impediments to performing the tasks and plans ways to overcome them. Ascertains retrospectively what obstacles occurred. Plans new or altered tasks to resolve the obstacles, including actions the practitioner will take on the client's behalf

I. Summarizes the task specificly

(23) Restates or asks the client to restate the formulated task

Includes the details of implementation in this reiteration

J. Reviews task progress in detail

(24) Explores, in interviews following task formulation, to learn what the client did with respect to task performance and what the results were

Does so for all tasks and obtains specific data on progress

V. *Work with others—practitioner tasks*

A. Consults and involves family appropriately

(25) Secures information from family members

Includes family members in treatment to the extent determined by the target problem and the wishes of the client and family

B. Consults and involves others appropriately

(26) Secures information from others in the social network in which the problem occurs

Includes them in treatment and treatment planning to the extent determined by the target problem and the wishes of the client and others

C. Secures resources

Resources can be classified as either concrete or intangible. Concrete resources include public assistance, homemakers, special education, medical or psychiatric care, visiting nurses, placements, social security benefits, and similar "in-kind" provisions. Intangible resources include counseling, advice, personal support, and the like. Obtaining either kind of resource entails use of the same practice skills. If the resource exists or can be organized by combining several existing resources, it must be procured

1. Consults, requests, or orders resources

(27) Confers with agency staff (colleagues, supervisors) to obtain information on types of available resources, procedures for procuring them, conditions for providing them, and evaluation of their usefulness. Asks for and requisitions the particular resource. This is the usual manner of obtaining resources available within the practitioner's agency. Resources from other agencies can sometimes be obtained this way, too

Resources are also obtainable from family members, friends, private-practitioner professionals, and local neighborhood organizations. Such nonagency resources should be secured by request, not order

2. Negotiates for resources	(28)	Arranges conferences between representatives from different agencies and reaches agreements or contracts that cause resources from other agencies to become available. This is done when boundaries between agencies and differences among them in the manner of provision necessitate negotiating for resources. Resources can be purchased from providers when the necessary agreements and funding are available
3. Provides interagency or intraagency feedback with respect to the provision of resources		Reports back to the provider, interpreting the client's use of the resource, and defining the provider's conditions for use of resource to the client. This step is not always necessary for resources provided routinely within the practitioner's own agency
4. Advocates the client's interest	(30)	Advocates the client's interests if a resource to which he is entitled by law, policy, or custom is not provided. Advocacy is negotiation with a difference; namely, that social pressures are brought to bear to release the desired resource. Advocacy steps of a mild sort are often necessary and should be carried out. However, where power conflicts are apparent so that strong advocacy is likely to involve an agency in an official or public conflict, such steps must be sanctioned by key administrators.

ing guide the student described the various steps of task planning and implementation, including the one given in example 12.1.

In the right-hand column of the guide, the instructor can comment on the student's work and rate the skills that are demonstrated. The relevant skills are identified by their numbers on the profile. Thus, in the example the number (9) refers to "Plans details of task implementation thoroughly" on the profile. The student is given a rating of 2, indicating performance at an acceptable but not at an advanced level. As the instructor notes, the student might have helped the client be more explicit about where she should keep the study sheet, since children frequently misplace or lose aids of this kind. The U rating would have been circled if the skill need not have been used in this instance and was not.

At the end of each of the three quarters of the academic year,

Example 12.1

b. Details of task implementation as they
were planned with client.

(9)

```
Amy is to use multiplication
fact sheet (the one developed
as a part of task in session
6) whenever she has difficulty
in remembering the facts. This
sheet is to be taken out and
used every time she does math.
```

3 ②1 U

```
Where should she
keep the sheet?
```

summary ratings are prepared by the instructor. Most instructors
have their students make their own summary ratings independently. The two are compared and necessary adjustments made
before the evaluation is completed.

Reliability Study

The criteria for evaluating performance of task-centered practice
evolved through experience between 1973 and 1977. A pilot study
of the reliability of judgments made about the skills was undertaken by Eleanor Tolson in 1976.

The plan of the study called for the random selection by date
of two recording guides from each student. One of the recording
guides was based on an interview, which was tape-recorded. The
practice skills were rated from the recording guides by two independent judges. (The tape recording will, at a later date, be used
to determine the accuracy of the recording guides.)

The judges rated the skills on a more elaborate version of the
scale described above. They were asked to make two decisions
about the use of each skill. The first decision concerned whether or
not the skill should have been used. The second decision con-

cerned the level of skill actually used: unacceptable, acceptable, or advanced. Cohen's (1960) coefficient of agreement for nominal scales (Kappa) was used to measure the reliability between the ratings of the two judges with respect to the first decision. Kendall's Tau was used to determine the reliability with regard to the second decision.

Of a total of 27 skills analyzed,*, the two judges were able to agree beyond a chance level (Kappa, $p < .05$) on the *appropriateness* of use of 15. In other words, for the majority of skills judges were able to agree that the skill should or should not have been used in a given situation. Agreement tended to be highest when the skill was one that was to be uniformly used at a particular point in the application of the model and when its presence or absence was easy to discern. Not surprisingly, agreement on appropriateness tended to be highest for such skills as identifying target problems, making an early assessment, determining problem prioritiies, setting treatment duration, eliciting task agreement, and reviewing task progress. By the same token agreement was relatively poor on a number of skills in which time or discretion in use were important factors, such as formulating tasks and planning details of task implementation, or in which practitioner performance was difficult to evaluate, such as disciplining feelings.

Judges agreed on skill *level* (unacceptable, acceptable, advanced) with respect to 13 skills (Tau $< .05$), not necessarily the same skills on which agreement on appropriateness of use was obtained. Significant agreement on level was found for most skills reflecting major activities of the model with the notable exceptions of task formulation and task review. The median inter-judge correlation (Tau) for skills on which significant agreement occurred was .49.

Although the results of the pilot study indicate that we have a long way to go toward the goal of achieving reliable measures of skill, we were able to demonstrate, at least, that obtaining such measures is a realizable goal. It will not be simple to attain, how-

---

* When the study was conducted, specific skills under "Securing Resources" had not been sufficiently delineated to permit separate ratings.

ever. Not only are skills difficult to assess when they occur but, as has been shown, it is necessary to make a prior judgment about whether or not their use is appropriate in given circumstances. Judges may agree on one aspect but not the other. For skills to be reliably assessed, concurrence on both is needed. We also need to determine the relation of assessments made on the basis of written records to those made on the basis of mechanical recordings of the practitioner's activities.

Adaptation of the Profile for Social Agency Purposes

The profile and rating system have been developed for use in a graduate training program. In its present state, the skill-assessment package is too time-consuming for immediate transfer to the conditions of agency practice.

Nevertheless, this material is presented in order to inform the field about a system that has proven practical for its particular purposes. This system, we think, can be simplified for use in social agencies. The rating system could be applied to key skills that might be in evidence in the kind of structured recording guide presented in chapter 11, or following practice in some agencies, workers could be asked periodically to submit more detailed samples of their recording—perhaps on more extensive recording guides of the type used by our students.* Tapes of interviews so recorded might also be supplied for use at the assessor's discretion.

Even if it were not to be used for rating of particular skills in the ways suggested, the profile could still serve two important functions in agencies or programs that have adopted the task-centered approach: (1) it would set forth a common standard for evaluation of skill regardless of the method of assessment used; (2) it would provide staff with skill descriptions that should prove useful in their work. But however they are employed, the profile and

* Copies of these recording formats can be obtained from the School of Social Service Administration.

related methods of skill assessment obviously need much further development before their potential can be realized.

It is also hoped that our work on skill assessment will facilitate comparable efforts with respect to other models of practice. Our methods of linking skill ratings to recordings and of delineating different skill levels within the same profile are examples of features that can be used within the framework of other practice systems.

Appendix I
Typology of Target Problems

The unit of classification is a psychosocial problem that the client and practitioner agree to work on in treatment. Usually it should be possible to classify problems from problem statements (one-sentence summaries of the problems), though in some cases additional information may be required. The categories of the typology are defined below. Each definition is followed by illustrative problem statements.*

1. *Interpersonal Conflict.* This category applies to problems of overt conflict between two individuals—usually, but not always, family members. It requires the agreement of *both* partners to the conflict that a problem exists—that is, the problem must be defined in terms of, and by, a two-person system. In the case of three-person or more complex forms of conflict, separate problems are identified. Thus, in a triangular conflict between father, mother, and son, conflict between father and mother would be classified as one problem; conflict between father and son as another; between mother and son as a third.

Subcategories by type and relationship in conflict: marital; parent-child; sibling; peers; other

---

* The reliability of the typology (or verification of it) has been assessed by having independent judges code the same target problems from practitioner-written recordings of task-centered cases. Interjudge agreement on major categories has generally exceeded 85 percent.

Illustrative problem statements:
   Mr. and Mrs. A argue constantly about the children.
   Mrs. B and her daughter, Sonia, quarrel about Sonia's domestic responsibilities.
   Harry and his teacher, Mrs. R., disagree about the amount of makeup work that he needs to do.

2. *Dissatisfaction in Social Relations*. In problems of this kind, the client usually perceives deficiencies or excesses in his interactions with others. For example, he may feel he is not sufficiently assertive, that he is excessively shy or dependent, or that he is overly aggressive. He may feel generally isolated and lonely. He may be dissatisfied with his relations with a particular group, such as members of the opposite sex or people in authority. In some cases, the client may see his own behavior as responsible for his dissatisfaction ("I am too dependent on my family"). In other cases, the source of the difficulty may be placed in the behavior of others ("My coworkers are prejudiced against me").

This category, instead of *interpersonal conflict,* should be used when a problem of "conflict" is defined by one client only. In such situations the problem to be solved, in effect, is the client's dissatisfaction over his relations with the other.

Subcategories by type of relationship providing source of dissatisfaction: marital; parent-child; other family; peer; generalized other

Illustrative problem statements:
   Mr. M finds it difficult to establish relationships with women.
   Miss A does not have an adequate social life.
   Joan's boyfriend is overly critical of her.

3. *Problems with Formal Organizations*. Problems of this type, like problems of interpersonal conflict, occur between the client and a specified other, although in the present instance the client's antagonist is more properly viewed as an organization rather than an individual. The client may find his interactions with

individuals in the organization troublesome, but their behavior is best viewed as an expression of an organizational position: that is, the client might expect to experience the same kind of difficulty with a different set of individuals occupying the same organizational slots.

Illustrative problem statements:
   The Welfare Department is not giving Mrs. A the amount for her children's winter clothing she thinks she is entitled to.
   Jackie has been expelled from school.

   4. *Difficulties in Role Performance.* If the client's major concern is his difficulty in carrying out a particular social role, his problem falls in this category. Most problems of this type that practitioners are apt to deal with concern family roles (usually spouse or parent) and roles of student, employee, and patient. Our use of the term ''role'' is limited to achieved roles, those the client has attained, rather than those ascribed to him because of his biological characteristics, such as his age or sex.
   It may sometimes be difficult to decide between this category and the first two in problems involving family relationships. If two partners define the problem as involving their behavior toward one another, *interpersonal conflict* should be used, even though role performance of family roles may be a major issue. *Dissatisfaction in social relations* should be used whenever the problem is (a) defined by just one family member, and (b) the focus is on some aspect other than that member's performance deficiencies in a family role.

Subcategories by type of role: spouse; parent; student; employee; patient; other

Illustrative problem statements:
   Harold gets out of his seat without the teacher's permission.
   Mrs. C is inconsistent in her disciplining of her son, Bobby.
   Mr. L spends too much time socializing with his caseworker.

5. *Decision Problems*. The focus of this problem is the client's need to make a particular decision, often but not necessarily involving a major life change. The issue to be resolved is the client's uncertainty about what to do in a particular situation, not a general problem of indecisiveness. If the decision to be made involves two partners who have contrary positions, the problem should be classified as *interpersonal conflict*.

Illustrative problem statements:
   Mrs. E can't decide whether to leave her husband.
   Mr. and Mrs. Y can't decide which method of birth control to use.

6. *Reactive Emotional Distress*. Anxiety, depression, or other expressions of disturbed affective states are likely to accompany each of the problems that have been described thus far. A client experiencing interpersonal conflict or undergoing a difficult social transition can hardly be expected to remain unperturbed. Still, the client who has such problems does not present his being upset as his primary concern. He may feel distressed about this relationship with his spouse, but he wants help primarily with his marital difficulty and not his feelings about it.

In problems of reactive emotional distress, however, the client's major concern is with his feelings themselves rather than the situation that may have given rise to them. This may be so not only because of his distress but also because there may be little he can do about the precipitating events, either because they have already occurred or because they are beyond his control. In order to be classified in the present category, however, his distress must be reactive to a specific event or set of circumstances that can be readily identified, such as the death of a family member, loss of status, separation from a loved one, financial difficulties, or illness.

Subcategories according to type of emotional distress: anxiety; depression; other

Illustrative problem statements:
Miss C is worried about the outcome of her pending operation.
Mr. T has been depressed over the recent loss of his job.

7. *Inadequate Resources.* The problem to be resolved involves lack of tangible resources, such as money, housing, food, transportation, child care, or job. If the client's access to a resource is being blocked by an organization, the preferred classification would be a *problem with a formal organization.*

Subcategories by type of resource needed: money; housing; job; etc.

Illustrative problem statements:
Mr. and Mrs. G are unable to remain in their own home without outside assistance.
Mrs. V lacks transportation to get to the clinic.

8. *Psychological or Behavioral Problems Not Elsewhere Classified.* This residual category is designed to cover any cognitive, emotional, or behavioral problem that cannot be classified into any of the preceding categories of the system. The problem must still be client-acknowledged, capable of relief through his independent actions, and relatively specific. Habit disorders, addictive behavior, phobic reactions, concerns about self-image, and thought disturbances are examples of problems for which this code may be used. Many such problems can be classified elsewhere. Thus, school-related behavior problems of children would be normally classified as *difficulties in role performance: student;* concerns about self-image are often an aspect of *dissatisfaction in social relations;* and so on.

Illustrative problem statements:
Mr. G is afraid of leaving his apartment.
Mr. L is unable to moderate his drinking.

9. *Other and Unclassifiable*. When it is used as a coding instrument, this typology needs to account for all problems that are identified as target problems, even though they may not fall within the domain of the model. Coded here are problems that fall outside the scope of the model as it is defined in the preceding categories, or that are incorrectly or inadequately identified.

Illustrative problem statements:
    Mr. J suffers from chronic low-back pain.
    Harriet is all mixed up inside.

Appendix II
Activities and Techniques Coding Schedule

This schedule is designed for the coding of practitioner and client activities and practitioner techniques from tape recordings of task-centered interviews. The basic categories of the coding system are described below. In actual coding, the schedule needs to be used in conjunction with supplementary materials which include instructions for making distinctions among categories, for identifying problems and tasks, for establishing coding units, and for coding multiple-client interviews.

Outline of Activities and Techniques

Activities (A)

A1. Problem Specification (PS)
A2. Task Planning
    Generating alternatives (GA)
    Task agreement (TA)
    Planning Details of
      Implementation (PDI)
    Summarization (SUM)
A3. Establishing Incentives and
    Rationale (EIR)
A4. Analyzing Obstacles (AO)
A5. Simulation (SIM)

Techniques (T)

T1. Exploration (EPL)
T2. Structuring (STR)
T3. Encouragement (ENC)
T4. Direction (DIR)
T5. Overt Understanding (OU)
T6. Explanation (EXP)
    EXP 1—Environment
    EXP 2—Significant others
    EXP 3—Client behavior
    EXP 4—Interactions
T7. Modeling (MOD)

Activities (A)	Techniques (T)
A6. Guided Practice (GP)	T8. Role-Playing (RP)
A7. Structuring Interview time (SIT)	T9. Other (OTH)
A8. Planning Practitioner task (PPT)	
A9. Review Client Task (RCT)	
A10. Review Practitioner Task (RPT)	
A11. Orientation to Treatment (OT)	
A12. Other (OTH)	

Practitioner–Client Activities

Unit of Classification

The unit to be classified is the "practitioner-client activity," which is defined as a set of closely related practitioner and client responses designed to facilitate accomplishment of problem-solving actions. For example, a social worker may pose a series of questions in order to help the client define exactly what the nature of his problem is. This activity would be classified as *problem specification*. Or the client might ask the worker what the point is in carrying out a certain task, in which case the worker might respond by pointing out or eliciting from the client potential benefits to be gained from task completion. This practitioner-client activity would be coded as *establishing incentives and rationale*.

In coding, the focus should be on indicators that are distinct for each activity. Coding of an activity begins when the social worker or client start to engage in the activity as denoted by the indicators and continues until another activity begins. The indicators of activities are described and illustrated below.

Categories

A1. Problem Specification (PS)

This activity involves identification and specification of a problem and monitoring of the progress of the problem. Once a problem has been identified, the worker asks questions or elicits information from the client regarding the characteristics and duration of the problem. This process of specification involves pinpointing characteristics such as behavioral manifestations of the problem; when, where, and with whom the problem occurs; the particular events immediately preceding or following problem occurrence. Additional data on these characteristics and changes in them are elicited as treatment proceeds.

P: Tell me first of all, how have you been sleeping this week?

C: Monday I slept very well, Tuesday I slept all right, Friday—it was not good.

P: When you say "not good," do you mean that you didn't sleep at all?

C: I wouldn't say I didn't sleep at all—but I woke up when my roommate turned the radio on.

P: Did you say anything to her about it?

C: I did once, and she turned it up.

P: She turned it up? What did you do after that?

C: I walked out.

A2. TaskPlanning (TP)

The practitioner helps the client plan problem-solving actions to alleviate the problem.

Generating alternatives (GA). In carrying out this activity, the worker and the client explore the various possible tasks or courses of action to alleviate the target problem. The worker asks questions, elicits alternatives, and makes suggestions. The category includes initial statements of tasks and statements of possible actions even though they do not become tasks.

This category should not be used after practitioner and client begin detailed consideration of a task on the assumption that the client will attempt it, even if there is no explicit task agreement. Such discussion, including consideration of ways of carrying out the task, should be coded as Planning Details of Implementation (below).

P: So you want to do something about the problem of kids teasing you on the playground. What do you think you can do?
C: I could just stay in at recess.
P: But that wouldn't be any fun. What else could you do?
C: I could go to the playground teacher if they messed with me.

Task agreement (TA). The client acknowledges that he is willing to work on the designated task. The category includes practitioner activity designed to elicit and clarify agreement.

P: I'd like for you between now and next time to keep track of all the times you get upset. No matter what it is. Do you think you can do it?
C: I think so . . .
P: Sure?
C: Yes.

Planning details of implementation PDI). This category refers to discussion of how the task is to be carried out, and includes generation of data about client's problems, behaviors, and motives needed for purposes of planning a task under consideration. Consideration of alternative ways of proceeding with the task would be coded PDI if the practitioner and client appear to be operating on the assumption that the task will be attempted. This aspect of task planning also includes "obstacle scanning"—that is, the identification of possible difficulties that may be encountered in carrying out the task and discussion of what the client might do should such occur.

The task being discussed is that Donna will talk to her mother about having a friend come over to play from 7:30–8:30.

P: You can bargain. If you tell your mother you'll clean up your room, will she let you have a friend over? What kind of response will she give you? Remember what she says, think hard. You tried that recently.
C: I can't remember.
P: You can. Come on. Does she say, "Hey, that's a great idea. Why don't you call her and tell her to come over?" No, that's what we would like her to say.
C: She'd say she has to talk to her mother.
P: If she could do that would she let you have her over?
C: She would want to know my friend and meet my friend's mother.
P: What's her name?
C: Michele.
P: What time would you have her over?
C: Come over when they aren't eating.
P: What time do you go to bed?
C: 9:00.
P: Why don't you ask your mother if it's o.k. to have her come over from 7:30–8:30.

Summarization (SUM). This code is to be reserved for recapitulation of the task agreement and details of how the client is to proceed. Summarization usually occurs at the end of task planning or at the end of the interview.

A3. Establishing Incentives and Rationale (EIR)
In carrying out this activity, the worker and client attempt to specify a rationale or purpose in carrying out the task. For instance, either the worker or the client might first consider the benefits to be gained from carrying out the task. What good will come of it? The practitioner reinforces or encourages realistic benefits and may point out positive consequences that the client may not have perceived.

C: Yes, I'll visit Tommy, if it will help him.
P: I think it will. But what will it do for you?

A4. Analysis of Obstacles (AO)

In analysis of obstacles, the worker and client consider reasons why the client is experiencing or is likely to experience difficulty in carrying out a task. The reasons may have situational or psychological origins.

For this category to be applied there must be an identified task that the client has tried to carry out or is considering. Further, there must be an explicit attempt to explore reasons why the task has been, or may be, difficult to implement. The identification of a possible obstacle should be coded PDI. Consideration of why the obstacle is occurring and related discussion should be coded AO.

C: It will be hard for me to tell my mother that I plan to move out. (PDI)
P: Why is that? (AO)
C: Because she'll begin to tell me how lonely she'll be. (AO)
P: How will that make you feel? (AO)
C: As guilty as hell. (AO)
P: What else? (AO)

In the example above, coding of AO would begin with the practitioner's first question. The code would continue to be used as long as discussion concerned reasons for the client's anticipated difficulty or factors contributing to these reasons.

A5. Simulation (SIM)

The worker and client simulate proposed task behavior through role-play, practitioner modeling, and client rehearsal. Simply asking the client to indicate what he might say or do under particular circumstances would be PDI. Simulation would involve a more extensive "dry run" of the client's performance.

A6. Guided Practice (GP)

Guided practice is the performance of the actual (as opposed to simulated) task behavior by the client during the interview; thus, a child may practice reading or a marital pair more constructive forms of communication, with the worker taking a coaching or teaching role.

A7. Structuring Interview Time (SIT)

This activity incudes any discussion related to how or when the interviews are to be conducted. For example, discussion related to any of the following topics would be coded SIT: scheduling time; location of next interview; frequency or duration of contacts; who is to be included in the interview. Also included in this activity category are reviews or planning of topics for discussion for the current or future interviews.

A8. Planning Practitioner Task (PPT)

One step toward problem reduction may involve a course of action to be carried out by the social worker. For example, the worker might agree to write a letter to the client's landlord, find a tutor, explore school resources, or verify medication. All discussion related to the development of such practitioners' tasks is coded PPT.

A9. Review Client Task (RCT)

This activity involves discussion to ascertain what the client has done to carry out a task agreed upon in a previous interview.

The task is for the client (who has a sleeping problem) to go to bed at a later hour.

P: Have you been going to bed later?
C: Yes.
P: Good. Were you able to stay up 'til midnight every night?
C: There were only two days when I didn't.

A10. Review Practitioner Task (RPT)

See RCT (A9, above; substituting practitioner for client.

A11. Orientation to Treatment (OT)

Discussion of general purpose and nature of treatment falls in this category.

A12. Other (OTH)

This category includes any discussion unrelated to problem reduction, e.g., greetings and other preliminary amenities, the weather, current events, movies, or TV shows last seen.

P: What did you do this past week?
C: I went shopping.
P: Did you buy anything?
C: Clothes and books. My birthday's coming up!
P: What day? . . .

Practitioner Techniques

Unit of Classification

The basic unit to be classified is the "practitioner response." In general, a practitioner response refers to all practitioner communication that occurs between two client communications. What is meant becomes readily apparent when the interview is put into dialogue form:

C: You know how it is.
P: No, tell me. (Practitioner response)
C: Well, it's hard for me . . .

Worker communications that open or terminate interviews are also to be regarded as responses. To be classified as such, a response should contain at least one word that conveys a unit of thought. Thus, "Good!" or "Why?" would qualify as responses. Utterances that do little else than inform the client that the worker is listening—"Um," "Mm," "Yeah," "Yes" (in some cases)—should be disregarded, as well as interrupted fragments that do not express thought units ("but I want to uh . . ."). Also to be ignored are certain background comments made while the client is talking, such as, "Oh," "I see," etc., which do not interrupt the client's flow of communication.

The same considerations apply to minimal, fragmentary, or background communications from the client. Thus, a speech fragment made by the client while the worker is talking should not be seen as breaking up a continuous, single worker response into smaller units.

Some responses contain more than one technique. For example, the practitioner may begin a response with explanation, then shift to direction. In such cases, code the technique that first appears, then code each successive technique as it appears. For example, "In order to obtain food stamps next month you have to be recertified [EXP-1]. You should go to the district office as soon as possible" (DIR).

Categories

T1. Exploration (EPL)

Exploration is used to obtain a fuller picture of the client's behavior or situation, or to help the client pursue a particular line of thought. Whatever its immediate purpose, exploration is designed to *elicit rather than to convey information.*

"Where do you work?"
"How have things been this past week?"

Exploratory questions or comments may be used to facilitate or clarify the client's communication. Included here would be (a) "echoes" or simple restatements or reflections of what the client has said:

C: I was up all night with my sick kid.
P: All night, you say.

or (b) questions or comments to help the worker understand the manifest meaning of what has been said:

C: They fried my brain!
P: You mean they gave you electric shock treatment?

T2. Structuring (STR)

This technique consists of the practitioner's explicit efforts to structure the treatment relationship and to provide the client with guidelines for communication. The immediate objective is to enhance the client's functioning in the role of client *within the interview situation* rather than to affect problems in his life situation *outside* the interview.

Structuring communication. Responses in this category *explicitly* direct or focus the client's communication. This may be done when the client is reluctant to continue with a particular topic; or when the worker wishes to change the subject, to suggest topics for future discussion, or to explain why a specific line of communication is necessary:

"Let's stick to this topic."
"Perhaps we need to discuss your relationship with your husband."
"Let's go back to the point you made about John."
"We need to talk about this to understand why you are having this problem."

Structuring the treatment relationship. This category includes explanations of the nature and purpose of treatment, statements of the practitioner's expectations of the client, discussion of the reasons for treatment decisions, consideration of the advisability of continuing or terminating treatment, and the like: "I think it best if I could work with both you and your husband."

Practitioner statements about own intentions. Any practitioner response that clarifies what the practitioner has done, is doing, or will do in or outside the interview situation and the reasons for the worker's actions are coded as structuring, e.g., "I'll write that letter for you this week," or "I'm stressing this point because I really feel it's important."

T3. Encouragement (ENC)
These responses most often take the form of supportive statements expressing praise or approval of the client's behavior, attitude, or feelings:

"You're doing a great job at completing your homework assignments."
"Good work!"
"It seems to me that you're quite capable of handling this responsibility."

T4. Direction (DIR)
The practitioner uses his professional knowledge and authority to make recommendations for the guidance of the client's decisions and behavior *outside* the interview situation. Within this category should be included *leading questions* that have the effect of giving advice, such as, "Why don't you try to do this?" Giving a professional opinion that would serve to guide the client's behavior in a specific direction should also be classified here. Thus, the practitioner might say, in response to the client's question about telling her child about her divorce plans, "I think a child of this age should be told." Other examples:

"Perhaps you need to talk these plans over with your husband."
"Don't you think scolding Johnny aggravates this behavior?"

Also included in this category are statements that express the worker's opinion about something but that contain no informational content based on the worker's professional knowledge. For example, "Parties can be fun," although expressing no more than the practitioner's opinion, may have direct influence on the client's attitudes or beliefs.

T5. Overt Understanding (OU)
Responses in this category consist of explicit expressions of understanding, sympathy, concern, acceptance, or appreciation with re-

spect to the client's feelings, situation, etc. The apparent purpose is not to encourage any particular behavior, as in "Encouragement," above, or to add to the client's cognitive grasp of his behavior or situation as in, "Explanation," below, but rather to show the client that the practitioner understands what the client is going through or has gone through:

"I can see how you must have felt."
"Your anger is quite understandable."

т6. Explanation (EXP)

This technique consists of the practitioner's efforts to enhance the client's awareness of others, situation, and self. To achieve this, the practitioner typically presents to the client *formulations* concerned with his functioning or his interactions, or relating to other persons or to his environment. These formulations are derived from a synthesis of the worker's professional knowledge and his knowledge of the case. As such, they provide the client with a new way of viewing or thinking about himself and his world. The formulations may be in the form of declarative statements or leading questions. They may be stated as facts, hypotheses, or evaluations. Whatever their form, their major function is to inform the client. Although they may contain directive, encouraging, or empathic elements, they should be coded as "EXP" if their primary apparent purpose is to provide the client with presumably new information (concepts, data, etc.) about his behavior or environment.

Explanations concerning the environment (EXP-1). This category consists of formulations designed to increase the client's understanding of his environment or social situation (exclusive of behavior of significant others, covered below). For example, explanations might concern services, organizations, or the client's physical functioning or situation in general:

"There are a number of clinics to which you may apply."
"The principal and the vice-principal get together with the teacher to decide who should be promoted at the end of the year."
"A vasectomy is a very simple operation."
"Your job seems to be pulling you one way; your family another."

Explanations concerning significant others (EXP-2). In the use of this technique the client is presented with formulations designed to help him understand the behavior, motives, attitudes, etc., of specific others with whom he is in contact. The focus is on the other rather than the client:

"Perhaps your mother isn't really angry with you but is merely trying to express her concern for you."
"I think that your teacher is overreacting to the situation."
"Isn't this an example of your wife's tendency to hesitate to take responsibility?"

Explanations concerning client's behavior (EXP-3). In this category the practitioner's formulations are concerned primarily with the client's own functioning or his interactions with others. The practitioner's comments may be addressed to the meaning, causes or consequences of the client's actions or interactions:

"Perhaps you are really shy about reading alone in front of the class."
"I think that you're overly sensitive to your teacher's bad moods."
"What you seem to be saying is that you really want to stop taking the medicine."
"If you stop tattling, the other kids will like you more."
"Did you act in this way because you were afraid of creating a bad impression?"

Explanations concerning interactions (EXP-4). Explanation of this type refers to interpretations of interactions of two or more clients, when it is not possible to distinguish whose behavior is the primary object of the explanation. This category is to be used in multiple interviews where there is an explanation of the interaction of the clients present. In coding EXP-4 it should be clear that the explanation of the interaction is on a system level, i.e., balanced, rather than focused on the consequence of one or the other behavior, which would be coded as EXP-3: (To couple) "Here again you seem to be subtly insulting one another."

T7. Modeling (MOD)

This technique includes any responses made while the practitioner is modeling proposed or hypothetical task behavior for the client. For example, if the practitioner demonstrates to the client how to call up tutoring agencies to inquire about services, all worker responses made during the demonstration would be coded as modeling. This includes only those responses made by the worker when he assumes the role of model. The code does not apply to discussion carried on with the client outside of the modeled role or responses in the discussion after the modeling.

T8. Role-play (RP)

This technique includes any responses made while the practitioner is in a role-play situation with the client. For instance, if the practitioner and the client rehearse how the client will talk to his teacher concerning his math homework, and the practitioner takes on the role of teacher, any responses made while assuming this role would be classified as role-play. The code does not apply to responses made outside of the role or in the discussion following the role-play.

T9. Other (OTH)

Those responses that cannot be coded or classified in the preceding categories of techniques should be designated as "other." In coding "other," use the following subcategories:

Responses inaudible on tape
Miscellaneous responses outside the context of treatment, e.g., conventional greetings, comments on weather, time, etc.

Any treatment responses that involve practitioner self-disclosure, e.g., "I do that kind of thing all the time"; "I tried that at home too, and it really helped me."

Any other treatment responses that cannot be classified elsewhere

References

Alexander, James F. and Bruce V. Parsons. 1973. "Short-Term Behavioral Intervention with Delinquent Families: Impact on Family Process and Recidivism." *Journal of Abnormal Psychology* 81(3)219–25.

Azrin, Nathan H., Barry J. Naster, and Robert Jones. 1973. "Reciprocity Counseling: A Rapid Learning-Based Procedure for Marital Counseling." *Behaviour Research and Therapy* 11:365–82.

Bandura, Albert. 1971a. "Analysis of Modeling Processes." In Bandura, ed., *Psychological Modeling: Conflicting Theories*.

—— 1971b. "Psychotherapy Based upon Modeling Procedures." In Bergin and Garfield, eds., *Handbook of Psychotherapy and Behavior Change*.

Bandura, Albert, ed. 1971. *Psychological Modeling: Conflicting Theories*. New York: Lieber-Atherton.

Bartlett, Harriet M. 1970. *The Common Base of Social Work Practice*. New York: National Association of Social Workers.

Bass, Michael. 1977. "Toward a Model of Treatment for Runaway Girls in Detention." In Reid and Epstein, eds., *Task-Centered Practice*.

Beck, Aaron T. 1967. *Depression: Clinical, Experimental, and Theoretical Aspects*. New York: Harper and Row. Republished as: *Depression: Causes and Treatment*. Philadelphia: University of Pennsylvania Press, 1972.

—— 1970. "Cognitive Therapy: Nature and Relation to Behavior Therapy." *Behavior Therapy* 1:184–200.

—— 1976. *Cognitive Therapy and the Emotional Disorders*. New York: International Universities Press.

Beck, Dorothy Fahs and Mary Ann Jones. 1973. *Progress on Family Problems: A Nationwide Study of Clients' and Counselors' Views on Family Agency Services*. New York: Family Service Agency of America.

Bem, Daryl J. 1970. *Beliefs, Attitudes, and Human Affairs.* Belmont, Calif.: Brooks/Cole.

Bergin, Allen E. and Sol L. Garfield, eds. 1971. *Handbook of Psychotherapy and Behavior Change.* New York: Wiley.

Bergin, Allen E. and Michael J. Lambert. "The Evaluation of Therapeutic Outcomes." In Garfield and Bergin, eds., *Handbook of Psychotherapy and Behavior Change.* 2d ed.

Berkowitz, Barbara P. and Anthony M. Graziano. 1972. "Training Parents as Behavior Therapists: A Review." *Behaviour Research and Therapy* 10:297–317.

Bijou, Sidney W., Robert F. Peterson, and Marion H. Ault. 1968. "A Method to Integrate Descriptive and Experimental Field Studies at the Level of Data and Empirical Concepts." *Journal of Applied Behavior Analysis* 1(2):175–91.

Bogatay, Alan and Frank Farrow. 1977. *An Assessment of the Management Impact of the Task-Centered Model in Public Welfare Agencies.* Washington, D.C.: Lewin and Associates.

Boies, Karen G. 1972. "Role Playing as a Behavior Change Technique: Review of the Empirical Literature." *Psychotherapy: Theory, Research, and Practice* 9(2):185–92.

Bowlby, John. 1969. *Attachment and Loss.* 2 vols. New York: Basic Books.

Brand, Myles, ed. 1970. *The Nature of Human Action.* Glenview, Ill.: Scott, Foresman.

Briar, Scott. 1973. "The Age of Accountability." *Social Work* 18(1):2.

Brown, Lester B. 1977a. "Client Problem Solving Learning in Task-Centered Social Treatment." Dissertation research in progress, School of Social Service Administration, University of Chicago.

—— 1977b. "Treating Problems of Psychiatric Outpatients." In Reid and Epstein, eds., *Task-Centered Practice.*

Buckley, Walter. 1967. *Sociology and Modern Systems Theory.* Englewood Cliffs, N.J.: Prentice-Hall.

Burrill, George C. 1976. "The Problem-Oriented Log in Social Casework." *Social Work* 21(1):67–68.

Butcher, Allen E. and Mary P. Koss. "Research on Brief and Crisis-Oriented Therapies." In "The Evaluation of Therapeutic Outcomes." In Garfield and Bergin, eds., *Handbook of Psychotherapy and Behavior Change.* 2d ed.

Callahan, E. J. and Harold Leitenberg. 1970. "Reinforced Practice as a Treatment for Acrophobia: A Controlled Outcome Study." Paper presented at the Annual Meeting of the American Psychological Association, Miami.

Carkhuff, Robert R. 1972. "The Development of Systematic Human Resource Development Models." *Counseling Psychologist* 3:4–10.

"Chicago 1973 City Workers' Standard Budget." 1975. U.S. Bureau of Labor Statistics. *Handbook of Labor Statistics*. Reference edition. Superintendent of Documents, U.S. Government Printing Office, Washington, D.C.

Christophersen, E. R., S. K. Rainey, and J. D. Barnard. 1973. *The Family Training Program Manual*. Lawrence, Kans.: University Printing Service.

Cohen, Jacob. 1960. "A Coefficient of Agreement for Nominal Scales." *Educational and Psychological Measurement* 20(1):37–46.

Cormican, Elin J. 1977. "Task-Centered Model for Work with the Aged." *Social Casework* 58(8):490–94.

Corsini, Raymond. 1966. *Role Playing in Psychotherapy*. Chicago: Aldine.

Corson, John A. 1976. "Families as Mutual Control Systems: Optimization by Systematization of Reinforcement." In Mash, Hamerlynck, and Handy, eds., *Behavior Modification and Families*.

Davidson, Stephen M. 1976. "Planning and Coordination of Social Services in Multiorganizational Contexts." *Social Service Review* 50(1):117–37.

Dewey, John. 1938. *Logic: The Theory of Inquiry*. New York: Holt.

D'Zurilla, Thomas J. and Marvin R. Goldfried. 1971. "Problem Solving and Behavior Modification." *Journal of Abnormal Psychology* 78:107–26.

Eisler, Erhard and Michel Hersen. 1973. "Behavioral Techniques in Family-Oriented Crisis Intervention." *Archives of General Psychiatry* 28:111–16.

Ellis, Albert. 1962. *Reason and Emotion in Psychotherapy*. New York: L. Stuart.

Epstein, Laura. 1976. "Task-Centered Treatment after Five Years." In Bernard Ross and S. K. Khinduka, eds., *Social Work in Practice*. New York: National Association of Social Workers.

Ewalt, Patricia L. 1977. "A Psychoanalytically Oriented Child Guidance Setting." In Reid and Epstein, eds., *Task-Centered Practice*.

Fanshel, David. 1975. "Parental Visiting of Children in Foster Care: Key to Discharge?" *Social Service Review* 49(4):493–514.

—— 1977. "Parental Visiting of Foster Children." *Social Work Research and Abstracts* 13(3):2–10.

Fein, Edith. 1975. "A Data System for an Agency." *Social Work* 20(1):21–39.

Festinger, Leon A. 1957. *Theory of Cognitive Dissonance*. Evanston, Ill.: Row, Peterson.

Fischer, Joel L. 1978. *Effective Casework Practice: An Eclectic Approach*. New York: McGraw Hill.

Fischer, Joel L. and Harvey L. Gochros. 1975. *Planned Behavior Change: Behavior Modification in Social Work*. New York: Free Press.

Fischer, Joel, ed. 1976. *The Effectiveness of Social Casework*. Springfield, Ill.: Charles C. Thomas.

Fortune, Anne E. 1976. "Tasks in Relation to Client Problems." Mimeographed. Chicago: School of Social Service Administration, University of Chicago.

—— 1977. "Practitioner Communication in Task-Centered Treatment." Dissertation research in progress, School of Social Service Administration, University of Chicago.

Frank, Jerome. 1974. *Persuasion and Healing*. Rev. ed. New York: Schocken Books.

Freitag, Gilbert, Elaine Blechman, and Philip Berck. 1973. "College Students as Companion Aides to Newly Released Psychiatric Patients." In Specter and Claiborn, eds., *Crisis Intervention*.

Gambrill, Eileen D. 1977. *Behavior Modification: Handbook of Assessment, Intervention, and Evaluation*. San Francisco: Jossey-Bass.

Garfield Sol. L. and Allen E. Bergin, eds. In press. *Handbook of Psychotherapy and Behavior Change*. 2d ed. New York: Wiley.

Garvin, Charles D. 1974. "Task-Centered Group Work." *Social Service Review* 48:494–507.

—— 1977. "Strategies for Group Work with Adolescents." In Reid and Epstein, eds., *Task-Centered Practice*.

Garvin, Charles, D., William J. Reid, and Laura Epstein. 1976. "Task-Centered Group Work." In Roberts and Northen, eds., *Theoretical Approaches to Social Work with Small Groups*.

Golan, Naomi. 1977. "Work with Young Adults in Israel." In Reid and Epstein, eds., *Task-Centered Practice*.

Goldberg, E. Matilda, and James Robinson. 1977. "An Area Office of an English Social Service Department." In Reid and Epstein, eds., *Task-Centered Practice*.

Goldfried, Marvin R. and Anita P. Goldfried. 1975. "Cognitive Change Methods." In Kanfer and Goldstein, eds., *Helping People Change*.

Goldman, Alvin I. 1970. *A Theory of Human Action*. Englewood Cliffs, N.J.: Prentice-Hall.

Goldstein, Arnold P. 1973. *Structured Learning Therapy*. New York: Academic Press.

Goldstein, Howard. 1973. *Social Work Practice: A Unitary Approach*. 1st ed. Columbia: University of South Carolina Press.

Gottman, John, Cliff Notarius, Howard Markman, Steve Bank, Bruce Yoppi and Mary Ellen Rubin. 1976. "Behavior Exchange Theory and Marital Decision Making." *Journal of Personality and Social Psychology* 34:14–23.

Grinnel, Richard M., Jr. and Nancy S. Kyte. 1975. "Environmental Modification: A Study." *Social Work* 20(4):313–18.

Grossman, Leona. 1973. "Train Crash: Social Work and Disaster Services." *Social Work* 18(5):38–43.

Group for the Advancement of Psychiatry. 1970. *The Field of Family Therapy*. Report No. 78:525–644.

Gurman, Alan S. and David P. Kniskern. In press. "Research on Marital and Family Therapy." In Garfield and Bergin, eds., *Handbook of Psychotherapy and Behavior Change*. 2d ed.

Guzzetta, Roberta A. 1976. "Acquisition and Transfer of Empathy by the Parents of Early Adolescents through Structured Learning Training." *Journal of Counseling Psychology* 23:449–53.

Haley, Jay. 1963. *Strategies of Psychotherapy*. New York: Grune and Stratton.

—— 1976. *Problem-Solving Therapy*. San Francisco and London: Jossey-Bass.

Hallowitz, David. 1974. "Advocacy in the Context of Treatment." *Social Casework* 55(7):416–20.

Hamilton, Gordon. 1951. *Theory and Practice of Social Casework*. 2d ed., rev. New York: Columbia University Press.

Hasenfeld, Yeheskel, and Richard A. English, eds. 1974. *Human Service Organizations: A Book of Readings*. Ann Arbor: University of Michigan Press.

Heinicke, Christoph, and Ilse Westheimer. 1965. *Brief Separations*. New York: International Universities Press.

Hersen, Michel and David W. Barlow. 1976. *Single Case Experimental Designs*. New York: Pergamon Press.

Hoehn-Saric, Rudolph et al. 1964. "Systematic Preparation of Patients for Psychiatry, I: Effects on Therapy Behaviors and Outcomes." *Journal of Psychiatric Research* 2:267–81.

Hollis, Florence. 1972. *Casework: A Psychosocial Therapy*. 2d ed. New York: Random House.

Jackson, Don D. 1965. "Family Rules: *The Marital Quid Pro Quo*." *Archives of General Psychiatry* 12:589–94.

Jacobson, Neil S. and Barclay Martin. 1976. "Behavioral Marriage Therapy: Current Status." *Psychological Bulletin* 83:540–56.

Johnson, David W. and Ronald P. Matross. 1975. "Attitude Modification Methods." In Kanfer and Goldstein, eds., *Helping People Change*.

Kahn, Alfred J. 1976. "New Directions in Social Services." *Public Welfare* 34(2):26–32.

Kane, Rosalie A. 1974. "Look to the Record." *Social Work* 19(4):412–19.

Kanfer, Frederick H. and Arnold P. Goldstein eds. 1975. *Helping People Change*. New York: Pergamon Press.

Karoly, Paul. 1975. "Operant Methods." In Kanfer and Goldstein, eds., *Helping People Change*.

Kiesler, Donald J. 1971. "Experimental Designs in Psychotherapy Research." In Bergin and Garfield, eds., *Handbook of Psychotherapy and Behavior Change*.

Kifer, Robert E., Martha Lewis, Donald R. Green, and Elery L. Phillips. 1974. "Training Predelinquent Youths and Their Parents to Negotiate Conflict Situations." *Journal of Applied Behavioral Analysis* 7:357–64.

Klein, Zanvel K. 1973. "Bibliographies on Behavior Modification: An Annotated Listing." *Behavior Therapy* 4:592–98.

Korbelik, John and Laura Epstein. 1976. "Evaluating Time and Achievement in a Social Work Practicum." In *Teaching for Competence in the Delivery of Direct Services*. New York: Council on Social Work Education.

Korman, Abraham K. 1974. *The Psychology of Motivation*. Englewood Cliffs, N.J.: Prentice-Hall.

Korner, Ija N. 1973. "Crisis Reduction and the Psychological Consultant." In Specter and Claiborn, eds., *Crisis Intervention*.

Krasner, Leonard. 1971. "The Operant Approach in Behavior Therapy." In Bergin and Garfield, eds., In *Handbook of Psychotherapy and Behavior Change*.

Lake, Martha and George Levinger. 1960. "Continuance Beyond Application Interviews at a Child Guidance Clinic." *Social Casework* 41:303–9.

Leitenberg, Harold. 1976a. "Behavioral Approaches to Treatment and Neurosis." In Leitenberg, ed. *Handbook of Behavior Modification and Behavior Therapy*.

Leitenberg, Harold, ed. 1976b. *Handbook of Behaviour Modification and Behavior Therapy*. Englewood cliffs, N.J.: Prentice-Hall.

Levy, Rona L. and Robert D. Carter. 1976. "Compliance with Practitioner Instigations." *Social Work* 21(3):188–93.

Liberman, Robert P. 1972. "Behavioral Methods in Group and Family Therapy." *Seminars in Psychiatry* 4(2):145–56.

Lish, Raymond. 1973. "Verbal Techniques in Casework with Children." Dissertation, School of Social Service Administration, University of Chicago.

Lemert, Edwin M. 1967. *Human Deviance, Social Problems, and Social Control*. Englewood Cliffs, N.J.: Prentice-Hall.

Litwak, Eugene. 1970. "Toward the Theory and Practice of Coordination Between Formal Organizations." In Rosengren and Lefton, eds., *Organizations and Clients*.

Loeb, Armin, Aaron T. Beck, and James Diggory. 1971. "Differential Effects of Success and Failure on Depressed and Nondepressed Patients." *Journal of Nervous and Mental Disorders* 152:106–14.

Luborsky, Lester, Barton Singer, and Lise Luborsky. 1975. "Comparative Studies of Psychotherapy." *Archives of General Psychiatry* 32:995–1008.

Lukton, Rosemary Creed. 1974. "Crisis Theory: Review and Critique." *Social Service Review* 48(3):384–402.

Maddi, Salvatore R. 1972. *Personality Theories: A Comparative Analysis*. Rev. ed. Homewood, Ill.: Dorsey Press.

Mahoney, Michael J. 1971. "The Self-Management of Covert Behavior: A Case Study." *Behavior Therapy* 2:575–78.

—— 1974. *Cognition and Behavior Modification*. Cambridge, Mass.: Ballinger.

Maluccio, Anthony N. 1974. "Action as a Tool in Casework Practice." *Social Casework* 55(1):30–35.

Maluccio, Anthony N. and Wilma D. Marlow. 1974. "The Case for the Contract." *Social Work* 19(1):28–36.

Marcia, James E., Barry M. Rubin, and Jay S. Efran. 1969. "Systematic Desensitization: Expectancy Change or Counterconditioning?" *Journal of Abnormal Psychology* 74:382–87.

Martens, Wilma M. and Elizabeth Homstrup. 1974. "Problem-Oriented Recording." *Social Casework* 55(9):554–561.

Martin, Barclay and Craig Twentyman. 1976. "Teaching Conflict Resolution Skills to Parents and Children." In Mash, Handy, and Hamerlynck, eds., *Behavior Modification Approaches to Parenting*.

Mash, Eric J., Leo A. Hamerlynck, and Lee C. Handy, eds. 1976. *Behavior Modification and Families*. New York: Brunner/Mazel.

Mash, Eric J., Lee C. Handy, and Leo A. Hamerlynck, eds. 1976. *Behavior Modification Approaches to Parenting*. New York: Brunner/Mazel.

Mayer, John E. and Noel Timms. 1970. *The Client Speaks: Working Class Impressions of Casework*. New York: Atherton Press.

McBroom, Elizabeth. 1970. "Socialization and Social Casework." In Roberts and Nee, eds., *Theories of Social Casework*.

McFall, Robert M. and Craig Twentyman. 1973. "Four Experiments in the Relative Contribution of Rehearsal Modeling and Coaching to Assertion Training." *Journal of Abnormal Psychology* 81:199–218.

Meichenbaum, Donald. 1975. "Self-Instructional Methods." In Kanfer and Goldstein, eds., *Helping People Change*.

Meyer, Carol H. 1976. *Social Work Practice*. 2nd ed. New York: The Pree Press.

Miller, George A., Eugene Galanter, and Karl H. Pribram. 1960. *Plans and the Structure of Behavior*. New York: Holt, Rinehart, and Winston.

Mitchell, Kevin M., John K. Bozarth, and Charles C. Krauft. 1977. "A Reappraisal of the Therapeutic Effectiveness of Accurate Empathy, Nonpossessive Warmth, and Genuineness" in Gurman and Razin, eds., *Therapists Handbook for Effective Psychotherapy*. New York: Pergamon Press.

Morris, Robert. 1977. "Caring For versus Caring About People." *Social Work* 22(5):353–359.

Morris, Robert and Delwin Anderson. 1975. "Personal Care Services: An Identity for Social Work." *Social Service Review* 49(2):157–74.

Mullen, Edward J. 1968. "Casework Communication." *Social Casework* 49(9)546–51.

Mullen, Edward J., James R. Dumpson, and associates. 1972. *Evaluation of Social Intervention*. San Francisco: Jossey-Bass.

Murray, Edward J. and Leonard I. Jacobson. 1971. "The Nature of Learning in Traditional and Behavioral Psychotherapy." In Bergin and Garfield, eds., *Handbook of Psychotherapy and Behavior Change*.

National Association of Social Workers. 1958. "Working Definition of Social Work Practice." *Social Work* 3(2):5–9.

—— 1977. Papers on Conceptual Frameworks for Social Work Practice. *Social Work* 22(5).

Olson, David H. 1970. "Marital and Family Therapy: Integrative Review and Critique." *Journal of Marriage and the Family* 32(4):501–38.

Osborn, Alfred F. 1963. *Applied Imagination: Principles and Procedures of Creative Problem Solving*. 3d ed. New York: Scribner's.

Oxley, Genevieve. 1973. "A Life-Model Approach to Change." *Social Casework* 52(10):627–633.

Parad, Howard J., ed. 1965. *Crisis Intervention: Selected Readings*. New York: Family Service Association of America.

Patterson, Gerald R., and Hyman Hops. 1972. "Coercion, a Game for Two: Intervention Techniques for Marital Conflict." In Ulrich and Mountjoy, eds., *The Experimental Analysis of Social Behavior*. New York: Appleton-Century-Crofts.

Perlman, Helen Harris. 1957. *Social Casework: A Problem-Solving Process*. Chicago: University of Chicago Press.

—— 1963. "Some Notes on the Waiting List." *Social Casework* 44:200–5.

—— 1970. "The Problem-Solving Model in Social Casework." In Roberts and Nee, eds., *Theories of Social Casework*.

—— 1975. "In Quest of Coping." *Social Casework* 56(4):213–25.

Pilivian, Irving. 1968. "Restructuring the Provision of Social Services." *Social Work* 13:34–41.

Pincus, Allen and Anne Minahan. 1973. *Social Work Practice: Model and Method*. Itasca, Ill.: F. E. Peacock.

Pinkus, Helen. 1968. "A Study of the Use of Casework Treatment as Related to Selected Client and Worker Characteristics." Doctoral dissertation, School of Social Work, Columbia University.

Polansky, Norman A. 1975. *Social Work Research: Methods for the Helping Professions*. Rev. ed. Chicago and London: University of Chicago Press.

Polemis, Bernice. 1976. "Is the Case Closed?" In Fischer, ed., *The Effectiveness of Social Casework*.

Polster, Richard A. 1977. "Self-Control Procedures in the Development of a Delivery System to Improve the Academic Performance of Seventh and Eighth Grade Underachievers." Doctoral dissertation. School of Social Service Administration, University of Chicago.

Raimy, Victor. 1975. *The Misunderstandings of the Self*. San Francisco: Jossey-Bass Publishers.

Rapoport, Lydia. 1970. "Crisis Intervention as a Mode of Brief Treatment." In Roberts and Nee, eds., *Theories of Social Casework*.

Rappaport, Alan F., and Harrell, Jan. 1972. "A Behavioral-Exchange Model for Marital Counseling." *Family Coordinator* 21(2):203–12.

Reid, William J. 1967. "Characteristics of Casework Intervention." *Welfare in Review* 5:11–19.

—— 1972. "Target Problems, Time Limits, Task Structure." *Journal of Education for Social Work* 8(2):58–68.

—— 1974. "Developments in the Use of Organized Data." *Social Work* 19(5):585–93.

—— 1975a. "A Test of a Task-Centered Approach." *Social Work* 20:3–9.

—— 1975b. "Applications of Computer Technology." In Polansky, ed., *Social Work Research: Methods for the Helping Professions*.

—— 1976. "Needed: A New Science for Clinical Social Work." In Fischer, ed., *The Effectiveness of Social Casework*.

—— 1977a. "Process and Outcome in the Treatment of Family Problems." In Reid and Epstein, eds., *Task-Centered Practice*.

—— 1977b. "Social Work for Social Problems." *Social Work* 22:374–381.

—— 1977c. *A Study of Characteristics and Effectiveness of Task-Centered Methods*. Report of the Task-Centered Services Project, vol. 2. Chicago: School of Social Service Administration.

Reid, William and Laura Epstein, eds. 1977. *Task-Centered Practice*. New York: Columbia University Press.

—— 1972. *Task-Centered Casework*. New York: Columbia University Press.

Reid, William J. and Ann Shyne. 1969. *Brief and Extended Casework*. New York: Columbia University Press.

Resnick, Jerome H. and Thomas Schwartz. 1973. "Ethical Standards as an Independent Variable in Psychological Research." *American Psychologist* 28:134–39.

Rhodes, Sonya L. "Contract Negotiation in the Initial Stage of Casework." 1977. *Social Service Review* 51(1):125–40.

Rimm, David and John Masters. 1974. *Behavior Therapy: Techniques and Empirical findings*. New York: Academic Press.

Ripple, Lillian. 1964. *Motivation, Capacity, and Opportunity: Studies in Casework Theory and Practice*. School of Social Service Administration, University of Chicago.

Risley, Todd R. and Donald M. Baer. 1973. "Operant Behavior Modification: The Deliberate Development of Behavior." In Bettye M. Caldwell and Henry N. Ricciuti, eds., *Review of Child Development Research*, Chicago: University of Chicago Press.

Roberts, Robert W. and Robert H. Nee, eds. 1970. *Theories of Social Casework*. Chicago: University of Chicago Press.

Roberts, Robert W. and Helen Northen, eds. 1976. *Theories of Social Work with Groups*. New York: Columbia University Press.

Rooney, Ronald H. 1977a. "Adolescent Groups in Public Schools." In Reid and Epstein, eds., *Task-Centered Practice*.

Rooney, Ronald H. 1977b. "Prolonged Foster Care: Toward a Problem-Oriented Task-Centered Practice Model." Dissertation research in progress, School of Social Service Administration, University of Chicago.

Rose, Sheldon D. 1975. "In Pursuit of Social Competence." *Social Work* 20(1):33–39.

Rosenberg, Blanca N. and Jacqueline Stackhouse Short. 1970. "Differential Treatment of the Pseudoneurotic Client." *Social Casework* 51(9):556–65.

Rosengren, William, and Mark Lefton, eds. 1970. *Organizations and Clients: Essays in the Sociology of Service*. Columbus, Ohio: Merrill.

Rosenthal, Robert. 1967. "Covert Communication in the Psychological Experiment." *Psychological Bulletin* 67:356–67.

Ross, Dorthea M., Sheila A. Ross, and Thomas A. Evans. 1971. "The Modification of Extreme Social Withdrawal by Modeling with Guided

Participation." *Behavior Therapy and Experimental Psychiatry* 2:273–79.

Rossi, Robert B. 1977. "Helping a Mute Child." In Reid and Epstein, eds., *Task-Centered Practice*.

Rotter, Julian B. 1972. "Beliefs, Social Attitudes, and Behavior: A Social Learning Analysis." In Rotter, Chance, and Phares, eds., *Applications of a Social Learning Theory of Personality*.

Rotter, Julian B., Joan E. Chance, and E. Jerry Phares, eds. 1972. *Applications of a Social Learning Theory of Personality*. New York: Holt, Rinehart, and Winston.

Saxon, William W., Jr. 1976. "The Behavioral Exchange Model of Marital Treatment." *Social Casework* 57(1):33–40.

Scheff, Thomas J. 1966. *Being Mentally Ill*. Chicago: Aldine.

Schur, Edwin. 1971. *Labeling Deviant Behavior: Its Sociological Implications*. New York: Harper and Row.

Schwartz, Arthur and Israel Goldiamond. 1975. *Social Casework: A Behavioral Approach*. New York and London: Columbia University Press.

Schwartz, Edward E. 1977. "Macro Social Work: A Practice in Search of Some Theory." *Social Service Review* 51(2):207–27.

Seaberg, James R. 1965. "Case Recording by Code." *Social Work* 10(4):92–98.

Seabury, Brett A. 1976. "The Contract: Uses, Abuses, and Limitations." *Social Work* 21(1):16–21.

Shelton, John L. and J. Mark Ackerman. 1974. *Homework in Counseling and Psychotherapy*. Springfield, Ill.: Charles C. Thomas.

Shorkey, Clayton T. 1977. "Bibliography: Social Learning Theory Approaches to Social Work Practice (1968–Spring, 1977)." Mimeographed. Austin: University of Texas at Austin.

Sieveking, Nicholas A. 1972. "Behavioral Therapy—Bag of Tricks or Point of View? Treatment for Homosexuality." *Psychotherapy: Theory, Research, and Practice* 9(1):32–35.

Silverman, Phyllis R. 1970. "A Reexamination of the Intake Procedure." *Social Casework* 51:625–34.

Siporin, Max. 1975. *Introduction to Social Work Practice*. New York: Macmillan.

Sloane, R. Bruce, Fred R. Staples, Allen H. Cristol, Neil J. Yorkston, and Katherine Whipple. 1975. *Psychotherapy versus Behavior Therapy*. Cambridge, Mass. and London: Harvard University Press.

Sluzki, Carlos E. 1975. "The Coalitionary Process in Initiating Family Therapy." *Family Process* 14:67–77.

Smalley, Ruth E. 1970. "The Functional Approach to Casework Practice." In Roberts and Nee, eds., *Theories of Social Casework.*

Snyder, Veronica. 1975. "Cognitive Approaches in the Treatment of Alcoholism." *Social Casework* 56(8):480–85.

Specter, Gerald A. and William Claiborn, eds. 1973. *Crisis Intervention.* New York: Behavioral Publications.

Stotland, Ezra. 1969. *The Psychology of Hope.* San Francisco: Jossey-Bass.

Stuart, Richard B. 1969. "Operant-Interpersonal Treatment for Marital Discord." *Journal of Consulting and Clinical Psychology* 33(6):675–82.

—— 1970. *Trick or Treatment.* Champaign, Ill.: Research Press.

—— 1971. "Behavioral Contracting within the Families of Delinquents." *Journal of Behavior Therapy and Experimental Psychiatry* 2:1–11.

Stuart, Richard B. and Leroy A. Lott, Jr. 1972. "Behavioral Contracting with Delinquents: A Cautionary Note." *Journal of Behavior Therapy and Experimental Psychiatry* 3:161–69.

Studt, Eliot. 1968. "Social Work Theory and Implications for the Practice of Methods." *Social Work Education Reporter* 16(2):22–46.

Taffel, Suzanne J., K. Daniel O'Leary, and Sandra Armel. 1974. "Reasoning and Praise: Their Effects on Academic Behavior." *Journal of Educational Psychology* 66(3):291–95.

Taylor, Carvel. 1977. "Counseling in a Service Industry." In Reid and Epstein, eds., *Task-Centered Practice.*

Thomas, Edwin J. 1970. "Behavioral Modification and Casework." In Roberts and Nee, eds., *Theories of Social Casework.*

—— 1976. *Marital Communication and Decision Making: Analysis, Assessment, and Change.* New York: Free Press.

Thomas, Edwin J., Kevin O'Flaherty, and Joyce Borkin. Rev. ed., in press. ".'Coaching Marital Partners in Family Decision Making." To appear in J. D. Krumboldtz and C. Thoresen, eds., *Counseling Methods.*

Thoresen, Carl E. and Michael J. Mahoney. 1974. *Behavioral Self-Control.* New York: Holt, Rinehart, and Winston.

Thorndike, Edward L. and the staff of the Division of Psychology of the Institute of Educational Research, Teachers College, Columbia University. 1935. *The Psychology of Wants, Interests, and Attitudes.* New York and London: D. Appleton-Century.

Truax, Charles B. 1967. "A Scale for the Rating of Accurate Empathy." In Carl R. Rogers, ed., *The Therapeutic Relationship and Its Impact.* Madison: University of Wisconsin Press.

Truax, Charles B. and Kevin M. Mitchell. 1971. "Research on Certain Therapist Interpersonal Skills in Relation to Process and Outcome." In Bergin and Garfield, eds., *Handbook of Psychotherapy and Behavior Change.*

Tolson, Eleanor. 1977. "Alleviating Marital Communication Problems." In Reid and Epstein, eds., *Task-Centered Practice.*

Ullman, Leonard P. 1970. "On Cognitions and Behavior Therapy." *Behavior Therapy* 1:201–4.

U.S. Dept. of Health, Education, and Welfare. 1975. Social and Rehabilitation Service. *Social Service U.S.A.* October–December Publication No. SRS–76-03300.

Valins, Stuart and Alice Allen Ray. 1967. "Effects of Cognitive Desensitization on Avoidance Behavior." *Journal of Personality and Social Psychology* 7:345–50.

Vinter, Robert D. 1974. "Analysis of Treatment Organizations." In Hasenfeld and English, eds., *Human Service Organizations.*

Volland, Patricia. 1976. "Social Work Information and Accountability Systems in a Hospital Setting." *Social Work in Health Care* 1(3):277–285.

Watzlawick, Paul, Janet Helmick Beavin, and Don D. Jackson. 1967. *Pragmatics of Human Communication.* New York: Norton.

Watzlawick, Paul, John Weakland, and Richard Fisch. 1974. *Change: Principles of Problem Formulation and Problem Resolution.* New York: Norton.

Waxler, Nancy E. 1974. "Culture and Mental Illness: A Social Labeling Perspective." *Journal of Nervous and Mental Disease* 159(6):379–95.

Weed, Lawrence L. 1969. *Medical Records, Medical Education, and Patient Care: The Problem-Oriented Record as a Basic Tool.* Cleveland: Case Western University Press.

Wexler, Phyllis. 1977. "A Case from a Medical Setting." In Reid and Epstein, eds., *Task-Centered Practice.*

Weiss, Robert L. 1975. "Contracts, Cognition, and Change: A Behavioral Approach to Marriage Therapy." *The Counseling Psychologist* 5(3):15–26.

Weiss, Robert L., Gary R. Birchler, and John P. Vincent. 1974. "Contractual Models for Negotiation Training in Marital Dyads." *Journal of Marriage and the Family* 36:321–30.

Weissman, Andrew. 1976. "Industrial Social Services: Linkage Technology." *Social Casework* 57(1):50–54.

—— 1977. In the Steel Industry." In Reid and Epstein, eds., *Task-Centered Practice*.

Werner, Harold R. 1974. "Cognitive Theory." In Francis J. Turner, ed., *Social Work Treatment*. New York: Free Press.

White, Alan R., ed. 1973. *The Philosophy of Action*. London: Oxford University Press.

White, Paul E., and George J. Vlasak, eds. 1970. *Proceedings: Conference on Research on Interorganizational Relationships in Health*. Baltimore, Md.: John Hopkins University Press.

White, Robert W. 1963. "Ego and Reality in Psychoanalytic Theory." *Psychological Issues* 3(3).

Wise, Frances. 1977. "Conjoint Marital Treatment." In Reid and Epstein, eds., *Task-Centered Practice*.

Wolberg, Lewis R. 1967. *Technique of Psychotherapy: Part Two*. 2d ed. New York: Grune and Stratton.

Author Index

Ackerman, J. M., 154
Alexander, J. F., 215
Armel, S., 156
Ault, M., 129
Azrin, N., 203; quoted, 212

Baer, D. M., 71
Bandura, A., 70, 159
Barlow, D. W., 129
Barnard, J. D., 215
Bartlett, H., 109
Bass, M., 214
Beavin, J. H., 73, 191, 192, 216
Beck, A., quoted, 50, 52, 54, 67, 163
Bem, D., 45, 46, 47
Bergin, A. E., 136
Bijou, S., 129
Birchler, G. R., quoted, 206
Bogaty, A., 295
Boies, K., 159
Bowley, J., 15
Bozarth, J. K., 88
Brand, M., 59, 60
Briar, S., 9
Brown, L. B., 36, 67; quoted, 149, 183
Buckley, W., 73
Burrie, G. C., 274
Butcher, A. E., 136

Carkhuff, R. R., 88
Callahan, E. J., 162
Carter, R. D., quoted, 269
Chance, J. E., 47
Christophersen, E. R., 215

Claiborn, W., 102, 103
Cohen, J., 306
Cormican, E. J., 7
Corsini, R., 159
Corson, J. A., 215

Davidson, S. M., 80
Dewey, J., 48
Dumpson, J. R., 8, 25
D'Zurilla, T. J., 66

Efran, J. S., 56
Ellis, A., 54, 163
English, R. A., 78
Epstein, L., 4, 5, 7, 17, 18, 20, 29, 35, 87; quoted, 88, 97, 98, 136, 177, 190, 218n, 224, 225, 264, 265, 299
Evans, T. A., 154
Ewalt, P. L., 36, 87, 99, 151, 152, 189

Fanshel, D., 13
Farrow, F., 295
Fein, E., 274
Festinger, L. A., quoted, 53
Fisch, R., 150
Fischer, J. L., 2, 8, 42, 88, 89, 154
Fortune, A. E., 257n, 259, 290
Frank, J., quoted, 46, 50, 56

Galanter, E., quoted, 45, 62
Gambrill, E. D., 154
Garvin, C. D., 7, 190, 218n, 224
Gochros, H. L., 2, 154
Golan, N., 296

Goldfried, M. R., 66
Goldiamond, I., 2, 154
Goldman, A. I., 18, 26, quoted, 27, 45
Goldstein, A., quoted, 86, 135, 154
Goldstein, H., 107
Gottman, J., 194
Grinnel, R. M., 36
Grossman, L., 100
Group for the Advancement of Psychiatry, 216; quoted, 217
Gurman, A. S., 136
Guzetta, R. A., 66, 211

Haley, J., 149; quoted, 150, 191, 193
Hamilton, G., 2; quoted, 115
Harrel, J., quoted, 198, 202
Hasenfeld, Y., 78
Hersen, M., 129
Hoehn-Saric, R., 135
Hollis, F., 2, 4; quoted, 58, 92, 259, 260
Holmstrup, E., 274
Hops, H., quoted, 201

Jackson, D., 73, 191, 192, 194, 216
Jacobson, N. S., 45, 54, 56, 57, 206
Johnson, D., 54
Jones, R., 203; quoted, 212

Kahn, A. J., 111
Kane, R. A., 274
Kanfer, F. H., 154
Kifer, R. E., 66
Klein, Z., 154
Kniskern, D. P., 136
Korbelik, J., 7
Korman, A. K., 47, 54, quoted, 58
Koss, M. P., 136
Krauft, C. C., 88
Kyte, N. S., 36

Lake, M., 32
Lefton, M., 78
Leitenberg, H., 67, 154, 162
Lemert, E. M., 77
Levy, R., quoted, 269
Lish, R., 259, 260

Litwak, E., 80
Levinger, G., 32
Lott, L. A., 214
Luborsky, Lester, 136
Luborsky, Lise, 136
Lukton, R. C., quoted, 16

Mahoney, M. J., 47, 129; quoted, 163, 166
Maluccio, A. N., 61, 133
Marcia, J. E., 56
Marlow, W. D., 133
Martens, W. M., 274
Martin, B., 206, 215
Matross, R. P., 54
Mayer, J. E., 21, 32, 68
McBroom, E., 159
McFall, R. M., 271
Miller, G. A., quoted, 45, 62
Minahan, A., quoted, 23, 39, 107, 109
Mitchell, K. M., quoted, 87, 88
Morris, R., 9
Mullen, E. J., 8, 25, 259, 260
Murray, E. J., 45, 54, 56, 57

Naster, B., 203; quoted, 212
National Association of Social Workers, quoted, 9, 108
Northen, H., 189

O'Leary, K. D., 156
Olson, D. H., 216
Osborn, A. F., 142
Oxley, G., 61

Parad, H. J., 2, 103
Parsons, B., 215
Patterson, G. R., quoted, 201
Perlman, H. H., 2, 4; quoted, 25, 39, 89, 159
Peterson, R. F., 129
Phares, E. J., 47
Piliavin, I., 9
Pincus, A., quoted, 23, 39, 107, 109
Pinkus, H., 259, 260
Polemis, B., 8
Polster, R. A., 38
Pribram, K. H., quoted, 45, 62

Raimy, V., 54, 163, 165
Rainey, S. K., 215
Rapoport, L., 2
Rappaport, A. F., quoted, 198, 202
Ray, A. A., 56
Reid, W. J., 4, 5, 7, 13, 17, 18, 20, 25, 29, 35, 74, 76, 87, 88, 97, 98, 136, 177, 185, 189, 190, 196, 218n, 224, 225, 236n, 259, 260, 264, 265, 269, 274, 287, 293
Resnick, J. H., 72
Rhodes, S., 21
Ripple, L., quoted, 44, 99
Risley, T. R., 71
Roberts, R. W., 189
Rooney, R. H., 98, 146n, 190, 218, 222n, 223, 224, 295
Rose, S. D., 66, 159
Rosenberg, B. N., quoted, 77
Rosengren, W., 78
Rosenthal, R., quoted, 268
Ross, D., 54
Ross, S., 54
Rossi, R. B., 67
Rotter, J. B., 47; quoted, 65
Rubin, B., 56

Scheff, T. J., 77
Schur, E., 78
Schwartz, T., 2, 72, 107, 108, 154
Seaberg, J. R., 274
Searbury, B. A., 133
Shelton, J. L., 154
Shorkey, C. T., 154
Short, J. S., quoted, 77
Shyne, A., 4, 5, 25, 74, 76, 136, 185, 196, 259, 260, 265
Sieveking, N. A., 67
Silverman, P. R., 21, 32
Singer, B., 136

Siporin, M., 107, 109
Sloane, R. B., 25, 88
Smalley, R. E., 2
Snyder, V., 163
Specter, G. A., 102, 103
Stotland, E., 145
Stuart, R. B., 77, 213; quoted, 214
Studt, E., 4

Taffel, S. J., 156
Taylor, C., quoted, 124
Thomas, E. J., 2, 66, 209
Thoreson, C. E., 129, 166
Thorndike, E. L., 26
Timms, N., 21, 32
Tolson, E., 189, 207, 299
Truax, C. B., quoted, 87, 88
Twentyman, C., 215, 271

Ullman, L. P., 61
U.S. Department of Health, Education, and Welfare, 111

Valins, S., 56
Vincent, J. P., quoted, 206
Vlasak, G. J., 80
Voland, P., 274

Watzlawick, P., 73, 150, 191, 192, 216
Waxler, N. E., 77
Weakland, J., 150
Weed, L. L., 274
Weiss, R. L., 189, quoted, 206
Weissman, A., 173, 187
Werner, H. R., 163
Wexler, P., 189
White, A., quoted, 59
White, P., 80
White, R., 44
Wolberg, L. R., quoted, 77

Subject Index

Action, client: behavior, and, 59-68; feedback, as, 63-65; importance of plans,
62-63; incremental, 67-68; response to,
70-72; sequence, 65; skill, need for, 65-67;
task-centered treatment, relation to, 61,
84-85, 89, 321
Activities, practitioner and client: definition
of, 177-78; emphasis on, 177-78; interrela-
tionship of, 174-76; *types of:* analysis of
obstacles, 163-66, determining desired
changes, 129-30, forming the contract,
133-37, other in-session activities, 166-67,
planning task implementation, 144-45,
problem definition and explication,
126-29, problem specification, 115-23,
summarization, 146, task agreement, 144,
task planning, 138-44; *see also* Appendix
II
Adaptations of the task-centered model,
150-54; alcoholism, 104; child welfare,
94-96, 98; family interaction, 215-18;
formed groups, 218-24; foster care, 98;
marital interaction, 96, 190-212; mental
health, 97, 164-65; parent-child interaction, 212-15; public welfare, 102-3; residential treatment center, 97-98; schools,
100-2, 132, 142-43; state department of
social services, 152-55
Agency, social: in-service training in,
295-98; role in task-centered approach, 90
Analysis of obstacles, 163-66
Assessment, 92; action requirement, 92-94;
constraints, 92-95; marital treatment, in,
196-201; obstacles, 92-95, 110-11

Behavioral treatment: sources from literature,
154; use in task-centered approach, 104-7
Behavior rehearsal, *see* Simulation
Beliefs and belief systems: as guides to
action, 48-49; emotion, in relation to,
54-57; nature of, 45-47; obstacles, as,
163-66; *points of leverage in, 49:* accuracy, 50-51, consistency, 53-54, scope,
51-52; role of the unconscious in, 57-59;
wants, relation to, 47-48
Brief treatment, 4-5; *see also* Planned brevity; Termination of treatment

Case information, systematic, 272-93; recording approaches, 273-75; task-centered
practice, recording of, 275-93
Casework, task-centered, *see* Task-centered
system
Client, definition of, 39-41
Communication, basic types of: direction,
325; encouragement, 325; exploration,
323; structuring, 323-24; *see also* Practitioner techniques
Conjoint treatment, 189-90; with families,
215-18; with formed groups, 218-24; with
marital pairs, 190-212
Contracts: conversion to open-ended treatment, 186-87; essence of, 136-37; formu-

Contracts (*Continued*)
lation of, 133-36; oral vs. written, 137; recontracting, 183-86
Core conditions, 87-89

Diagnosis, *see* Assessment
Dissemination of task-centered treatment: aspects of, 294-98; definition of, 294; Profile of practice skills, 298-308; teaching and supervision, 295-98
Duration of service, *see* Termination of treatment and Planned brevity

Effectiveness, study of: activities in, 254-58; case assignment, 230-31; case characteristics, 239-48; client evaluation of service in, 264-66; content analysis of service interviews, 252-54; follow-up findings, 261-63; interview characteristics, 251-52; phase I of, 231-34; practitioners and settings, 229-30; problem change, measurement of, 235-48, 262-63; problem reviews, 234-35; study purpose, design, and method, 226-29; task characteristics and progress, 248-51; techniques in, 258-60; work with collaterals in, 260-61
Emotion, 54-57
Empathy, 87-88
Empirical orientation, 107-225
Expressive needs, 99-100

Families (practice field), 190-218; *adaptations of the model for:* family interaction, 215-18, marital interaction, 190-212, parent-child interaction, 212-15
Field of practice, *see* Practice field
Focus, specificity in treatment, 115; lack of problem focus, 102-3; resistance to, 100-2

Goals in treatment, 134-35
Group treatment and practice systems, 189-90; use in task-centered approach, 218-24
Guided practice, 162-63, 320

Incentives and rationale, 319; *see also* Task
Intake, *see* Problem specification
Involuntary clients: problem specification with, 118-23; protective situations, 103

Labels and labeling: in social systems, 76-78; risks of, 76-77
Long-term treatment, 97-99; *see also* Termination of treatment

Marital treatment (practice field): adaptations of the model, 190-212; communication in marital problems, 207-12; initial phase, 196-201; task implementation in, 206-12; tasks, use of, 201-5; uses of the model, 195-96
Mental health (practice field): adaptations of the model, 97, 164-65

Obstacles, 110-11, 163-66, 320; *see also* Social systems

Planned brevity: advantages, 136; in task-centered treatment, 5, 136; research on, 136
Post-treatment planning, 182-88
Practice fields: child welfare, 94-96, 98; elderly, 7; families, 212-18; foster care, 98; marital treatment, 96, 190-212; mental health, 97, 164-65; public welfare, 102-3, 152-55; school social work, 100-2, 132, 142-43
Practitioner task, 167-74
Practitioner techniques, 322-29; direction, 325; encouragement and reinforcement, 325; explanation, 326-28; exploration, 323; modeling, 328; other, 328-29; overt understanding, 325-26; practitioner response, 322-23; role play, 328; structuring, 323-24; *see also* Appendix II
Problem review: contents of, 179-81; final, 179-80
Problems: client acknowledgment of, 20-23; common problems, 34; formation and resolution of, 42-82; interdependent problems, 34-35; manifestations of, 32-34;

nature of psycho-social problems, 20-41; relief through independent action, 23; specificity in, 23-25; unsatisfied wants, as, 25-30; *see also* Target problems

Problem-solving experience, 90-92

Problem specification: applicants, with, 115-18; determining desired changes, use in, 129-30; exploration, 123-26; identification of potential problems, 115-23; marital treatment, in 196-201; person-situation context, 130-33; problem definition, in, 126-29; respondents, with, 118-23; task-centered groups, with, 221-23

Profile of practice skills, 298-308; adaptations for agency purposes, 307-8; reliability study of, 305-7

Psychoanalytic approach, 99

Psychodynamic treatment theory, 99; use with task-centered approach, 103-4

Public welfare, *see* Practice field

Range of application, 96-103; contraindications, 98-99; limitations in, 99-103

Recording: approaches to, 273-75; of task-centered practice, 275-83

Referral, 187-88

Relationship, practitioner-client, 86-89

Research, *see* Effectiveness, study of

Role play, *see* Practitioner techniques; Simulation

School social work (practice field): adaptations of the model, 100-2, 132, 142, 160-62 case examples, 100-2, 160-62; target problems, 159; task formulation, 159

Service delivery: breakdowns and shortcomings in, 78-80; multi-organizational involvement, 80-81; task-centered practice as part of social services, 111-12

Short-term treatment, *see* Planned brevity; Termination of treatment

Simulation, 160-62, 320; *see also* Task

Skill: as form of client action, 65-67; in task-centered practice, *see* Dissemination

of task-centered treatment; Profile of practice skills

Social services and task-centered treatment, 111-12

Social system: action sequences, relation to, 72-74; effect on beliefs, 69-70; labels in, 76-78; relevance to maintenance or resolution of problems, 68-69; responses to client action, 70-72; role of organizations in, 74-75

Social work and task-centered treatment, 7-11

Social work education, 294-98

Social work practice systems, 1-4

Structure in treatment, 174-77

Supervision, *see* Dissemination of task-centered treatment

Target problems: *alleviation of, 83-88*: client's role, 84-86, practitioner's role, 84-86, 88; contract, as part of, 113-14; decision problems, 36, 312; emotional distress, reactive, 36, 312-13; exploration of, 42-82; interpersonal conflict, 35, 309-10; major groupings, 35-38; organization, formal, with, 35, 310-11; other and unclassifiable, 314; psychological or behavioral not classified elsewhere, 36, 313; resources, inadequate, 36; role performance, difficulty in, 35-36, 311; selection of, for groups, 220-22; social relations, dissatisfaction with, 35, 310; social system, relation to, 68-69; specificity in, 23-25, 113-14 (*see* Problem specification); treatment model addressed to, 88-89

Task: accomplishment of, 147-48; agreement reached on, 139-44; analysis of obstacles, 163-66, 320; defined, 109-10; 139-41; degree of achievement, 174, 279-81; establishing incentives and rationale, 155-58, 319; facilitation, 168-71; feasibility of, 139; generating alternatives, 141-44; guided practice, 162-63, 320; in relation to target problem, 83-87; planning, formulation, and selection, 138-44, 317-18; practitioner's activities in relation to,

Task (*Continued*)
  84-85, 110, 167-74, 321; recording, 146;
  simulation, 160-62, 320; task plans and
  strategies, 144-54, 167-68, 318
Task achievement scale, 174, 279-81
Task-centered system: action, client emphasis on, 59-68, 70-72, 84-85, 89, 321;
  application for use with lower-class
  clients, 86-87; as part of social work,
  107-8; basic strategy in, 84-85, 174-76;
  contracts in, 133-37, 183-86; empirical
  orientation, 107, 225; focus, treatment,
  specificity in, 100-3, 115; guidelines for
  development of, 7-11; origins of, 4-5;
  planned brevity, 5, 136; practitioner con-
  formity to, 85; review of past literature on,
  4-5; structure in, 174-77; study of effectiveness, 226-66; target problems, addressed to, 35-38; techniques used in, 90-
  92, 315-16; termination of treatment, 179-
  88; use of theory in, 12-19
Task planning, 138-44, 155, 167-68, 317-19
Task review schedule, 174, 279-83
Tasks, types: general, 139-40; individual,
  140, 205-6; joint problem-solving, 204;
  mental, 100; operational, 139-40; reciprocal, 140, 202-3; two-sided, 149-51; unitary vs. complex, 140
Teaching of task-centered treatment, *see* Dissemination of task-centered treatment
Techniques, *see* Practitioner techniques
Termination of treatment, 179-88; agreement
  on in initial phase, 179; *see also* Brief
  treatment; Duration of service
Theory: *problem-oriented theory, 12-19;* for
  task-centered, 17-19, need for, 13-15,
  testability, 15-17; systems theory, 215-17
Treatment, long-term vs. short-term, *see*
  Planned brevity; Termination of treatment
Treatment relationship in task-centered practice, 87-89

Unconscious, in relation to task-centered
  system, 57-59

Wants: assessment of, 43-45; conflicted, 45;
  constrained, 30-32; definition of, 43-45;
  occurrent, 44-45; problems as unsatisfied,
  25-30; relation to beliefs, 47-49; standing,
  44